Po

EASTERN
WETLANDS

T. TRAVIS AND SHANDA BROWN

STACKPOLE
BOOKS

0 11557 01173   9

To future generations

Copyright ©2014 by Stackpole Books

Published by
STACKPOLE BOOKS
5067 Ritter Road
Mechanicsburg, PA 17055
www.stackpolebooks.com

Printed in USA

10 9 8 7 6 5 4 3 2 1

FIRST EDITION

Cover design by Wendy Reynolds
Photos by T. Travis Brown

Library of Congress Cataloging-in-Publication Data

Brown, T. Travis.
    The pocketguide to Eastern wetlands / T. Travis and Shanda Brown. —
  First edition.
        pages cm
    Includes bibliographical references.
    ISBN 978-0-8117-1173-9
    1. Wetland ecology—East (U.S.)   2. Wetlands—East (U.S.)   I. Brown,
Shanda.   II. Title.
QH104.5.E37B76   2014
577.680974—dc23
                                                              2013030840

Contents

Introduction

It is our hope that this guide takes you to some incredible places. If you have the opportunity to watch 10,000 geese settle on a prairie marsh; to stand at the edge of a vernal pool while the calls of spring peepers wash over you in waves of sound; or to take a closer look at the brilliant colors of a dragonfly or the iridescence of a fish, then you will understand what is so special about wetlands. The purpose of this book is to help you identify the common plants, animals, and physical characteristics of wetlands, and to help you figure out more of the story behind the ecology of your favorite wetland haunts. Hopefully, this book will provide knowledge and inspiration that will allow you to enjoy and protect wetlands wherever you find them in the eastern United States.

HOW TO USE THIS GUIDE

Field guides are often organized according to taxonomy and presumed evolutionary history. The most primitive groups are usually at the beginning and the most advanced groups are toward the end. This works well if you are very familiar with the particular kind of organism (for instance, birds), but makes little sense if you are a complete novice. Because few people are likely to be familiar with the taxonomy of so many different groups (and since most of us just flip through the pictures anyway), this guide is organized according to the most intuitive methods we could come up with. The organization of each identification section is discussed at the beginning of those sections.

This guide is designed to be page-flipper-friendly. We have attempted to put the taxa that look the most alike together. In some cases, animals are covered at a taxonomic level that includes many species (i.e., at the order, family, and genus levels). Where it is beyond the scope of this book to differentiate the species from all lookalikes, we have attempted to list important anatomical features. These would be good features to photograph or take notes on so that you can confirm the identification later with the help of the internet or specific taxonomic references.

Some groups, such as oak trees and sunfish, are particularly common in wetlands and their general ecology is similar. In these cases we have elected to include a general description of their ecology as a group, along with abbreviated summaries of several species' distinguishing characteristics. Where visual characteristics, such as leaf shape and coloration, are particularly useful we have included photos of as many common species as space will allow.

Unless otherwise noted, all lengths reported are total lengths (including the tail).

CHAPTER 1

What are Wetlands and What are They Good For?

WHAT IS A WETLAND?

We know many types of wetlands when we see them. Most of us can look at a cypress swamp, a large bog, or a salt marsh and say, "Yep, that's a wetland." But what about that low spot that floods periodically down by the creek or that corner of your yard where water stands for days after a rain? Because wetlands are federally protected by the Clean Water Act and by various state laws, an enormous amount of time and money goes into answering the question "Is this a wetland?" every year.

There are a number of ways to define a wetland. However, the U.S. Army Corps of Engineers is the major agency charged with identifying the boundaries of wetlands, and it defines a wetland as an area that has these three components:

Wetland Hydrology: The area remains saturated or flooded for a long time, usually for more than two weeks at a time.

Hydric Soils: Over time, saturated or flooded soils develop certain characteristics because of anaerobic conditions in the upper part of the soil.

Hydrophytic Vegetation: Plants that adapt to survive in very wet locations.

There are also aquatic habitats that are not normally referred to as wetlands. Deepwater habitats such as lakes are not traditionally considered "wetlands," but they are under the jurisdiction of clean water protection laws. In general, wetlands have rooted vegetation, while deepwater habitats are too deep to harbor vegetation rooted in the bottom. While streams are also important aquatic habitats and often interact with wetlands, they are typically catalogued separately. Streams are usually confined to a channel with a streambed and banks and have flowing water. The wetland types that we cover in this guide are those that have most traditionally been considered wetlands. They typically have standing or very slowly flowing water with vegetation rooted in the bottom.

WHAT IS NOT A WETLAND?

Most areas that are not wetland are considered upland. Water does not stay in upland areas long enough to produce the characteristic plants and soils that develop in places where there are long periods of saturation.

WHY ARE WETLANDS DELINEATED?

The Clean Water Act, along with many state and local laws, prohibits development in wetlands without certain permits. In order to understand where the jurisdiction of these laws applies, it is necessary to identify the boundaries of wetlands.

WHY SHOULD I CARE ABOUT WETLANDS?

At this point you may be wondering why so many protections are needed for wetland ecosystems, or you may be one of those people who get asked, "What are wetlands good for anyway?" Whether the question is asked by a policymaker or an elementary school student, it is important to be able to give an answer that includes a description of the huge amount of wetlands that we've lost, and what we could lose if wetlands are not protected. Some of the main reasons that our remaining wetlands are important are bulleted below for ease of reference.

- Over half of the wetland acreage in the lower forty-eight states has been drained or destroyed since the American Revolution.
- Seven states have lost more than 80 percent of their wetlands (California, Illinois, Indiana, Iowa, Kentucky, Missouri, and Ohio). With six of the seven states located in the Midwest, some of the most drastic wetland drainage occurred there. However, the Atlantic coastal region also has lost 65 percent of its wetland acreage.
- Wetlands filter our water supply, removing harmful chemicals and fertilizers that contribute to algal blooms and, ultimately, dead zones downstream. In fact, constructed wetlands have been successfully used to partially treat municipal wastewater and remove agricultural chemicals from field outflows.

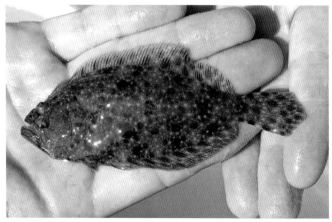

Wetlands are important nursery areas for seafood species like this flounder.

- Some wetlands provide an area for water to slowly soak into the ground and recharge aquifers.
- Wetlands hold water from storms and flooding, helping to prevent flash floods.
- Wetlands provide coastal buffers that help to lessen the effect of storm surge on people and property.
- The lush vegetation in many wetlands produces oxygen and sequesters carbon, lessening the effect of greenhouse gases on our climate.
- Wetlands are important nurseries for many of our seafood species.
- Wetlands are home to many game and fish species.
- Wetlands are home to some of the most endangered species on the planet. When we drain, clear, or fill these habitats we also eliminate species that are adapted to live in them.
- Our wetlands are visited each year by huge numbers of eco-tourists who search for birds, reptiles, amphibians, orchids, dragonflies, butterflies, flowers, and a growing number of other species that have managed to attract a devoted following. People are increasingly attracted to the quality of life and adventure that our natural wonders provide and they spend money in the communities near those wetlands.

The spotted turtle has become rare in much of its range because of loss of wetlands.

Below: Many species, like this orange fringed orchid, require special wetland conditions that are difficult to replace once they have been lost.

The eastern massasauga rattlesnake lost vast areas of habitat as prairie marshes were drained for agriculture.

Wetlands like this one have been eliminated from many river corridors, leaving few undeveloped places for floodwaters to be stored.

For some of us, the intrinsic value of wetlands is reason enough to protect them. We have been lucky enough to see the sun rise over a marsh filled with waterfowl or set over a swamp filled with calling frogs, and have felt the power of life in those places. Some of us, by necessity, have to be very realistic. The ecosystem services and potential monetary values of our remaining wetlands should be enough to convince even the most practical person of the importance of wetlands. Whether you are a farmer who wants to keep drinking the water from your well, a developer who would like to continue eating seafood, or a coal miner who likes hunting ducks, it should be easy to understand why we need to protect and restore our wetlands.

CHAPTER 2

Basics of Wetland Ecology

Studying the natural history and ecology of a wetland can be a way to tell the story of a landscape. Understanding more about wetland ecology can also help you to find plants or animals that you are particularly interested in, or to understand how wetlands may be restored to their former glory. This chapter covers some of the basic concepts that are useful in learning more about wetlands, including where to find them, how they are formed, and some of the characteristics that make each wetland unique. We only have space to skim the surface of wetland ecology, but this chapter should provide you with an intuitive introduction to the foundations.

HOW AND WHERE ARE WETLANDS FORMED?

Wetlands form in a number of ways. A good rule of thumb when looking for these habitats is to head to low ground. However, a number of wetland types form at higher elevations, even on steep slopes. Most wetlands form in depressions or flat areas, and the soil is often underlain by some sort of restrictive layer (rock, clay, or a mix of both) that prevents water from soaking farther down into the soil.

The fringes of larger bodies of water, such as lakes, ponds, or even the ocean, are some of the most common places to find wetlands. These larger bodies of water often have unique stories of formation. For instance, many of the bogs and lakes across our northern states were created by glaciers. As the glaciers receded, enormous chunks of ice fell off and melted, leaving behind the depressions that we call kettle lakes and prairie potholes. In the Atlantic coastal plain, lakes and wetlands often occupy large depressions called Carolina bays (also known as Grady ponds, Maryland bays, or other names depending on the location). The formation of these waterbodies has been a source of mystery and argument, but one commonly accepted theory is that they were formed by ocean currents thousands of years ago. In much of the eastern U.S., the most common waterbodies are the human-made lakes and ponds that have either been excavated or created by damming streams. Most of these have at least some wetlands around the edges.

Many types of wetlands are also associated with rivers and streams. Floodplain depressions, abandoned stream channels, and oxbows often become sloughs and swamps. On very flat land streams may only form an actual stream channel periodically, consisting instead of a wide, slowly flowing series of wetlands. Extensive wetlands often form at the mouths of rivers where they empty into the ocean or large lakes. Historically, many small stream valleys were filled with extensive wetland areas because of beaver dams. However, trapping for the fur trade eradicated beavers from much of the U.S. in the past, and many beaver ponds continue to be eliminated because they cause flooding in areas where it is unwanted by humans.

Wetlands also occur where groundwater seeps to the surface. Seeps often form where rock layers prevent water from traveling farther underground or where breaks in less-permeable underground layers allow upwelling of water. In karst areas, ponds and wetlands often form where water has dissolved the underlying limestone layers, leaving sinkholes and springs where water collects or seeps to the surface.

TELLING THE STORY OF A WETLAND LANDSCAPE

Telling the story of a wetland involves weaving together the geological history of an area with local topography, climate, and other physical characteristics. These physical factors help to explain why certain plants and animals are present today and how those plant and animal communities may have changed over time. In essence, two simple questions can be the first thread in a much larger landscape story—what are you seeing and why is it there?

Wetlands share several basic characteristics; however, there are many different types of wetlands. Below, we will discuss a few of the basic ecological characteristics and processes that are shared by virtually all wetlands. Then, we will cover some of the major factors that work together to make each wetland's appearance and ecology unique.

All wetlands have wet land (obviously). The soil is saturated, at least for part of the year. This saturation leads to the other characteristics that wetlands share. First, most wetland soils are low in oxygen. Oxygen diffuses much more slowly into saturated soil, and microbes quickly use up the available oxygen, so wetland soil quickly becomes anoxic (without oxygen). Second, the saturation and anoxic conditions found in wetland soil lead to colonization by hydrophytic (water-loving) vegetation. These plants are specially adapted to live in soil that is low in oxygen and constantly saturated. Third, wetland soils develop certain colors and textures that result from constant saturation (called redoximorphic features—see the soils section in chapter 5).

This is largely where the similarity of wetlands ends and the diversity begins. Each type of wetland has a character all its own because of its hydrology, geology, nutrient availability, geographic position, microtopography, pH, salinity, climate, and other physical and chemical characteristics. Many of these characteristics affect each other; however, some of them can be very useful in describing the character of a wetland and understanding its ecology.

Hydrology is one of the most important factors influencing the ecology of a wetland. As it applies in this context, hydrology is the study of how

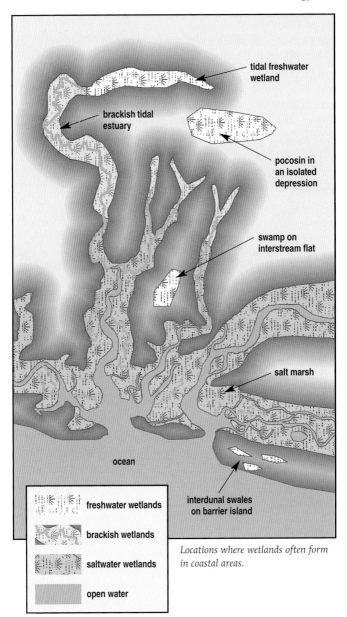

Locations where wetlands often form in coastal areas.

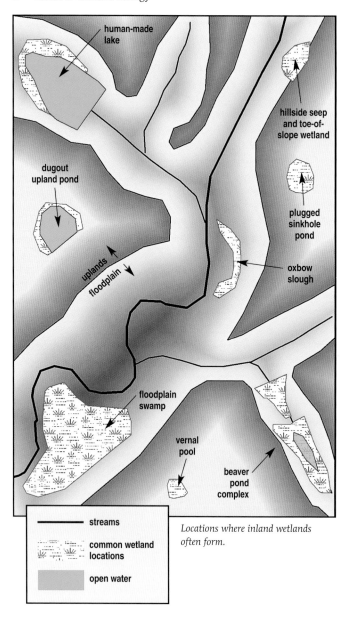

Locations where inland wetlands often form.

water gets to a wetland, how long it stays there, and how it leaves. Some wetlands, such as vernal pools and true bogs, are supplied with water mainly from precipitation. Others, such as fens, karst wetlands, and seeps, receive most of their water from underground sources. Sloughs, beaver ponds, and human-made impoundments trap water from overland flows, and many types of coastal wetlands receive salt water from the ocean. The water found in vernal pools and bogs may be very static, while some marshes are actually slowly flowing, and wetlands on the edges of larger bodies of water are affected by waves and tides. Water leaves wetlands through a variety of means. Evapotranspiration (the combination of direct evaporation of water and transpiration of water absorbed by plants) can be the major egress of water from small vernal pools. Subsurface flow, overland flow into streams, and tides are other common means by which water leaves wetlands. Hydroperiod is a term used to describe the period of time that a wetland's soil is saturated. Vernal pools may have a relatively short hydroperiod, while swamps may have a hydroperiod that is nearly year round.

Nutrient availability is another important factor shaping the character of a wetland. It is important to realize that while many wetlands have a thick layer of dead organic material, this material can't really be used by plants until it is broken down further by bacteria. It must be transformed into inorganic molecules of carbon, nitrogen, phosphorous, and other nutrients that can actually be absorbed by the plants, and this process is very slow under anoxic conditions. Some wetlands, such as marshes, have abundant nutrients provided by nutrient-laced flowing water and organic matter that has been broken down. Accordingly, these wetlands are filled with lush growth of highly competitive vegetation, such as cattails. Other wetlands are very nutrient poor. For instance, bogs are too acidic for the efficient conversion of organic material to the inorganic forms of nutrients that are useful to plants. Vegetation in these areas may be very stunted or may consist of plants that are specially adapted to deal with limited nutrient availability. Nutrient-poor wetlands can be very interesting communities of highly adapted species, such as carnivorous plants, that exist in delicate concert with one another.

Wetlands with a short hydroperiod are ideal for amphibians because predatory fish like this gar cannot survive.

Where a wetland is found in the landscape (its geographic position) has a lot to do with its character. At a broad geographic scale, the part of the country where a wetland is located shapes its plant and animal community. For instance, brackish coastal wetlands are much different from freshwater inland wetlands, and cold-tolerant species are not usually found in southern swamps. Local topography is often more interesting because it explains more of the story of a specific wetland. Is the wetland in a wide floodplain and probably the result of an old river channel? Is it isolated high on the side of a hill and fed by a small woodland seep?

Microtopography within a wetland can also provide interesting stories relating to the flora and fauna. In many of our shallow wetlands, a few inches in elevation change can make a huge difference in the plant and animal community present. For instance, when a large tree falls down it often leaves a pit where the root mass pulled out of the ground, and an adjacent mound where the stump and root mass rotted away. The pit is a little deeper than the surrounding area and may be the last place to dry up during the summer. This provides an important refuge for amphibian larvae, invertebrates, and even fish. In contrast, the mound left by the old stump can become an important sunning area for reptiles and dragonflies. Additionally, many of the trees that grow in swamps cannot initially sprout and grow while inundated. The stump mound provides a place for trees to begin growing. This is just one example of how the structural diversity provided by microtopography can lead to plant and animal diversity.

Finding out how the local, underlying geology influences a wetland's hydrology, nutrient content, pH, and other characteristics can be a very informative way to expand your knowledge of a wetland. Wetlands can be the result of a restrictive layer of rock or clay that prevents water from seeping farther into the ground. They can also occur where the water table nears the ground surface for some reason or where water percolates out because of some underlying geological feature. If water percolates through limestone to get to a wetland, the result may be a mineral-rich fen; however, if the wetland is located in an area of organic soil that simply catches rainwater, the result is an acidic bog. If the wetland is in a depression made of solid granite, then its water may be very low in nutrients, but if the underlying substrate consists of alluvial deposits on a river floodplain, then there are likely to be high levels of nutrients present.

Salinity is another important wetland characteristic, especially in coastal areas. There are also rare eastern inland wetlands with relatively high salinity. Few freshwater plants and animals are able to survive in very salty environments; therefore, saltwater wetlands are inhabited by species that are specially adapted to live in high salinity. The effects of salinity are particularly evident at the mouths of coastal rivers. In salt marshes, which have direct connections to the ocean and the highest salinity, only plants and animals that are adapted to high salinity can survive. As you move upstream in coastal wetlands, you enter a zone where fresh water and salt water mix

Glacial lake in an eastern forest.

Prairie pothole.

(brackish water). Water in these areas may flow toward the ocean or away from it, depending on whether the tide is coming in or going out. In this estuarine environment, there is an interesting mixture of species that can tolerate saltwater along with freshwater inhabitants. In some areas, fairly sharp zonation of plant species can be seen where freshwater plants give way to more salt-tolerant plants.

Climate is another major factor determining the community of plants and animals that inhabit a wetland. For instance, many of our northern lakes and bogs occupy depressions that were produced when large chunks of ice fell off of glaciers as they receded at the end of the last ice age. While both the prairie potholes and the northwoods lakes farther east were formed this way, the prairie potholes are in a relatively arid region. They dry down significantly in the summer and are surrounded by grasslands. Conversely, the many lakes and bogs farther east are surrounded by forest and more of them contain water year round. Even similar wetlands may be inhabited by different species because of the temperature tolerance of those species. For instance, a northern swamp forest might be inhabited by northern white cedar, tamarack, and black ash, while a swamp with very similar hydrology would be forested with bald cypress and water tupelo in the south. Microclimates are also an important part of wetland ecology. For instance, cool groundwater can allow cold-loving northern species to grow in certain fens that are farther south than those species typically grow. Similarly, plants that typically only grow in cool northern wetlands can grow at high elevations in the southern Appalachian Mountains.

Seasonal changes are an essential part of any wetland's story. During the dry times of year, some wetlands leave only subtle clues that water was ever present. Many types of seasonal wetlands are at their wettest from autumn to early spring, but by the end of summer they may be dry. In some years these seasonal wetlands may have standing water for only a very short time. This dry period is essential to some plants that cannot sprout underwater, and certain plants cannot survive being inundated for the entire year.

Following a wetland through an entire year of its life can be an extremely valuable exercise. Beginning in spring, most wetlands explode with life. They are often filled with the deafening calls and bold colors of amphibians that come there to breed. Permanently inundated areas may have fewer amphibians in spring, but often have spawning fish. Insects change from larvae to adults and many emerge to fly in the terrestrial environment. During the summer, plants flourish and bloom, insects continue to emerge, and many areas are filled with the calls of breeding birds. Some wetlands dry down and become meadows or flats of cracked earth in the summer. By late summer and fall the last plants of the year may be blooming, and the transition to winter begins. Seasons mean different things to different kinds of wetlands in various parts of the country. For example, many parts of the southern U.S. are wintering grounds for birds, while those same species spend the summer months breeding on the arctic tundra or in the prairie pothole region.

Dry periods are essential for many plants to sprout in wetlands.

The most visually evident difference between wetland types is usually their plant community. An important part of a wetland's story is to deter-

During some seasons, certain kinds of wetlands may look like little more than a meadow with patches of cracked earth.

mine why the plant community is what it is. What are the physical characteristics that have allowed certain plants to thrive at that location? To the practiced eye, plants give important clues about how long the wetland holds water in a typical year, salinity, pH of the soil, amount of nutrients available, history of disturbance, and many other aspects of wetland ecology. For instance, salt marsh plants are specially adapted to high salinity and tides, bog plants often have special adaptations to deal with acidity and low nutrient availability, and most plants prefer a certain amount of sun or shade.

While we may talk about each aspect of wetland ecology separately, they are quite connected to each other. Thinking about what factors are in play at a wetland site can often yield a rich story. With a little thought, exploration, and perhaps investigation of more resources specific to your area, you may be able to answer important questions about your wetland's story, such as: Where does the water come from? Where does the water go? How long does the water stay? Why do the plants found here like it so much? What would this area have looked like before Europeans dominated the landscape? What animals are here? Why are some animals not here?

ZONATION

Zonation is an important concept in wetland ecology. It is the tendency of plants to grow in different zones determined by their tolerances of water depth, sun/shade, salinity, and other physical characteristics. Wetlands with relatively deep water usually have a zone in the middle where only floating vegetation and submerged plants grow. As one travels into shallower water, there may be floating plants that are rooted in the soil. Next, in still shallower water, are the emergent plants that grow in water year round. Finally,

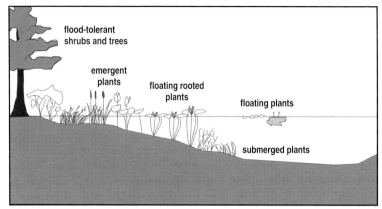

Typical zonation of water plants in response to water depth.

one encounters plants that are on dry land, but these plants often have their roots in the water table and may be flooded occasionally (see figure above). Similar patterns of zonation can be seen in relation to salinity in coastal wetlands. The most salt-tolerant species grow in the lower marsh, while less salt-tolerant species grow farther back from the salty tides where freshwater makes up a larger proportion of the available moisture.

ADAPTATIONS FOR LIVING IN WETLANDS

While the previous section involved telling the story of a wetland ecosystem as a whole, this section focuses more on telling the story of how individual plants and animals are adapted to survive in wetlands. These include adaptations for dealing with challenges that are common to almost all wetlands and adverse conditions that are only found in certain kinds of wetlands.

One of the major adversities that wetland organisms have to overcome is low oxygen availability. By definition, wetland soils are very low in oxygen (see explanation in the soil indicators section of chapter 5), and even the water found in wetlands can be low in oxygen because the decomposition of organic matter uses up so much of it.

Because plants produce oxygen through photosynthesis, it might seem strange that they have trouble living where their roots cannot get oxygen. Plants use sunlight and carbon dioxide to produce sugars, and they produce oxygen as a byproduct. However, plants still use oxygen and sugars to generate energy through respiration. Some of the oxygen needed for this process is obtained through the roots, which is why plants that are not adapted to low-oxygen soils die when they are over-watered. Wetland plants deal with low oxygen in a number of ways. Some plants have special structures that absorb atmospheric oxygen and carry it to the roots, acting like a snorkel for the plants' roots. For instance, mangroves have pneumatophores that stick up from the soil surface; the knees of cypress trees are thought to serve the same function. Many hydrophytic plants also have tissue (called aerenchyma) that is filled with air chambers. These chambers allow air to travel from the above-water portions of the plant to the roots. Some plants even have pressurized systems that push oxygen down into the roots.

Animals also have adaptations that allow them to survive low-oxygen conditions in wetland water. For many animals, this simply involves conservation of energy. They remain still much of the time, hiding in vegetation and avoiding energy expenditure that would cause them to increase their breathing rate. Many wetland fishes, such as topminnows and mosquitofish, have adapted to life at the water's surface, where there is a layer of more oxygen-rich water. Some fish, like the bowfin and mudminnow, have a modified swim bladder that acts like a lung and actually allows them to use air gulped from the water's surface. Similarly, many aquatic salamanders can use their gills, skin, and lungs to absorb oxygen. Many reptiles and amphibians can

Aerenchyma, or air chambers that help provide oxygen to a plant's roots in anaerobic soil.

Below: Cypress knees are thought to assist in providing oxygen to the tree's roots.

drastically lower their heart rate, which allows them to use less oxygen when resting, and they can even stay buried in mud for long periods of time.

Invertebrates also display a number of adaptations that allow them to live in low-oxygen water. One of the most visually evident adaptations is hemoglobin, a red pigment found in the blood of midge larvae (and human blood as well). This pigment gives them bright red coloration and increases their blood's ability to carry oxygen. Many other invertebrates simply carry their air supply with them. Often, aquatic beetles and true bugs carry a bubble of air with them as they swim, or carry a layer of air that sticks to their body when they dive. As in vertebrate animals, many invertebrates simply remain inactive much of the time, thereby reducing their need for respiration.

One of the most interesting and weird adaptations of any plant to wetland conditions is a carnivorous one. Carnivory enables plants to live in some wetlands—especially bogs—that have very few nutrients (such as nitrogen) available to growing plants. Carnivorous plants capture invertebrates and digest them to obtain essential nutrients.

Perhaps the most famous example of a carnivorous plant is the Venus flytrap (*Dionaea muscipula*). Several plant monsters have been modeled after this species, and many people readily recognize it even though it is native to a relatively tiny area in the southeastern U.S. When a small insect or arachnid touches the inside of the plant's jaw-like modified leaf two times over about a twenty-second interval, the jaws close. This delayed trigger prevents the plant from wasting energy on wind-blown debris. Bladderworts (*Utricularia* spp.) similarly trap tiny insects and microcrustaceans. When tiny hairs at the mouth of their underwater bladders are triggered the bladder snaps open, sucking the plant's prey inside where it is digested. Sundews (*Drosera* spp.) and butterworts (*Pinguicula* spp.) have semi-active means of catching prey. When tiny insects or arachnids get stuck in the sticky secretions on their leaves, these plants curl the leaf around the tiny carcass and digest it. Our last group of carnivorous plants, the pitcherplants (*Sarracenia* spp.), passively trap their prey. Insects and arachnids that are attracted to the plant's color and nectar fall into the watery mixture in the plant's pitcher, where they are digested by enzymes.

Plants and animals living in brackish and saltwater wetlands have to deal with additional challenges. Too much salt can be toxic to living things, so organisms in brackish wetlands often have ways to rid their bodies of excess salt. Plants can excrete excess salt through their roots and leaves, and some plants exclude salt from uptake by the roots. Several birds and reptiles have salt glands that excrete excess salt. Most fish are adapted to either salt water or fresh water, but certain species show a remarkable ability to change the way they osmoregulate (regulate the salt concentration in their body), and move between salt water and fresh water for different parts of their life cycle.

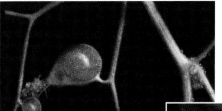

Bladderwort bladder.

Flypaper-like leaves of butterwort.

Pitcherplant pitcher.

Sundew leaf with sticky "dew."

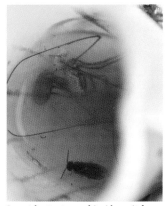

Jaw-like modified leaves of a Venus flytrap.

Invertebrates trapped inside a pitcher-plant.

Wetlands are essential to many amphibian larvae.

WETLAND NURSERY GROUNDS

Wetlands are nurseries for a variety of animals. One of the most commonly referenced ways that wetlands act as nurseries is for seafood. Many of our most commercially important seafood species spend their early life in coastal wetlands. Shrimp, crabs, and many fish, such as flounder and anchovies, may be caught in the open ocean, but these fisheries would collapse without the coastal rivers and wetlands where the young species develop. In coastal wetlands, young fish and crustaceans can find high concentrations of the invertebrates and organic matter that they eat. They also find shallow habitats with ample vegetation, which provides cover from predatory animals that they would face in the open ocean.

Farther inland, wetlands provide important nursery areas for amphibians, insects, waterfowl, and many other animals. Amphibians need an aquatic environment where their larvae can develop, yet most permanent waterbodies contain fish, which eat the eggs and young. Seasonally flooded wetlands provide an environment that doesn't support fish, and where amphibian larvae can develop without being eaten. Aquatic insects, many of which only need to live in water as larvae, also find many niches in rich wetland environments, as well as plenty of organic matter and other invertebrates for them to eat. For waterfowl, wetlands provide lush plant forage, plenty of invertebrates to eat, and water that can protect their young from land-based predators. Besides those that use wetlands directly as nurseries, there are numerous animals that raise their young next to wetlands where they can capture the rich abundance of food coming out of the water.

CHAPTER 3

Wetland Classification

The physical characteristics that shape a wetland (as discussed in chapter 2) work together to create some recognizable categories of wetlands. In general, wetlands are most easily described by the plant communities that inhabit them. For instance, we recognize marshes by their grasses, sedges, and rushes, and easily identify swamps by their trees.

Numerous wetland classification systems have been developed over the last several centuries, and various state, federal, and international organizations classify wetlands in different ways. Perhaps the most widely used system in the eastern U.S. is that developed by the U.S. Fish and Wildlife Service (*Classification of Wetlands and Deepwater Habitats of the United States* by Cowardin et al., 1979). This method is used to classify wetlands by various categories and sub-categories that eventually yield a code consisting of letters and numbers describing a wetland or waterbody type. This is a useful way of creating an abbreviated description of a wetland. This system is also helpful because it uses geographical terms and descriptions of vegetative structure that require very little knowledge of specific plant species. We have chosen not to recreate the entire USFWS classification system here, but several of the most useful terms are defined below.

The five types of wetland "systems" according to the USFWS wetland classification:

Palustrine: Freshwater (ocean-derived salinity of less than 0.5%), non-tidal wetlands, usually with rooted vegetation. If vegetation is lacking, palustrine wetlands are always less than 8 ha (20 ac) in size, lacking evidence of wave action, and less than 2 m (6.6') in depth. Most freshwater wetlands we discuss in this book fall into this category.

Lacustrine: Deepwater lake habitats with little rooted vegetation and at least 2 m (6.6') of water at the deepest point during low water. These habitats often have wave action and can be tidal or non-tidal, but always have an ocean-derived salinity of less than 0.5%.

Estuarine: Deepwater tidal habitat and surrounding wetlands mostly enclosed by land, but with access to the open ocean at least part of the time. Ocean water in these habitats is, at least occasionally, diluted by freshwater runoff from adjacent land.

Marine: Open-ocean habitats overlying the continental shelf and including the coastline.

Riverine: River and stream habitats. Any wetland or deepwater habitat confined to a channel, except for those dominated by trees or emergent vegetation, and those with ocean-derived salinity greater than 0.5%.

Several terms that are used in the USFWS classification to describe the vegetational structure of wetlands:

Aquatic Bed: Wetlands containing many plants growing on or below the surface of the water for most of the growing season during most years. Examples: ponds and coastal submerged aquatic vegetation beds.

Moss–Lichen Wetland: A saturated wetland with few emergent trees and shrubs where lichens or mosses cover a substrate other than rock. Example: bogs.

Emergent Wetland: A wetland characterized by rooted, emergent, hydrophytic vegetation, excluding mosses and lichens. Example: marshes.

Scrub–Shrub Wetland: A wetland characterized by woody vegetation less than 6 m (19.7') tall. Examples: pocosins and shrub swamps.

Forested Wetland: A wetland characterized by woody vegetation more than 6 m (19.7') tall. Examples: swamps and pine flatwoods.

In the following sections we discuss a number of wetland types. The types of wetlands discussed here are often easy to distinguish, and the names for these wetlands are commonly used by non-scientists. However, it is important to remember that identification of habitat types is nowhere near cut and dry. In reality, most wetlands are mosaics or complexes of many different habitat types. For example, freshwater marshes often contain areas of shrubby wetland, and many swamps have gaps in their canopy that allow shrubs and marsh vegetation to flourish. The following wetland types are only simple categories useful in discussing associations of plants and animals found in wetlands and furthering your understanding of the story of a wetland seen before you. As with any classification of the natural world, these wetland types can be endlessly divided into subtypes based on dominant plant species, pH, water regime, and various other characteristics. We provide brief discussions of the way these wetland types can be further divided; however, you should look into more regional publications to find out what wetland types exist in your area. Seeking out unique wetland types and the animals and plants that inhabit them can be a fascinating way to explore the natural world.

WETLAND TYPES
Human-made Wetlands

Throughout much of the country, the most common types of wetlands that people encounter have been created by humans. These include roadside ditches, rain gardens, lake fringes, farm pond fringes, stormwater retention basins, and many other areas. These habitats typically have plants and animals that do well in disturbed situations, and are often home to invasive plants introduced from other countries. Most human-made wetlands have

A small wetland designed to absorb stormwater.

Cranberry beds in the Great Lakes region.

emergent vegetation and shrubs, but some are forested. Common plants include cattails, rushes, bulrushes, sedges, common reeds, and other species of emergent plants and shrubs. Animals that are tolerant of turbidity and pollution, such as mosquitofish, fly larvae, and certain snails, can be common in the most marginal of these habitats (such as roadside ditches).

Certain human-made wetlands serve important functions for both people and wildlife. Across our urban landscape, stormwater ponds store water that would otherwise flood our streets and buildings. In a few places, human-made wetlands are used to harvest crops, such as cranberries and wildrice. Some wetlands can even replace some of the habitat that has been lost to the march of "progress." High-quality human-made wetlands mimic the function of natural lakes, vernal pools, swamps, and marshes, and these areas may be home to plants and animals more typical of the wetland types described below.

Pond/Lake Fringe

Ponds and lakes may be formed by glaciers, ancient ocean currents, karst topography, river oxbow abandonment, beaver activity, human dams, human digging, or other means. The center of these features often consists of open water that is permanent and too deep for rooted vegetation to grow, but in more shallow areas and at the edges a wetland fringe often grows. The vegetation here is similar to a marsh or shrub swamp. There may even be backwater areas of swamp, bog, or other wetland types. Pond/lake fringes are some of the best places to see plant zonation illustrated (see pages 13–14). You may see submerged, rooted floating, emergent, scrub-shrub, and forested wetland vegetation at the edge of a single lake. The fish community is not limited to species that can withstand low oxygen because during high temperatures (which deplete oxygen) fish can retreat to the cool depths of the lake or pond. True frogs, cricket frogs, and toads are common along the banks, as are pond slider turtles, painted turtles, and water snakes. Waterfowl, wading birds, muskrats, beavers, and mink may also be common. A colorful array of dragonflies can often be seen along pond/lake fringes.

Freshwater Marshes

Marshes are dominated by herbaceous plants. Freshwater marshes are generally found where flooding, fire, or other disturbances prevent woody vegetation from becoming dominant. Surface water, or at least saturated soil, is often present throughout the year. Marsh vegetation consists mostly of

A lake fringe.

A prairie pothole.

The Everglades.

emergent grasses, sedges, rushes, and forbs. Common native plants include broadleaf cattail, yellow pond-lily, bur-reeds, bulrushes, and many other sun-loving species. Cattails are perhaps the most ubiquitous freshwater marsh plant; however, other plants dominate marshes in certain areas. A marsh in your area may be dominated by monocultures of one plant or a diverse mixture of emergent species.

A variety of animals also inhabit marshes. Mind-boggling numbers of waterfowl, wading birds, shorebirds, rails, and songbirds inhabit marshes at certain times of the year. Muskrats, mink, and many small mammal species are characteristic of these habitats. A huge variety of reptiles and amphibians can also be found in marshes or along their fringes; however, several species, such as the eastern massasauga rattlesnake, have become scarce because many marshes have been converted to agricultural land.

There are many different types of marshes. For example, on the northern plains, prairie potholes are the most common type of marsh and are usually filled with cattails and other grasses. In southern Florida the Everglades dominate the landscape with huge expanses of sawgrass. Even within a single landscape there are different types of marshlike plant communities. In areas with saturated soil but no standing water a wet meadow may form. These damp communities are often dominated by sedges, in which case they are called sedge meadows. In deeper areas cattails may dominate the marsh, and in still deeper areas submerged plants may be most common. Many areas with marshy vegetation are actually fens fed by seeping groundwater (see the bog/fen section on page 26).

Few people realize that much of the Midwest was once covered with vast marshes equal to the Everglades in grandeur. Ditches, channelized streams, and networks of buried drainage tiles drained vast areas of the Midwest. Today the Midwest has some of the most fertile farmland in the world.

Northern lake.

A freshwater marsh in New England.

However, it came at the cost of millions of acres of marsh that were once breeding grounds for unfathomable numbers of waterfowl and home to many now-rare plants and animals.

Relatively large examples of natural freshwater marshes still exist along our coasts and in some of the ancient glacial lakes of northern states. Throughout much of the country this wetland type occurs in old strip mine depressions, at the edges of lakes, and on our wildlife refuges where specially designed impoundments (called moist soil units) mimic natural marshes.

In addition to the agricultural drainage that has already eliminated many natural marshes, freshwater marshes are in danger from invasive plants. Common reed, hybrid cattails, and reed canarygrass are just a few of the plants that tend to take over marshes, smothering native plants and making the marsh too thick for certain wildlife species.

Vernal Pools

Vernal pools typically form in small woodland depressions. They are usually filled by rains, but some receive water that overflows from nearby streams.

Sun-loving, obligate wetland plants, such as cattails and bulrushes, are often absent from vernal pools because they can be found in the deep shade of woodlands.

In the summer, a vernal pool may simply be a concave area with sparse vegetation and water-stained leaves, or there may be a thick growth of some plant that is tolerant of moist soils.

Vernal pools usually dry up in the summer, which means they don't naturally contain fish. This is essential to the many amphibian species that lay their eggs in vernal pools where their larvae can develop into adults without being eaten by fish. Vernal pools often contain caddisfly larvae, various predaceous beetles, worms, fingernail clams, and many microcrustaceans that are essential foods for tiny salamander larvae.

In fall, these areas usually fill with water and become habitat for certain amphibians. Vernal pools are essential for eastern newts, chorus frogs, and many species of mole salamanders (*Ambystoma* spp.).

A vernal pool.

Bog/Fen Systems

Bogs and fens are lumped together here because they are both types of peat-lands (areas where organic matter builds up over time to form spongy deposits of peat). They can also have some of the same plant species and are often confused with each other. Peatlands can include areas that are technically fens and other areas that are bogs.

True bogs are usually found in isolated depressions with very little inflow of groundwater. Bogs receive most of their water from rainfall, which makes them acidic and ombrotrophic (having mineral-poor water that comes mostly from rainwater). In contrast, fens receive a substantial amount of inflow from groundwater, are neutral or basic in PH, and are minerotrophic (having mineral-rich water that comes from groundwater).

"Bog" is a term that is often used incorrectly when it comes to wetlands. Many wet areas are informally referred to as "boggy," and some fens have even been named bogs on maps. While fens tend to have marshy vegetation such as grasses and rushes, most bogs have spongy areas of sphagnum moss, which can build up over time into poorly decomposed layers of organic matter called peat. This un-decomposed material provides few nutrients to plants, so bog vegetation is often stunted. Carnivorous plants that trap small invertebrates to obtain nutrients are often present. Acid-loving plants are also usually present, including many species of shrubs in the Heath family

A black spruce bog in the Great Lakes region.

A bog in the southeastern coastal plain.

(Ericaceae), certain ferns, and many orchids. There is great variation between different types of bogs and fens, and the amount of terminology available for classifying each is therefore immense. Wetland scientists have been coining terminology for peatlands for more than a century.

Many of the bog and fen communities found in northern Europe and Asia are similar to ones found in northern North America. Bogs and fens are very common in our northern states, especially in the Great Lakes region and parts of Maine. Many of them occupy the margins of existing lakes or the depressions left behind by ancient lakes. Dominant tree species usually include black spruce, tamarack, and/or white cedar. Ericaceous shrubs, such as Labrador tea, leatherleaf, bog rosemary, sheep laurel, cranberry, and blueberry are common, as are sphagnum moss, pitcherplants, sundews, and a variety of sedges. The extensive peatlands of the north are often called patterned peatlands because their surfaces are marked with a series of features. For instance, patterned peatlands sometimes have an alternating pattern of flarks (mud-bottomed areas with standing water and aquatic plants) and strings (narrow low ridges covered in bog or fen vegetation).

Southern bogs are found in relatively flat areas and large depressions such as Carolina bays (depressions thought to have been created by ancient ocean currents). They can share many of the same species found in northern bogs, but are generally more speciose. For instance, there is one species of pitcherplant found in northern bogs, but nine species found throughout southeastern bogs.

Appalachian Mountain bogs are a particularly diverse, rare, and sensitive group of wetland types. While they are typically referred to as mountain or montane bogs, many of these wetlands receive groundwater, so they are actually fens. They generally form in small depressions on mountain slopes or in flat stream valleys. Beavers can be important in maintaining this wetland community. Because of cool temperatures found at high elevations, southern

A montane bog in the southern Appalachians.

A fen in the Midwest.

A pocosin.

Appalachian Mountain bogs can share many of the same species found in bogs of northern states.

Bog/fen systems are filled with interesting plant and animal life. Carnivorous plants, flowering shrubs, orchids, and globally rare plants can be found in these habitats. Animals ranging from moose and beaver to rare bog turtles and Pine Barrens treefrogs also make their homes here. Throughout the northern states and southeastern coastal plain these habitats can be quite extensive; however, in much of the rest of the eastern U.S., bogs and fens are like tiny islands of habitat for rare plants and animals.

Shrub Swamps

Shrub swamps often occur where conditions are too wet or too nutrient-poor for forested swamps to develop. Some types of shrub swamp are part of a larger wetland complex. They may be found adjacent to marshes, in swamp canopy openings, along the fringes of lakes, or in shallow depressions. Bottomland sloughs and stream valleys that have been dammed by beavers often develop shrub swamp areas.

In northern states, buttonbush, swamp loosestrife, and sweetgale are common in shrub swamps. Along the coasts, wax myrtle and eastern baccharis are often dominant shrubs in these wetlands. In deep southern states, fetterbush, inkberry, and other evergreen shrubs often predominate. Throughout the southeastern coastal plain, the pocosin is a major type of shrub swamp. Pocosins usually have a thick growth of evergreen shrubs and greenbrier, often with a sparse canopy of loblolly, longleaf, or pond pine.

Under the USFWS wetland classification system, these wetlands are referred to as scrub-shrub wetlands. However, this term can also be used to describe areas filled with saplings and shrubs, such as forested wetlands that are recovering from clear-cutting.

Pine Savannah/Flatwoods

The pine forests of the southeastern coastal plain go by many names and can be separated into a gradient of many distinct plant communities. They are lumped together here for ease of discussion. These are forested wetlands where pine species such as loblolly pine are the dominant canopy trees. Many of these forests are underlain by sandy soils, and water may seep to the surface or become trapped by an underlying layer of clay or rock. During the dry season it can be very challenging to determine what areas are actually wetlands within a southern pine forest. Soil indicators, such as dark organic layers and dark/light-streaked sandy soils, are essential to determine if a pine forest meets the technical definition of a wetland.

Fire is an important part of wet pine savannahs/flatwoods and the surrounding landscape. In many of these forests, fire regenerates the pines and maintains an open understory. Semi-evergreen trees and shrubs, including bay trees, water oak, fetterbush, blueberry, huckleberry, wax myrtle, and various other shrubs are common in the understory. The wettest areas, often occupying depressions with large buildups of organic matter, are dominated

A southern wet pine flatwoods.

by a thick undergrowth of evergreen broadleaf shrubs with scattered pond pines in the overstory (see pocosin, under the shrub swamps section). Pine savannahs/flatwoods can have a very high diversity of plants, insects, reptiles, amphibians, mammals, and birds.

Swamps

A swamp is most simply defined as a forested wetland. The cypress/tupelo swamps of the Southeast are iconic American wetlands. The buttressed trunks and boughs laden with Spanish moss are familiar to most people, even if they have only seen them in movies. These habitats may vary from the semi-permanently flooded cypress/water tupelo swamp to the more seasonally inundated areas canopied by oaks, bay trees, swamp tupelo, and red maples. These wetlands are often found in abandoned sections of river channel, in other floodplain depressions, or along the

A southern swamp.

A midwestern bottomland hardwood swamp.

margins of sprawling rivers. Southern swamps are essential wintering and migrating habitat for waterfowl. Other common species include prothonotary warblers, American alligators, anhingas, wood ducks, cottonmouths, and barred owls.

Northern states also have their share of forested wetlands. Northern swamps are often found in bottomlands adjacent to rivers and along the fringes of lakes and sluggish streams. Red maples, pin oaks, black ash, green ash, white cedar, black spruce, and other northern wetland trees are common in this community, and some of these wetlands can also be called bogs or bog forests. In some areas trees that normally inhabit uplands, such as eastern hemlock and white pine, may be dominant in northern swamps. Common animals include beavers, river otters, wood ducks, and barred owls.

Estuaries

An estuary is a partly enclosed area where fresh water from rivers and streams mixes with tidal salt water from the ocean (the mixed water is called brackish water). Often, barrier islands separate estuaries from the wave action of the open ocean. The estuaries of our Atlantic and Gulf coasts contain a variety of wetland types. Some areas are mostly open water with extensive beds of submerged aquatic vegetation. Other areas are salt marshes where species like smooth cordgrass, black needlerush, and glasswort flourish. Upstream of salt marshes, less salt-tolerant species thrive in brackish marshes and shrub swamps. Still farther upstream, many freshwater wetlands are influenced by high tides that push fresh water backward up rivers

A salt marsh mudflat exposed at low tide.

A coastal salt marsh.

A mangrove in southern Florida.

and tidal creeks. The most salt-tolerant species are found in the lower salt marsh where plants are constantly flooded with salty water and in salt pannes (areas where brackish water collects and evaporates, eventually producing very salty soils).

Mangroves

The word mangrove is a name for both the overall habitat type and the tree species that make up the habitat. In the U.S., mangroves are primarily limited to the Florida coast and scattered locations along the Gulf of Mexico. The many tropical plants and animals of these environs are not well represented in this guide because they occupy a relatively small part of the country; however, mangrove ecology is fascinating and a discussion of how mangroves build land can be found in the chapter 5 section about mangroves. Mangroves are filled with unique wildlife, and many of our more northern water birds spend the winter in these environs.

PHYSIOGRAPHIC REGIONS

Across the U.S. we can recognize regions that have similar characteristics in terms of climate, geology, and often land use. For instance, much of our southeastern U.S. consists of a flat, sandy coastal plain, while our mountains and piedmont have great changes in elevation and are often rocky. For this reason, the U.S. Army Corps of Engineers has developed different guides and lists of indicators for delineating wetlands in different physiographic regions. These physiographic regions are useful when attempting to understand the geologic history of an area and what types of wetlands are most common in the region. Throughout the eastern U.S. there are five major regions:

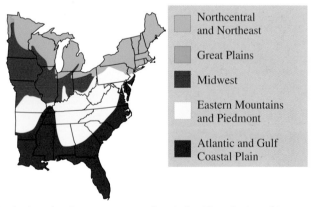

Northcentral and Northeast

Great Plains

Midwest

Eastern Mountains and Piedmont

Atlantic and Gulf Coastal Plain

Wetlands within the same region are often similar. These physiographic regions are used to identify areas with similar soils, topography, climate, and other physical characteristics.

Northcentral and Northeast: An area with many wetlands occupying glacially formed depressions. Many of our great northern forested wetlands are here. Bogs, fens, pond/lake fringes, northern swamps, shrub swamps, and marshes are common. Tidally influenced wetlands are found along the coasts of the Atlantic Ocean and Great Lakes, and estuarine wetlands are present along the Atlantic Coast.

Midwest: Once the home of vast prairie marshes but now mostly drained and used for row crop agriculture. Remnant marshes, bogs, fens, northern swamps, shrub swamps, and human-made wetlands can still be found.

Great Plains: This region barely enters the area covered by this book. It was once covered in a vast, tallgrass prairie; however, it is now mostly farmland. Prairie potholes and other types of marshes are common in this area, along with human-made wetlands.

Eastern Mountains and Piedmont: Many of the wetlands in this region are small and isolated. Small woodland seeps, bogs, and marshes occur occasionally, and larger wetlands occur near rivers, beaver pond complexes, human-made reservoirs, and a few natural lakes. Species diversity in much of this area is very high.

Atlantic and Gulf Coastal Plain: The coastal plain is home to vast areas of southern swamp and pine savannahs/flatwoods. There are also many shrub swamps, marshes, tidal wetlands, and coastal estuarine wetlands. Species diversity in this region is very high.

CHAPTER 4

Studying Wetlands

Exploring wetlands can be a challenging and interesting adventure. Indeed, one can even make a career out of delineating and restoring wetlands. In this chapter we will skim the surface of the equipment and techniques available to wetland ecologists.

Traveling in wetlands can be the biggest challenge many naturalists face. Some areas have developed boardwalks, allowing one to penetrate the heart of swamps and bogs while remaining suspended above the muck. This makes travel easier and prevents some small, fragile wetlands from being destroyed by human traffic. We would encourage readers never to pass up the chance to check out a wetland boardwalk. Kayak trips into the heart of a swamp or marsh are also extremely good ways to explore such wetlands, as long as you don't get lost. The rest of the time, waterproof waders and boots are the wetland naturalist's best friends.

Before going out to look at wetlands, a number of tools can give you a better idea of what you're getting into. Today, aerial photographs are so readily available that it is possible to gain an overhead view with your phone of the wetland in which you'll be standing. Aerial photos can show low areas with standing water, canopy gaps, and changes in vegetation. Exploring a natural area via an aerial photograph before heading out can help you to find wetlands more easily, determine the easiest way to access them, and identify different habitat types you may want to visit.

Another old standby for studying wetlands is the topographic map. These maps can help you to identify depressions, stream valleys, springs, and other likely wetland locations. Many marshes and swamps are also denoted on these maps. Other, more specialized maps can be indispensable to the wetland ecologist as well. National Wetland Inventory (NWI) maps show locations of many (but not all) wetlands and can help you find hidden ponds and swamps. Soil mapping can be used to identify areas that are frequently flooded and areas that were once wetlands before they were drained. The U.S. Department of Agriculture (USDA) Natural Resource Conservation Service (NRCS) maintains soil mapping and lists of soils that are hydric, or at least soils that once were hydric.

Obtaining all of these different types of maps once required visits to libraries or mail orders. Today, most of these maps can be downloaded after a simple internet search, and many can be opened using a smartphone. Some programs such as Google Earth can be used to overlay soils mapping, wetland mapping, stream lines, and other information directly onto aerial photos (from multiple years) of the wetland you are exploring.

As with any natural history endeavor, your best tools for studying wetland ecology are your senses and a field notebook to record your experiences in words and drawings. Binoculars, a camera, and other typical naturalist field gear are also very valuable for wetland explorations; however, there are a couple of items that are indispensable. A good dipnet can be essential—if you're not looking at what's below the water, you may be seeing only half of a wetland's story (or less). Running a dipnet through the leaves and vegetation in almost any type of wetland will provide you with a view of the many hidden and fascinating creatures living below the surface. A dipnet often works better than larger seines because it is not as likely to be snagged on sticks and logs. A clear jar, Ziploc bag, small aquarium, or other clear viewing device is also essential for getting a better look at invertebrates, fish, salamander larvae, and other creatures.

A second piece of equipment that is essential for understanding a wetland is some sort of digging tool. Wetland scientists often carry soil probes or augers for quick glimpses of soil in the field. One of the best tools is a spade, which can be used to slice large sections of soil and gain a more complete picture of the organic layers, depletions, and concentrations used to identify wetland soils. In a pinch, even a large knife can work for this purpose.

Also, a soil color chart is an essential tool for determining soil color changes that occur when an area is flooded for a prolonged period (see the soil indicators section in chapter 5). Many wetland scientists favor the Munsell Soil Color Chart, but other types are also available.

Terrariums and aquariums can be very interesting forums for studying wetland plants and creatures. Wetlands often have murky or tannin-stained water, whereas the clear water of your aquarium provides easy viewing of behaviors that would be missed in the wild. Many wetland fish and invertebrates are well suited to aquarium life. Their tolerance of low oxygen levels and low currents makes setting up a wetland aquarium simple. Generally, a few aquatic plants, an air stone, and a plant light are all you need to provide a home for wetland creatures. Some of our native wetland fish, such as blackbanded

Determining soil color with a color chart.

An aquarium can be an excellent place to study many wetland creatures.

sunfish, bluespotted sunfish, swamp darters, and many killifish and topminnows, can even be ordered from professional breeders.

We should be very clear that taking any organism from a nature preserve or protected area is wrong, as is taking animals that are rare, protected by law, or ill suited to captivity. In contrast, raising tadpoles from a backyard puddle that is doomed to dry out anyway is an almost magical experience that can teach you and/or your children valuable things. If you bring fish, plants, or other organisms into your aquarium, it is essential that you never release them in a different place from where you found them. In most cases, it is better not to return organisms into the wild at all. It may seem like the humane thing to do, but animals can carry disease, parasites, and invasive species back into wild habitats, which will kill many more animals. It is illegal to capture and/or keep certain wild animal species in an aquarium in many places, so carefully check the regulations in your area.

CHAPTER 5

Identification Guide

The following chapter is the heart of this field guide. The various sections will help you to identify physical indicators that tell you an area is a wetland, and to identify some of the plants and animals that make each wetland so unique. The U.S. Army Corps of Engineers (USACE) provides materials for completing the technical process of delineating wetlands (see the references section). While this guide does give generalized descriptions of some indicators used by the USACE, our primary goal is to provide understanding to the general public and supplementary information on identifying wetland species—not to recreate the USACE wetland delineation manuals.

HYDROLOGY INDICATORS

Wetlands have standing water or saturated soils for a substantial part of the year; however, a wetland can also be dry for months at a time. In general, most wetlands are flooded or saturated for more than two weeks during the growing season. The following section will help you to identify areas with wetland hydrology even when they are bone dry. Obviously, standing water and soil saturation are indicators of wetland hydrology, but if an area only floods for a day after a large storm, it is unlikely that this area will develop true wetland characteristics. Therefore, it is important to look for other indications of long-term inundation by water.

Understanding how water drains to or from an area is essential to knowing why an area is or is not a wetland. Understanding the local topography will help you to form an idea of how long water stands in the area. Is the local topography bowl shaped? Is the area in the floodplain of a stream? Is there a beaver dam or clogged culvert downstream? These kinds of questions, many of which can be answered with the aid of a topographic map or aerial photographs, will help you to identify the sources of water filling a potential wetland.

Watermarks

Watermarks are fairly self-explanatory. These are discolorations formed by standing water. They are often found as rings around trees or as sections of discoloration along embankments, rocks, or other fixed objects. However, a short-term flood can form watermarks in areas that do not stay wet long enough to become wetlands. An "ordinary high watermark" is an important indicator that water is found in an area on a regular basis. This happens

Watermarks.

Right: Moss trim line.

when water stays in an area long enough to kill the terrestrial vegetation. There is often a distinct line to which water typically extends.

Deposits

Wetland water carries a variety of minerals, tiny suspended particles, and large organic matter. When water dries or recedes, these things are often left deposited where the water was standing. Sediment is deposited on vegetation, fallen leaves, and debris. Larger deposits of leaves, sticks, and debris can often be seen at the upper limit of flooding or snagged by trees where water has flowed. Iron, which is typically leached from soils in wetland areas, is often seen deposited at the soil surface in saturated or recently dried wetland soils.

Algal Crust or Aquatic Fauna/Flora

A number of aquatic plants and animals can be left behind when a wetland dries. Often the most ubiquitous indicator is a film of algae that has dried over the soil surface and hangs in dried mats from vegetation. The presence of true aquatic vascular plants (plants that are typically submerged in or floating on water) is another indicator. Dead aquatic invertebrates are often lying around—particularly the shells of aquatic snails. The exuviae of aquatic

Iron deposit.

Algal mat.

insects such as dragonflies may be hanging from vegetation. In some areas that have recently dried there may be stressed tadpoles or salamander larvae confined to small pools or lying dried on the soil surface. In extreme droughts there may even be dead fish lying around.

Soil cracks and stunted/absent vegetation.

Left: Water-stained leaves.

Water-Stained Leaves
When fallen leaves have been submerged for a while they take on a darker color, and even when they dry, a grayish cast remains. Water-stained leaves indicating wetland hydrology will be obviously darker or grayer than leaves on nearby uplands that have not been inundated.

Secondary Hydrology Indicators
In addition to the primary indicators of wetland hydrology listed above, there are also several secondary indicators. Two or more secondary indicators are usually required to be confident that an area has wetland hydrology. Cracked soil, stunted vegetation, crayfish barrows, drainage patterns, and many other characteristics can be secondary indicators.

Other Indicators
Several hydrology indicators are also hydric soil indicators and therefore are covered in the following soils section. These include the presence of muck,

oxidized root channels, and soil/organic material that smells like sulphur (rotten eggs). If you find one of these, and if the area is also dominated by wetland plants, then you know that you have found a wetland.

SOIL INDICATORS

Soils can tell the skilled observer many things about the hydrology and history of a wetland. Understanding the processes that make soils change when they are submerged is essential to being able to identify a wetland. After being submerged for long periods of time, certain characteristics of soil begin to change. These changes are important indicators of hydric soil, and hydric soil indicators are among the most important and scientifically valid means of wetland delineation that we have. Still, we recognize that the average person does not get terribly excited about "dirt," and this section is quite short. Looking at wetland soils can be like looking into a window that shows the wetland's geological—and sometimes its seasonal—history. If that intrigues you, then we would encourage you to delve further into the many free resources available on hydric soils from the USDA and USACE.

Soil indicators vary depending on what type of soil was there to begin with and how long the area is saturated. For instance, brownish loam or clay soils may turn gray with orange blotches, while light-colored, sandy soils tend to gain a buildup of dark-colored organic material under hydric conditions.

When soil and organic matter are submerged in water, oxygen is very slow in diffusing from the atmosphere into these substrates. Microbes (bacteria) and other organisms quickly use up the oxygen that is present, and these aerobic organisms are replaced by microbes that can live in an anaerobic (no oxygen) environment. Anaerobic microbes don't need air for respiration, and instead their survival involves other kinds of chemical reactions (called oxidation-reduction or redox reactions). These redox reactions leave a number of telltale features in the soil (called redoximorphic features), many of which can be observed with the naked eye.

As a result of redox reactions, certain elements are changed to different forms. Nitrate, manganese, iron, sulphur, and carbon are changed to forms that are more water soluble. These changes first become apparent to us when manganese and iron are reduced (i.e., undergo redox reactions) to soluble forms that can be transported along with water as it moves through the soil. The areas from which these elements are removed are left gray and are called "redox depletions"; the areas to which they are transported are called "redox concentrations." Redox concentrations form orange, blackish, or purple mottles, and these elements often concentrate where oxygen is present, such as along living roots and at the soil surface during dry periods. Later, after the soil has been submerged for a long time (usually a month or more), sulphur and carbon may be reduced. This becomes apparent to us in the form of gas that smells like rotten eggs (hydrogen sulfide) and methane (a reduced form of carbon) bubbles that emerge from the bottom of the wetland when it is disturbed.

In addition to soil brightness and odor changes, there is another result of the anaerobic conditions found in wetlands. Anaerobic microbes are not as efficient at breaking down organic matter; therefore, there is often a buildup of un-decomposed organic matter. This may result in layers of muck, peat, and other organic material that build up over time.

Determining whether or not a soil is hydric can be a very complicated endeavor in disturbed wetlands, sandy soils, and very flat landscapes. Often, it is useful to compare the soil of a nearby upland area that never floods to the soil found in a wetland to observe the changes in soil characteristics that occur. Typically, soil color is determined using a color chart, and the chroma (brightness) and value (how light or dark the color is) of the soil are very important. For instance, dull gray soils with a chroma of 2 or lower are often hydric soils. Below are a few of the major categories of hydric soil indicators. However, this is by no means an exhaustive list of the soil conditions that can be present in a wetland. The USACE and USDA provide materials with detailed descriptions of many distinct soil indicators. It is also important to remember that soils can retain hydric soil characteristics for a long time after being ditched or tiled; however, these areas will not usually have wetland plant communities.

Organic Layers

Distinguishing Characteristics: A buildup of organic material may occur in varying stages of decomposition because decomposition is not a very efficient process in the anaerobic environment of wetland soils. Thick organic layers occur in the wettest wetlands. Peat (also called fibric soil material) is the least broken-down type of organic layer, and is composed of three-quarters or more of identifiable fibers of organic material (leaves, stems, etc.). Muck (also called sapric soil material) is the most broken-down form of organic layer. Less than one-sixth of organic fibers are recognizable in muck and it has a greasy feeling when rubbed between the fingers. Peaty muck (also called hemic soil material) and mucky

Peat—a lot of fibrous material remaining.

A chunk of sandy wetland soil placed on nearby upland sand.

Right: Muck—most fibrous material is broken down.

peat are recognized as intermediate organic layer types.

In sandy soils, a layer of organic material on top of the sand, layers of sand grains coated with black organic matter, or streaks of darker organic matter in the soil may be hydric soil indicators.

Sulphur Odor

A sulphidic odor (smells like rotten eggs) is a dead giveaway for wetland soils. Sulphur is one of the last elements to be used by microbes under anaerobic conditions, so the smell of rotten eggs is usually only found when one disturbs the substrate in one of our wettest wetlands.

Iron oxidized along living roots.

Left: Gleyed soil.

Depletions and Concentrations

As described above, colorful elements such as iron and manganese are transported from the soil matrix under anaerobic conditions, leaving a gray soil matrix. Wherever these elements are transported, concentrations of orange, purple, brownish, and/or blackish color form. One place where these elements often concentrate is near aerated pockets in the soil, such as along the roots of living plants. The scrolling orange lines produced along oxidized root channels are an excellent indicator of wetland soils and hydrology. Soils that have been submerged for the most extensive periods of time often have a grayish-blue caste, called gley. These gleyed soils can be found below the organic matter in many ponds and other permanently flooded soils.

Plants

This guide includes a substantial number of plants for several good reasons. Plants are the basis for many wetland classification systems (see chapter 3), and they are extremely important indicators of whether a questionable area is actually a wetland or not. Wetland plants display a fascinating array of adaptations for dealing with low-oxygen soil, frequent flooding, and sometimes low-nutrient conditions. In addition, there are many species that are only found in particular kinds of wetlands, and many animals require certain plants to survive.

In 1988, the U.S. Fish and Wildlife Service produced a list of plants that occur in wetlands, and each plant was given an indicator value based on experts' opinions of how indicative it was of wetland conditions. Recently, administration of this list was transferred to the USACE and plant indicator statuses were updated; however, the basic categories are still the same. In general, a plant that is almost always found growing in wetlands is considered to be an obligate wetland plant, while a plant that can grow either in uplands or wetlands is a facultative plant. Some plants such as red maple that are very common in certain kinds of wetlands are also very common on upland sites in other parts of the country. Different lists are available for various physiographic regions of the U.S. (see the physiographic regions map on page 34) because certain plants may grow in wetlands in one part of the country, but commonly grow in uplands elsewhere. We have included the most common status for each plant in the species descriptions. The possible statuses and their definitions are listed below.

OBL Obligate Wetland plant: Almost always occurs in wetlands.
FACW Facultative Wetland plant: Usually occurs in wetlands, but occasionally found in uplands.
FAC Facultative plant: Equally likely to be found in wetlands and uplands.
FACU Facultative Upland plant: Usually occurs in uplands, but occasionally found in wetlands.
UPL Obligate Upland plant: Almost always occurs in uplands. (The only reason it is in the list of wetland plants is because it occurs in wetlands in another region.)

NOTES ON ORGANIZATION

Plants in this guide are grouped by flower color. Within colors, plants are grouped by family. We have elected to cover many of the plants at the genus level, especially if no species is clearly more abundant than the other members of the genus over the majority of the eastern U.S. We did this because there are so many plant species found in wetlands, and many closely related plants have the same wetland indicator status.

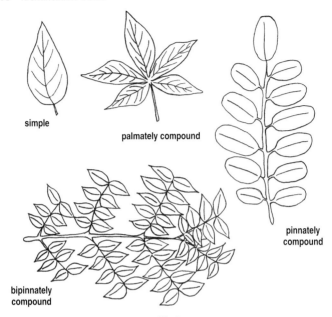

simple

palmately compound

pinnately compound

bipinnately compound

Common types of leaf arrangement.

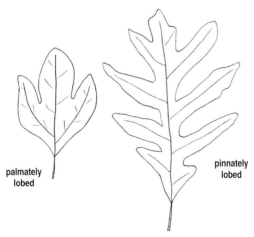

palmately lobed

pinnately lobed

Common types of leaf margins.

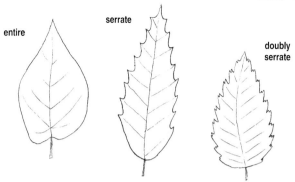

entire

serrate

doubly serrate

Common types of leaf margins.

Pondweeds   *(Potamogeton* spp.)

Above left:
Longleaf pondweed
(P. nodosus).

Left: Curly pondweed
(P. crispus).

Distinguishing Characteristics: Rooted in the bottom and usually submerged in less than 2 m (6.6') of water; height up to 2 m. The submerged leaves of many species of pondweeds are superficially similar to several other types of aquatic vascular plants and algae. The rather nondescript, submerged leaves are typically ribbon or threadlike, often branched, parallel-veined, and alternate. Unlike some very similar submerged plants, such as wigeon grass (*Ruppia* spp.) and other types of pondweeds, *Potamogeton* species have stipules that are either free from the leaf blade or attached along less than half of the stipule. Some species have larger leaves that float on the water surface.

Habitat and Remarks: Perennial. Native. OBL. About 42 species are native to the eastern U.S. Only one major invasive exotic species, curly pondweed (*P. crispus*), is in most of our area. The leaves and achenes are extremely important foods for waterfowl, and are also eaten by rails, shorebirds, muskrats, and even moose. The roots help to stabilize sediment, and the leaves provide important cover for many fish and invertebrates.

Coontail   *(Ceratophyllum demersum)*

Distinguishing Characteristics: Submerged growth up to about 4 m (13') long. The tight whorls of thin leaves give branches of this plant the shape of a raccoon's tail. Each leaf is very finely pointed and toothed only along 1 edge. These unique leaves separate coontail from superficially similar submerged plants such as Eurasian watermilfoil (*Myriophyllum spicatum*). Muskgrass (*Chara* spp.) is similar, but it is actually an algae and has a distinctive garlic/skunk-like odor when crushed. There are 2 other species of *Ceratophyllum*, but they have weaker leaves that split 3 to 4 times, whereas the leaves of coontail split only 1 to 2 times.

Habitat and Remarks: Perennial. Native. OBL. Also known as hornwort, this plant can be found in a variety of wetlands including marshes, swamps, pond fringes, and other semi-permanent water. Although it is often attached to the substrate, coontail can live and grow in a completely free-floating state and does well in aquariums. While tangled mats of coontail may be the bane of many fishermen, its beds form dense underwater growth that creates hiding places for many fish and a place for invertebrates to cling. This species is readily eaten by many ducks, which likely enjoy the vegetation and the loads of invertebrates that come attached to it.

Watermilfoil *(Myriophyllum spp.)*

Eurasian watermilfoil
(M. spicatum).

Distinguishing Characteristics: Submerged growth reaching more than 6 m (20'). Submerged plant, usually with whorls of 3 or 4 pinnate feather-like leaves at each node (sometimes 2 opposite leaves). These compound leaves separate watermilfoils from superficially similar species such as coontail. Unfortunately, non-native invasive species are the most common water-milfoils in many areas. Unlike native watermilfoil species, Eurasian water-milfoil (*M. spicatum*) leaves relax and fall against the main stem when the plant is lifted from the water. Also, Eurasian watermilfoil leaves typically have more than 10 pairs of leaflets per feather-like leaf, whereas native species typically have fewer than 10 pairs. Parrot's feather (*M. aquaticum*) is a similar invasive species, but it often has erect leaves that stick up out of the water (see photo).

Parrot's feather (M. aquaticum).

Habitat and Remarks: Perennial. Many species are invasive exotics. OBL. The exotic species produce large, choking beds of vegetation that crowd out native species. Watermilfoils favor nutrient-rich waters with low turbidity, but can grow under a variety of conditions. They produce seed, but can also produce new plants from small sections of stem. The plant is capable of breaking off and releasing small sections of stem even if not disturbed by an outside force such as waterfowl or human activity. Herbicide application may be the only effective means of eradication, although mechanical removal of large beds has been used. It is important to avoid spreading even tiny pieces of non-native species from one waterbody to another.

PLANTS

Sphagnum Moss   *(Sphagnum spp.)*

Sphagnum moss in various colors and wetness stages.

Distinguishing Characteristics: Height of living plant up to 25 cm (9.8"). Sphagnum moss species often form a very spongy green or reddish carpet on the floor of bogs. Mosses are non-vascular plants and lack the highly differentiated tissues of vascular plants (stem, leaves, and roots). Instead, the entire plant consists of spongy tissue attached to substrate via hair-like rhizoids. It might be mistaken for club-mosses (Lycopodiaceae), spike-mosses (Selaginellaceae), or other non-vascular mosses (Bryophyta). In most of the eastern U.S., sphagnum species have a greater tendency to form thick mats in wetlands than the other "mosses" listed above. Identification of individual species of sphagnum requires a microscope and includes cellular characteristics.

Habitat and Remarks: About 70 species native to the U.S. While sphagnum species are not on the official lists of wetland indicator plants, they are a fundamental part of certain types of wetlands. Also known as peat mosses, sphagnum species are most often associated with bogs, where they can form mats of organic material (peat) several meters thick. Sphagnum mosses resist decay via several methods. They live in wetlands where anaerobic conditions prevent efficient decomposition; they contain phenolic compounds (such as sphagnol) that inhibit the growth of microbes; and they have the ability to acidify their environment by taking up cations (such as calcium and magnesium) and releasing hydrogen ions. Because of their absorbent and antimicrobial qualities, sphagnum mosses have been used in baby diapers and bandages.

Horsetail   *(Equisetum spp.)*

Distinguishing Characteristics: Height up to 0.9 m (3'). Distinctive group of plants that may produce 2 types of stems. One type (the fertile stem) is cylindrical, hollow, easily pulled apart into short sections, and tipped with a strobilus that produces spores. The other stem type (sterile stem) has whorls of thin leaves coming from each node. Some species, such as scouring rush horsetail (*E. hyemale*), only produce fertile stems, and some, such as field horsetail (*E. arvense*), produce both types. There are about 11 species and several more hybrids of horsetail in the eastern U.S.

Habitat and Remarks: Perennial. Native. FAC-OBL depending on species. *Equisetum* is the only surviving genus of a group of plants that once dominated primitive forests. They may be found in marshes, swamps, fens, bog margins, pond/lake fringes, and some disturbed wetlands. Horsetails reproduce through spores, but also expand the size of their colony by pushing new stems up from underground rhizomes. The stems contain silicates, which give them a sandpapery feel. A handful of these plants can be used as a scouring pad for dishes, or they may be dried and used as fine-grain sandpaper. Several species make striking additions to rain gardens and other landscaped wetlands.

Glassworts *(Salicornia* spp.)*

*Virginia glasswort
(S. depressa).*

Distinguishing Characteristics: Height commonly up to 50 cm (20"). The leaves are reduced to tiny scales, and these plants appear to be made up of jointed, succulent, green stems approximately 0.6 cm (0.25") in diameter. They often turn reddish, especially in fall. There are 2 common eastern species. Virginia glasswort (*S. depressa*) has joints that are longer than they are wide, while dwarf saltwort (*S. bigelovii*) has joints that are wider than they are long (or nearly so). Perennial glasswort (*Sarcocornia perennis*) is similar, but has a woody stem.

Habitat and Remarks: Annual or perennial. Native. OBL. Also known as pickleweeds and saltworts. These are very common inhabitants of salt marshes. They often form large monocultures in the upper marsh, or may be found with other salt marsh plants, such as cordgrass. This plant can be plucked and eaten fresh as a lightly salty snack. It can also be pickled or added to cooked dishes. Snow and Canada geese often graze on glassworts. There is some interest in growing these species as crops in arid areas or where only saline water is available.

Duckweed Family   (Lemnaceae)

Distinguishing Characteristics: Height up to 1 cm (0.4"). A family of tiny plants, <2 cm (0.8") in length, that float on the water's surface or sit on top of saturated mud, often reaching high enough densities to create a uniform green surface on water and often mistaken for the seeds of some larger plant. The ecology of the duckweed family is relatively similar, so they are lumped together here. Stem and leaf are indistinguishable and fused into a thallus. The 5 genera can be distinguished as follows:

Watermeal (Wolffia): 4 species in our area; has a globoid thallus without roots; <2 mm (.08") long

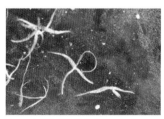

Bogmat (Wolffiella): 3 species in our area; has a linear thallus without roots; 4–14 mm (.16–.55") long

Common duckmeat (S. polyrrhiza): 1 species in our area; 7 to 21 roots per plant.

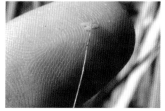

Duckweeds (Lemna): 9 species in our area; 1 root per plant

Dotted duckmeat (L. punctata): 1 species; 2 to 7 roots per plant.

Habitat and Remarks: Perennial. Both native and introduced species. OBL. This family contains the smallest flowering plants in the world—watermeal. Duckmeat is an appropriate common name for members of this family. The whole duckweed family is extremely important in the diet of waterfowl, and some species are very high in protein (almost as high as soybeans). This undoubtedly helps to support the transcontinental flights that many of our waterfowl undertake each year. Duckweed rafts often consist of several species, some of which can become a nuisance to fisherman and boaters.

Mosquito Fern *(Azolla caroliniana)*

Distinguishing Characteristics: Length up to 25 mm (1"). A red or green fern that floats on the surface of the water, with a small root hanging down from each stem. The fronds appear to be made up of small, overlapping scales and resemble a small piece of cedar leaf. In the shade these plants are green, but in the sun they turn red. Duckweeds (Lemnaceae), which also float on water, only have 1 to 3 leaves, instead of many overlapping scale-like leaves.

Habitat and Remarks: Annual. Native. OBL. Often found in swamps, sloughs, ponds, and other bodies of calm, open water. Mosquito fern is the only free-floating aquatic fern typically found in the eastern U.S. This plant may form thick mats that can reduce light penetration into the water below, but it is native to the U.S. and not typically considered to be invasive. Like other ferns it reproduces by spores, but plants also break apart to reproduce asexually. *Anabaena azollae*, a blue-green algae, is almost always found growing on this species. These 2 species have a mutualistic relationship in which the algae lives on byproducts of photosynthesis produced by the mosquito fern, and the fern receives nitrogen fixed by the algae (somewhat like the way nitrogen is fixed by symbiotic bacteria of legumes).

Eastern Marsh Fern *(Thelypteris palustris)*

Eastern marsh fern leaf margin.

Distinguishing Characteristics: Height up to 1 m (3.3'). Lance-shaped compound leaves similar to many other ferns. Margins of the leaflets are strongly curved downward. Leaves are glabrous and the rachis is finely pubescent. Leaves are deciduous. Prefers sunnier locations than most similar ferns, such as New York fern (*T. noveboracensis*).

Habitat and Remarks: Perennial. Native. OBL or FACW depending on region. Unusual among ferns for its love of open, sunny areas. This fern is most often found in sandy freshwater marshes and meadows, but it can grow along the fringes of brackish marshes, swamps, bogs, fens, and other sunny, damp habitats. It provides food and cover for many animal species, and is the only known host for the caterpillar of the marsh fern moth (*Fagitana littera*).

Cinnamon Fern *(Osmunda cinnamomea)*

Distinguishing Characteristics: Height up to 1.5 m (60"). Leaves made up of pinnae, which are cut deeply into lobes (almost bipinnate). Fertile leaves are modified into a cinnamon-colored sporophyll usually seen in late spring. Unlike Virginia chain fern (*Woodwardia virginica*), which has net venation, leaf veins extend straight from the mid-vein to the leaf edge. Might also be mistaken for ostrich fern (*Matteuccia struthiopteris*) or interrupted fern (*O. claytoniana*), but those species lack the light tan tufts of hairs that the cinnamon fern has at the base of each pinna.

Habitat and Remarks: Perennial. Native. FACW. It is typically found in swamps and along the shady fringes of bogs. It can grow in full sun as long as the soil remains wet year round. The furled sprouts or "fiddleheads" can be eaten raw in moderation or boiled briefly like spinach (just make sure not to mistake it for another plant such as poison hemlock). Deer and other animals also feed on fiddleheads.

Royal Fern   *(Osmunda regalis)*

Distinguishing Characteristics: Height up to 1.8 m (6'). An unusual-looking fern with bipinnately compound leaves composed of rounded leaflets. At first glance this species resembles some sort of flowering plant, but the fertile fronds or sporophylls reveal its true identity as a fern. They start out green and then turn brown after the spores are released. There are no ferns that closely resemble this species in the eastern U.S.

Habitat and Remarks: Perennial. Native. OBL. The royal fern is most often found in shaded wetlands such as swamps, beaver ponds, various streamside wetlands, and along the fringes of bogs. This species (or at least several very closely related species) is found on other continents, including Europe, Asia, Africa, and South America. The fibrous material crowning the rootstock of the royal fern and other *Osmunda* species (called Osmunda fiber) is used as a bedding material by orchid growers.

PLANTS

Netted Chainfern *(Woodwardia areolata)*

Distinguishing Characteristics: Height up to 46 cm (18"). The leaves of this plant do not resemble what one typically thinks of as a fern frond. Leaves are composed of about 10 pairs of pinnae with net venation and finely toothed edges. The netted chainfern is most similar to sensitive fern, which has leaflets with edges that are very wavy but not finely toothed. Sensitive fern leaves are triangular in outline because they lack the reduced lower leaflets that give netted chainfern a more ovular appearance. Sensitive fern also has very distinctive fertile fronds.

Habitat and Remarks: Perennial. Native. OBL in most regions, but FACW in eastern mountains. Netted chainfern is typically found in moist, acidic areas such as woodland seeps, swamps, and bogs. This species enjoys shade to part-sun. Like other ferns, it reproduces through spores held on the fertile fronds. In netted chainfern, the fertile fronds are thinner versions of the other fronds.

Sensitive Fern   *(Onoclea sensibilis)*

   Distinguishing Characteristics: Height up to 1 m (3.3'). Light green fern that does not resemble a "typical" fern. The sterile leaves are composed of up to 12 pairs of nearly opposite pinnae with net venation. The edges of pinnae may be very wavy but are not finely toothed, as are the leaves of netted chainfern. Pinnae of the fertile leaves are modified into very distinctive beaded structures that somewhat resemble rattlesnake rattles.

   Habitat and Remarks: Perennial. Native. FACW. The sensitive fern lives in wet meadows, wet forests, and along the margins of swamps and marshes. It is found in both shady and sunny habitats, and prefers acidic soils. Like other ferns, this species reproduces through spores, which are held in the beaded structures on the fertile fronds. Despite its name, this species is tolerant of a variety of habitat types and even occasional mowing, but it tends to wither and brown at the first hint of frost.

Spikerush (*Eleocharis* spp.)

Distinguishing Characteristics: Height up to 1 m (3.3'). Often mistaken for grasses or rushes, spikerushes are actually members of the sedge family (Cyperaceae). Unlike many other sedges, spikerush stems are round in cross section and there are no leaf blades. The leaves are reduced to tiny scales at the base of the plant, which consists almost entirely of a culm (the stem of grasslike plants) with a small, ovoid flower head at the top. Spikerushes often form dense, monospecific patches that resemble a lawn growing in much wetter places than where lawn grasses would normally survive.

Habitat and Remarks: Annual/Perennial. Over 50 species native to the eastern U.S. Most species OBL or FACW. Spikerushes typically inhabit the margins of ponds, wet meadows, marshes, fens, ditches, and other shallow wetlands. Some species are able to grow submersed under water. Some species flourish on the mudflats left by receding water. The seeds, foliage, and roots of these plants are commonly grazed upon by insects, waterfowl, and small mammals.

Carex Sedges   *(Carex* **spp.***)*

Left: *Fringed sedge (C.* crinita*).*

Right: *Gray's sedge (C.* grayi*).*

Distinguishing Characteristics: Height up to 1.5 m (5'). Grass-like plants with triangular stems. Members of the genus *Carex* are most often what is being referred to when someone mentions an unidentified sedge. Most *Carex* grow in low groupings, and resemble grasses to the untrained eye. However, members of the sedge family have a triangular stem (species in the grass and rush families have round stems). With a little practice, most people begin to identify the *Carex* sedges from a distance by their diverse and distinctive seedheads—even if they are not sure exactly which species they have encountered. The shapes of the seedhead and seeds are very important for identification of sedges. There are about 300 species of *Carex* found in the eastern U.S. Several of the more common, distinctive species are pictured here; however, even these have lookalikes too numerous to mention in the space we have available.

Tussock sedge (C. stricta*).*

Below: *Fox sedge (C.* vulpinoidea*).*

Right: *Hop sedge (C.* lupulina*).*

PLANTS

Habitat and Remarks: Perennial. Native. FACU through OBL depending on the species. *Carex* sedges are found in virtually all types of freshwater wetlands. They are the dominant plants in wetlands called sedge meadows, which are quite rare throughout most of their former range because of agricultural conversion. Look for the highest sedge diversity in sunny, shallow wetlands, but there are also several species found in the shade of forested wetlands. The seeds and shoots are eaten by a variety of birds and mammals.

Flatsedge Species   *(Cyperus* spp.)

Distinguishing Characteristics: Height up to 76 cm (2.5'). The triangular stem, which is typical of members of the sedge family (species in the grass and rush families have round stems), is very pronounced in flatsedges. The seedhead is an umbel made up of several stalks that extend from a single point. Spikelets occur at the ends of these stalks and are mostly 2-ranked (occurring in rows along 2 planes, resembling an "X" or "+" when viewed from the end of the stalk). There are many species of *Cyperus* and they are difficult to distinguish from each other, but most have this sort of seedhead, which distinguishes them from other sedges. In several cases characteristics of the roots are necessary to identify species.

Habitat and Remarks: Annual/Perennial. There are about 60 native species and 15 non-native species in the eastern U.S. FACU-OBL depending on species. Also commonly called umbrella sedge or nutsedge (because of the nut-like tubers attached to the roots of some species). *Cyperus* species are found in marshes, wet meadows, ditches, pond/lake fringes, and other sunny, moist areas. Some species are even found in lawns and other damp, disturbed areas. The "nutlets" or tubers attached to the roots of one species, yellow nutsedge (*C. strigosus*), are sweet and can be eaten raw or cooked, while the nutlets of some other species are bitter. Nutsedge seeds and tubers are eaten by rodents, waterfowl, and a variety of other birds.

Dark-Green Bulrush *(Scirpus atrovirens)*

Distinguishing Characteristics: Height up to 1.8 m (5.9'). Like other members of the sedge family, this species has a triangular stem (species in the grass and rush families have round stems), although it is somewhat more rounded than the stems of other sedges. The stem and leaves are fairly dark green and glabrous. The seedhead consists of a compound umbel. Each branch of the umbel ends in a small cluster of 6 to 26 short, dark brown, ovate spikelets.

Habitat and Remarks: Perennial. Native. OBL. This is a very common plant that is found in a variety of wet habitats including marshes, wet meadows, pond/lake fringes, and sunnier parts of forested wetlands. This species is very hardy, which makes it a good choice for wetland or stream restoration projects. The seeds of dark-green bulrush are eaten by a variety of songbirds, waterfowl, and small mammals. Some waterfowl graze on the shoots, and muskrats eat both the shoots and the roots.

Common Threesquare   *(Schoenoplectus pungens)*

Stem cross section.

Distinguishing Characteristics: Height up to 1 m (3.3'). Sturdy, strongly 3-angled stems with an inflorescence coming from the side of the stem. The stem appears to continue above the inflorescence (this is actually a bract) and ends in a slender pointed tip. *Schoenoplectus pungens* was once named *S. americanus*; however, that is now the name of a larger species that is more common along our coasts and in the western U.S.

Habitat and Remarks: Perennial. Native. OBL. Also known as basket grass, chairmaker's rush, and threesquare bulrush. This species inhabits marshes, fens, pond/lake fringes, and a variety of other wetlands over its extensive range. In some areas, particularly the Pacific Northwest, this plant is harvested and dried for basketry and floral arrangements. The seed, roots, and stems also provide food and structural cover for wildlife.

Woolgrass   *(Scirpus cyperinus)*

Distinguishing Characteristics: Height up to 1.5 m (4.9'). Like other members of the sedge family, this species has a semi-triangular stem (species in the grass and rush families have round stems), although the stem is not as sharply triangular as those of some sedges. Has drooping clusters of spikelets with wooly bristles that give the seedhead a distinctive, wooly appearance.

Habitat and Remarks: Perennial. Native. OBL in most regions, but FACW in the eastern mountains. A common plant of marshes, pond/lake fringes, wet meadows, disturbed wetlands, and sunny portions of swamps. A variety of birds eat the seeds, and muskrats and some waterfowl eat the roots and shoots. Woolgrass is an excellent species to plant to provide soil stabilization in wet areas and wildlife habitat.

Softstem Bulrush   *(Schoenoplectus tabernaemontani)*

Distinguishing Characteristics: Height up to 2.75 m (9'). Unlike most other members of the sedge family, which have triangular stems, soft-stem bulrush has a rounded, spongy stem. The seedhead is a compound umbel of spikelets, with a bract 12.7–76.2 mm (0.5–3") long that looks like a continuation of the stem. Might be mistaken for a *Juncus*, such as common rush (*J. effusus*), but *Schoenoplectus* species have cone-shaped clusters of seeds instead of the capsules found in *Juncus*.

Habitat and Remarks: Perennial. Native. OBL. Also known as great bulrush, this species is found in marshes, pond/lake fringes, ditches, and other sunny locations. A variety of birds eat the seeds, and muskrats dine on the rhizomes and stems. The young shoots are excellent eaten raw or cooked. The roots can be roasted and eaten, and the ground seeds and pollen can be used as flour. The stems are useful for weaving mats and baskets.

Sawgrass   *(Cladium mariscus ssp. Jamaiciense)*

Distinguishing Characteristics: Height up to 3 m (9.8'). Like other members of the sedge family, this species has a triangular stem (species in the grass and rush families have round stems). Sawgrass has small, sharp teeth on the edges and midrib of the leaves that slice skin readily. Forms dense, monospecific stands. There are several inflorescences spaced along the upper stem.

Habitat and Remarks: Perennial. Native. OBL. Although famous for being the dominant species throughout much of the Florida Everglades, this species is also found in many of our coastal freshwater and brackish marshes. The seeds are eaten by some waterfowl and wading birds, and the roots are used by muskrats. The foliage provides food for insects and structural habitat for many other species. Sawgrass is capable of thriving in a fairly nutrient-poor environment, but fertilizer runoff and other human-induced nutrient inputs are allowing cattails to take over large areas previously occupied by sawgrass. Conversion of delicately balanced, unique native plant communities to cattail monocultures is an important threat to biodiversity.

PLANTS

Bur-reeds   *(Sparganium* spp.)*

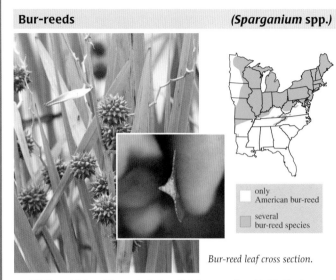

only
American bur-reed

several
bur-reed species

Bur-reed leaf cross section.

Distinguishing Characteristics: Height up to 2 m (6.6'). The leaves of bur-reeds are fairly similar to cattails, except they are keeled and form a low triangle in cross section. Some bur-reeds have limp leaves that may be submersed or floating. The seeds of bur-reeds easily distinguish them from cattails, irises, or other vegetatively similar plants. They consist of spiky balls, reminiscent of the fruits of a sweetgum tree. There are 10 bur-reed species in the eastern U.S., and they are relatively difficult to tell apart. American bur-reed is the primary species found throughout the Southeast, while numerous species inhabit northern areas.

Habitat and Remarks: Perennial. Native. All species are OBL. Bur-reeds provide food for a wide variety of animals. The seeds are eaten by waterfowl, the leaves are eaten by deer, and the whole plant is used by muskrats. The starchy roots are also edible to humans. Bur-reed is an excellent addition to wetland restoration projects or pond-edge plantings, and even competes well with cattails, which have a tendency to out-compete other plants.

Rushes   *(Juncus spp.)*

*Common rush
(J. effusus).*

    Distinguishing Characteristics: Height up to about 2 m (6.6'). This is a highly diverse group of grass-like plants with many species occurring in wetlands. Rushes usually have a solid, unjointed stem that is round in cross section and often filled with spongy material. These characteristics separate rushes from grasses (family Poaceae), which usually have a stem that is at least partially hollow with nodes or joints; and sedges (family Cyperaceae), which typically have stems that are very angular in cross section. Seeds consist of capsules. Bulrushes, which often cause confusion because of their name, are actually members of the sedge family.

    Habitat and Remarks: Most species are perennial. There are about 60 native eastern U.S. species and 5 introduced ones. Many species are OBL or FACW. Rush species are found in most types of wetlands, with the highest density and diversity usually occurring in sunny, shallow water. Marshes, pond/lake fringes, ditches, fens, and wet meadows are common places to find rush species. Common rush (*Juncus effusus*) is one of the most common freshwater wetland rushes, while black needlerush (*Juncus roemerianus*) is a very similar species indicative of brackish marshes. Photos of a few other examples are provided on the following page.

Needlepod rush (J. scirpoides)

Bog rush (J. biflorus).

Close-up of Juncus *capsules.*

Sweetflag (Acorus spp.)

Distinguishing Characteristics: Height up to 1.2 m (4'). Sweetflags have erect, sword-like green leaves superficially similar to cattail or iris; however, they are actually members of their own family (Acoraceae). When in flower, the yellowish spadix of sweetflags—which appears to stick out of the side of a leaf—quickly separates them from similar plants. When not flowering, sweetflags are easily identified by the sweet, pungent smell emitted by bruised leaves and roots. Several-vein sweetflag (*A. americanus*) is native to the northern U.S. and has several prominent veins in its leaves. Some experts consider single-vein sweetflag (*A. calamus*), which has a single, prominent vein in its leaves, to be an introduced Eurasian species. Both species have been widely planted by humans.

Habitat and Remarks: Perennial. OBL. Also known as calamus, these plants are commonly found around marshes, ponds, and streamside wetlands. The young, tender leaves obtained by peeling open the base of the flower stalk are edible, but *care must be taken to avoid eating similar-looking iris leaves, which are highly poisonous*. The roots of this plant can be used in making candy; however, they should be used sparingly because recent research indicates the presence of carcinogens that may be harmful in large amounts.

Cattails   *(Typha spp.)*

Distinguishing Characteristics: Height up to 2.1 m (7') above the water's surface. Leaves are flat and lack a midrib. The seedhead is large, distinctive, sausage-shaped, and brown when mature. In the summer the seedhead is green with a spike extending above it, which is covered in yellow or green pollen. Might be mistaken for irises (Iris spp.) or sweetflag (*Acorus* spp.) if the seedhead is not present, but those species have a midrib in each leaf near the leaf base. There is no bare space between the seedhead (pistillate head) and the pollen (staminate head) of broadleaf cattail (*T. latifolia*), as is the case in narrowleaf cattail (*T. angustifolia*) and southern cattail (*T. domingensis*). The latter 2 species are difficult to positively identify, and all 3 species may hybridize, particularly in disturbed habitats.

Habitat and Remarks: Perennial. Native, except for narrowleaf cattail and its hybrids. OBL. Usually found in marshes, sloughs, beaver ponds, pond/lake fringes, and various disturbed wetlands. Narrowleaf cattail is not native to the eastern U.S. but has been widely introduced. Hybrids between narrowleaf cattail and the other species are very vigorous, and can quickly change diverse and botanically unique wetlands such as the Everglades into a cattail monoculture. Cattail species spread rapidly through wind-blown distribution of their downy seeds and by rhizomes. Native cattail stands are important for a huge number of water birds, invertebrates, amphibians, fish, and mammals for food and structural habitat. Cattails are also useful to humans. The young shoots can be eaten raw (from areas that you know are not polluted), and the roots can be roasted and peeled for a potato-like vegetable. Flour can be produced from the peeled roots by crushing them in cold water. The starchy flour eventually settles to the bottom of the container, and the water can be poured off. The pollen also can be used as flour, and the green seedheads make a good green vegetable. The leaves are useful for weaving baskets, thatching shelters, and producing cordage.

Smooth Cordgrass   *(Spartina alterniflora)*

Distinguishing Characteristics: Height up to about 1.8 m (6'). Often found growing in almost pure stands in salt/brackish marshes. Leaves are approximately 1.5 cm (0.6") wide at the base, silvery on bottom and green on top. Flowers and seeds extend from only one side of the flowering stalk. Saltmeadow cordgrass (*S. patens*) is often found slightly higher in brackish marshes and may grow in a band directly uphill of smooth cordgrass marshes. Its leaves are rolled inward, stems are wispy, and flowers are more compact than smooth cordgrass, although flowers are also on only one side of the stem.

Habitat and Remarks: Perennial. Native in the eastern U.S., although it is an invasive introduced exotic on the West Coast. OBL. Found in the intertidal area of salt/brackish marshes. This species is an extremely important part of coastal ecosystems. It stabilizes coastlines, and the massive amount of organic matter produced from its stems builds peat deposits and fuels the biological productivity of our coastal marshes. This species will grow in fresh water, but persists best in the fluctuating water levels and high salinity to which it is adapted. Smooth cordgrass reproduces primarily through vegetative means rather than seeds and is often planted as an effective shoreline stabilizer in tidal areas.

Reed Canarygrass *(Phalaris arundinacea)*

Distinguishing Characteristics: Height up to 2.75 m (9'). Usually a fleshy, coarse grass forming monospecific stands in wet spots. Hairless stem. Leaves rough on top and bottom. Unlike some similar grasses, the ligule is membranous and transparent.

Habitat and Remarks: Perennial. Native (sort of). FACW in most regions, but OBL in the coastal plain. Found in wet meadows, marshes, ditches, and along the margins of swamps and ponds. This plant was probably native to the U.S., but the planting of aggressive agricultural cultivars and material from other continents has likely lead to the invasion of reed canarygrass that we see in certain areas. Large monocultures of canarygrass engulf and strangle native wetland plants, especially in disturbed areas. This grass has been used extensively to produce hay in lowland fields and to control erosion. It also provides habitat and food for some native animals, but there are many noninvasive grasses and sedges that provide far better habitat.

PLANTS

Rice Cutgrass *(Leersia oryzoides)*

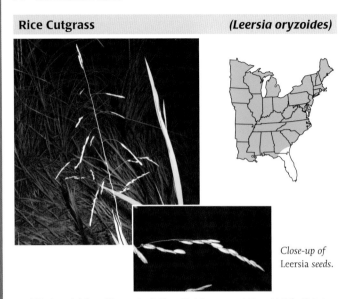

Close-up of Leersia *seeds.*

Distinguishing Characteristics: Height up to 1.5 m (4.9'). This is a rather nondescript grass with an open panicle of flowers that might be confused for several other grass species, such as mannagrass (*Glyceria* spp.) or Panicum (*Panicum* and *Dicanthelium* spp.). However, if you run your hand along cutgrass leaves, tiny teeth grab at your skin. They are even capable of cutting flesh and ripping very light clothing. The seed arrangement is also distinctive, with all of the seeds appearing on one side of the panicle branch. There are 5 *Leersia* species in the eastern U.S., but this is the most widespread and, in many areas, the most common species.

Habitat and Remarks: Perennial. Native. OBL. Rice cutgrass is often found in marshes, beaver dam ponds, bogs, and other wetlands that are partially shaded and often acidic. When a beaver dam is removed, this species often covers the resultant mudflats. The seeds and rhizomes of this plant are eaten by a variety of small mammals and waterfowl, and the vegetation provides cover for many more. The tendency of this species to grow in thick mats makes it a useful, native plant to use for erosion control and wetland restoration projects.

PLANTS

Fowl Mannagrass *(Glyceria striata)*

Distinguishing Characteristics: Height up to 1.1 m (3.5'). A nondescript, dark green grass with lax panicles of tiny seeds. Most likely to be confused for a bluegrass species such as fowl bluegrass (*Poa palustris*); however, fowl mannagrass has distinctively drooping seedheads. There are 11 other native *Glyceria* species (and several introduced species) found in the eastern U.S., but fowl mannagrass is one of the most common and widespread in wetlands.

Habitat and Remarks: Perennial. Native. OBL. Often found in woodland seeps, swamps, bogs, and the fringes of lakes. This species can often be seen in shady spots where other wetland grasses do not thrive. Despite its name, fowl mannagrass is not hugely important to waterfowl, which only occasionally eat the seeds. It does provide soil stabilization, structural cover, and food for small mammals and birds.

Wildrice   *(Zizania aquatica)*

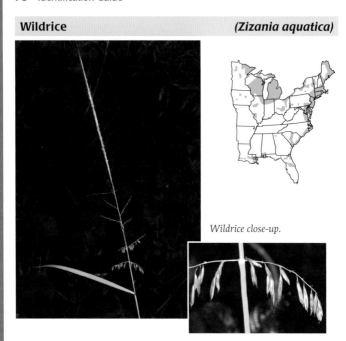

Wildrice close-up.

Distinguishing Characteristics: Height up to 3 m (9.8'). A large grass species with a distinctive panicle composed of 2 different types of flowers. The dangling male flowers are located below the erect tuft of female flowers, which eventually turn into elongate seeds. One might mistake this species for another large wetland grass, such as common reed, giant cutgrass (*Zizaniopsis miliacea*), or big cordgrass (*Spartina cynosuroides*), but the distinctive seedhead of wildrice serves to differentiate it from these species.

Habitat and Remarks: Annual. Native. OBL. Wildrice is best known in northern states where it inhabits marshes and other silty wetlands with some slight flow and up to about 2 feet of depth. It is traditionally harvested by beating the ripe seedheads with a stick over a canoe, and is harvested commercially in some northern areas. A huge number of animals, including many waterfowl species, feed on the seeds.

Common Reed *(Phragmites australis)*

Distinguishing Characteristics: Height up to 4 m (13'). Seedhead is a large, distinctive, glabrous, spreading plume. In the summer these plumes are purple, but turn grayish in the fall and winter. The stem is hollow. Native and introduced forms are difficult to differentiate. Often confused with giant reed (*Arundo donax*), which has more erect and fuzzy seedheads.

Habitat and Remarks: Perennial. Native (sort of). FACW. Often simply called Phragmites. Forms monospecific stands in damp areas. Commonly inhabits freshwater marshes, roadside ditches, brackish marshes, swamp margins, and disturbed wetlands throughout the world. Common reed is native to the U.S., but a highly aggressive variety has been introduced, most likely from Eurasia. Eradication efforts are being undertaken in some areas because this species crowds out many native wetland plants, including the native form of common reed. Increased salinity because of road salt runoff has been cited as one reason for the explosion of this salt-tolerant species into freshwater areas. Common reed is extremely useful. It can be used to make baskets, sleeping pads, straws, arrows, boats, thatching, paper, and many other items. All parts of the plant are edible, although new shoots are the most palatable. A variety of small mammals and birds feed on reeds, and many more inhabit the cover provided by this plant.

Swamp Dock   *(Rumex verticillatus)*

Swamp dock seeds.

Distinguishing Characteristics: Height up to 1.5 m (5'). Fleshy green plant with 1 to 4 racemes of whorled, dangling flowers that turn into dangling green fruits with 3 tubercles/achenes. Leaves are alternate, simple, lance-shaped, and flat when mature (not curly edged like some other docks). Habitat usually provides a good clue that you are looking at swamp dock and not 1 of the 55 others species of *Rumex*. However, an excellent identifying characteristic is swamp dock's fruit, which dangles on a pedicel 2 to 5 times the length of the fruit; the pedicels of other dock species are shorter.

Habitat and Remarks: Perennial. Native. OBL except FACW in the coastal plain. Swamp dock, as its name implies, is fond of partially shaded wetlands but can also be found in full sun. It inhabits vernal pools, swamps, marshes, and disturbed wetlands. A variety of birds eat dock seeds, and deer and the caterpillars of several butterfly and moth species seek out the foliage. The young leaves are edible for humans, but are best boiled in 2 changes of water. The dried seeds can be ground into rich brown flour.

Green Arrow Arum   (Peltandra virginica)

Green arrow arum fruit.

Distinguishing Characteristics: Height up to 76 cm (30"). Fleshy green emergent plant with arrow-shaped leaves. Might be mistaken for a large arrowhead (*Sagittaria* spp.); however, the flower is nothing like the white-petaled flowers of the arrowheads. Instead, this species has a slender, pointed, partially closed green spathe enclosing a spadix. The spadix eventually becomes a large, green, berrylike fruit that dangles in the water on its fleshy flower stalk. Eventually the fruits turn black and float away. There is another *Peltandra* species (*P. sagittifolia*), but it is rare, more southern, and has an open white spathe.

Habitat and Remarks: Perennial. Native. OBL. Often forms monocultures in marshes, lake fringes, and other shallow waters. The roots are edible if roasted or dried for an extremely long time, but like other arums, *fresh parts of this plant contain calcium oxalate crystals that cause an extremely intense burning inside the mouth if eaten.* The seeds are a favorite food of wood ducks, and are occasionally eaten by other waterfowl and rails.

Skunk Cabbage *(Symplocarpus foetidus)*

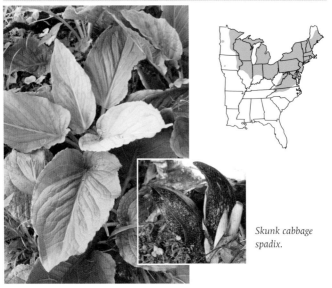

Skunk cabbage spadix.

Distinguishing Characteristics: Leaves up to 55 cm (21.6") long. The flowers are contained in a mottled purple hood-like structure (spathe) that comes out before the leaves in the spring, sometimes while snow is still on the ground. Leaves are large, ovular, fleshy, and smooth—resembling a large hosta—and have branched venation. Leaves superficially resemble those of young false hellebore (*Veratrum viride*), which has parallel leaf venation and a much different flower. This plant smells like a skunk if bruised or broken.

Habitat and Remarks: Perennial. Native. OBL. Skunk cabbage lives in forested wetlands and is often found around seeps, small streams, and northern swamps. The leaves are edible if dried for a long period of time, but *if eaten green, calcium oxalate crystals in this plant cause an extremely intense burning inside the mouth and may lead to breathing difficulty. The superficially similar false hellebore is toxic.* The flowers are very attractive to early spring insects.

Green Dragon and Jack in the Pulpit   (*Arisaema* spp.)

PLANTS

☐ only Jack-in-the-pulpit

☐ both species

Above left: Jack in the pulpit (A. triphyllum).

Left: Green dragon (A. dracontium).

Distinguishing Characteristics: Height up to about 47 cm (18"). Green dragon (*A. dracontium*) is a fleshy plant with leaves cut into 7 or more leaflets arranged in a rough half circle. With a little imagination, some of these leaves resemble a dragon's face. The flower is composed of a long, thin, cylindrical green structure (spadix) partially contained by a thin sheath (spathe). Jack in the pulpit (*A. triphyllum*) is the only other *Arisaema* species found in our area. It has 3 leaflets and a very distinctive flower. The flowers of both species become a clump of red berries in late summer.

Habitat and Remarks: Perennial. Native. FACW. Both plants inhabit moist, shady bottomland forests, often along the fringes of swamps. Jack in the pulpit corms (roots) can be thinly sliced, dried, and eaten like potato chips, but *if eaten fresh, calcium oxylate crystals in the root of these plants cause an extremely intense burning inside the mouth and may lead to breathing difficulty.* Varieties of these plants are sometimes used in ornamental landscaping for shady areas.

PLANTS

Water Arum *(Calla palustris)*

Distinguishing Characteristics: Height up to 30.5 cm (1') above water surface. What appears to be a flat white flower with a gold or white center is actually a white spathe enclosing a spadix covered in tiny yellow flowers. This spathe and spadix arrangement is typical of the arum family. The leaves are broadly heart shaped. Flowers become bright red berries in fall. Golden club (*Orontium aquaticum*) also has a golden spadix, but lacks the white spathe and is found in more southern marshes and swamps. White arrow arum (*Peltandra sagittifolia*) of the southeastern U.S. has similar flowers but arrow-shaped leaves.

Habitat and Remarks: Perennial. Native. OBL. Also known as wild calla, this is a common species usually found growing in standing water of northern bogs, marshes, and pond fringes. It is eaten by moose and other herbivores, and the tubers and seeds can be dried and ground into flour. *However, if eaten without being dried completely, calcium oxalate crystals in this plant cause an extremely intense burning inside the mouth.*

American Water Lotus (Nelumbo lutea)

American water lotus seedpod.

Distinguishing Characteristics: Height up to 1.5 m (5'), although a portion is usually submerged. A plant with large, circular leaves attached to the stem at the center (peltate) and huge white flowers that reach the size of a baseball cap. The leaves begin as floating circles, but eventually emerge from the water. The flowers eventually become very distinctive seedheads with many holes on the surface, each with a marble-sized seed in it. These are often seen floating or stranded on shore more than a year after they were produced.

Habitat and Remarks: Perennial. Native. OBL. Also known as water chinquapin and sacred bean, this species commonly inhabits the permanently inundated areas of marshes and lake fringes. The seedheads are popular in flower arrangements, and the seeds may be eaten green, roasted like a nut, or ground into flour. The tubers can also be baked or boiled for the table. Waterfowl eat the seeds and herbivores such as beavers and muskrats eat the whole plant. The range of this species may have been expanded by Native Americans, who are thought to have planted it because of its food value. It is valued by water gardeners for its beauty, but in some areas it is considered invasive because it forms monospecific stands.

PLANTS

Fragrant Water Lily   *(Nymphaea odorata)*

Distinguishing Characteristics: Flower height up to 15 cm (6") above the water surface, although the flat, circular leaves float directly on the water. Unlike the young floating leaves of the water lotus (*Nelumbo*), fragrant water lily leaves have a V-shaped cleft in one side. The fragrant flowers may be white or pink (rarely); however, there are numerous varieties of this species, including deep pink ornamentals. The fruits ripen underwater on a coiled stalk. Numerous varieties have been recognized as separate species, and there are a number of introduced species and hybrids, especially in coastal areas.

Habitat and Remarks: Perennial. Native. OBL. Found in the permanent waters of marshes, ponds, lake fringes, sloughs, and various streamside wetlands, especially in coastal areas. Ornamental cultivars of this species are frequently planted in water gardens. The seeds are eaten by waterfowl, and the whole plant is consumed by moose, beavers, and muskrats.

Water Plantains (*Alisma* spp.)

*American water plantain
(A. subcordatum).*

Distinguishing Characteristics: Height up to 0.9 m (3'). Leaves are oval shaped with parallel venation. Unlike similar plants in this family (Alismataceae) that have many whorls of pistols around a globose receptacle, the flowers of water plantains consist of a single whorl of pistols surrounding a flat receptacle. However, it is usually easy to identify mature specimens of water plantain by their erect, compound inflorescence (whorled branches at several nodes have whorled branches of their own). There are 3 similar species in this genus. Narrowleaf water plantain (*A. gramineum*) has very narrow leaves and often pinkish flower petals; American water plantain (*A. subcordatum*) has broad leaves and very small white flower petals about as long as the green sepals; and northern water plantain (*A. triviale*) has broad leaves and larger white flower petals that are longer than the green sepals.

Habitat and Remarks: Perennial. Native. OBL. Found mainly in marshes, pond/lake fringes, and sunny portions of swamps. Named for the similarity in shape of water plantain leaves to the common plantain (*Plantago major*) found in many of our yards. Roots are edible for humans, and the roots and seeds are eaten by wildlife such as muskrats and ducks.

PLANTS

Arrowheads   *(Sagittaria* spp.)*

Distinguishing Characteristics: Height up to 1.5 m (4.9'). Fleshy-stemmed plants with 3-petaled white flowers. The genus *Sagittaria* refers to the sagittate (arrowhead-shaped) leaves that many species of arrowhead have; however, leaves of some species are simply oval or lance shaped. Arrowhead leaves might be mistaken for green arrow arum (*Peltandra virginica*); however, the latter is easily identified by its flower and fruit. Arrowheads are similar to 2 other genera in the water plantain family (Alismataceae): burheads (*Echinodorus* spp.) and water plantains (*Alisma* spp.). However, these genera never have lobed/sagittate leaves, whereas many arrowheads do. Burheads often have angular petioles, while arrowhead petioles are smooth. Water plantains have a ring of pistils in the center of their flowers, while arrowhead pistils are in a dense head (usually yellow), and their flowers are usually much larger.

Habitat and Remarks: Perennial. About 20 species are native to the eastern U.S., with broadleaf arrowhead (*S. latifolia*) the most widespread and often the most common. OBL. Also known as duck potato or wapato, arrowhead species are common in marshes, along the edges of ponds, and in many other types of sunny wetlands that remain saturated with water for most of the year. The tubers were once a human food staple and are still important in some countries. The tubers provide a feast for muskrats and porcupines, while the seeds are very important for waterfowl and rails.

PLANTS

Lizard's Tail   *(Saururus cernuus)*

Distinguishing Characteristics: Height up to 76 cm (30"). Heart-shaped leaves with a very distinctive white, nodding spike of flowers. It's hard to mistake this plant for anything else if it is blooming.

Habitat and Remarks: Perennial. Native. OBL. Found in shady swamps, floodplain wetlands, ditches, and vernal pools. This is an attractive addition to shady wetlands after invasive plants have been removed, or to shady backyard rain gardens. Lizard's tail is also thought to have some medicinal potential as an anti-inflammatory.

Common Boneset   *(Eupatorium perfoliatum)*

Distinguishing Characteristics: Height up to 1.2 m (4'). Flower heads consist of broad, branching, flat-topped clusters (corymbs) of tiny grayish-white flowers. The stem is covered with hairs, and the leaves have a rough texture. The leaves serve to readily separate this species from similar-looking members of this genus. They are oppositely arranged and broadly joined at the base (especially the large lower leaves). This gives the appearance that the stem is growing through the middle of a single leaf (perfoliate).

Habitat and Remarks: Perennial. Native. FACW. Usually found in very wet soils in full to partial sun. Boneset often grows in wet meadows, marshes, pond/lake margins, and sunny openings of forested wetlands. It is a widely used remedy for fever, common cold, and influenza. Scientific research suggests that this plant has immune system-stimulating properties. However, if taken in large or concentrated doses, it has strong laxative and vomit-inducing properties, and extended use may cause liver damage. A tea made by steeping a small handful of the leaves in a cup of water for about 20 to 30 minutes and taken 3 times a day serves as a good cold-and-flu remedy.

Sundews   *(Drosera* spp.)

Above left:
Water sundew
(D. intermedia).

Left: Round-
leaved sundew
(D. rotundifolia).

Distinguishing Characteristics: Height up to 50 cm (20"). Basal rosette of leaves with swollen tips or longer filiform (threadlike) leaves covered with hair-like stalked glands. The dewy secretion on these glands often shines brilliantly in sunlight. Glands and leaves of several species are often red or pinkish. Flowers arise from a central stalk. Identification relies largely on leaf shape. For example, round-leaved sundew (*D. rotundifolia*) has very abruptly round leaf tips, while water sundew (*D. intermedia*) has more gradually widened, spoon-shaped leaves.

Habitat and Remarks: Perennial. Native. OBL. The 2 species listed above are the 2 most wide-ranging eastern U.S. species; however, there are about 8 eastern species and several hybrids, with particularly high levels of occurrence in northern and southeastern bogs. Sundews are found in wet meadows, savannahs, marshes, bogs, and the sunny margins of ponds and swamps. They are carnivorous, and the sticky, dew-like secretion on the leaves captures invertebrates. Once captured, the glands—and in some species the leaves—move to surround the animal more completely and digest it with enzymes secreted by some of the glands. In this way, sundews gain important nutrients that are often of limited availability in wetlands.

PLANTS

Pipewort Family (Eriocaulaceae)

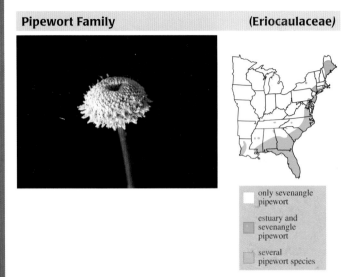

only sevenangle
pipewort

estuary and
sevenangle
pipewort

several
pipewort species

Distinguishing Characteristics: Height up to 1.1 m (3.6'). Often mistaken for grasses, sedges, or rushes. Superficially similar to spikerushes (*Eleocharis* spp.). Members of the pipewort family consist of a light-colored, roughly spherical flower head suspended on a stiff scape, with a basal rosette of grass-like leaves. There are 3 genera: the pipeworts (*Eriocaulon*), the bog-buttons (*Lachnocaulon*), and the hatpins (*Syngonanthus*). The species in these genera are difficult to distinguish; however, the majority of species are found in the Southeast. Only the pipeworts are found north of Virginia, and only 2 of these are found in New England and the upper Midwest: estuary pipewort (*E. parkeri*, flower head 4–10 mm, rare and only in the Northeast) and sevenangle pipewort (*E. aquaticum*, flower head 3–4 mm, widespread in the north).

Habitat and Remarks: Perennial. About 15 species native to the eastern U.S. Most species OBL, some FACW. Found in a variety of wetland types, including bogs, marshes, swamps, wet meadows, and estuaries. Southeastern species may be found in wet pine savannahs, ditches, wet meadows, pineland ponds, and various other wetlands. Pipeworts are susceptible to competition from more aggressive plants, and several species are rare.

Pennyworts and Marshpennyworts *(Hydrocotyle spp.)*

Large-leaf pennywort
(H. bonariensis).

Distinguishing Characteristics: Height up to 61 cm (2'). Fleshy green plant composed of a horizontal stem with roots at nodes and round or kidney-shaped leaves that stick up like little umbrellas. Leaves are scalloped along the margin. Some species have leaves that are peltate (center of leaf attached to petiole), while others have leaves attached along the margin. The flowers are small umbels of greenish or white flowers.

Habitat and Remarks: Perennial. Six native eastern U.S. species, and a few more introduced ones. Most species are OBL or FACW. Often found in swamps and marshes, and along the fringes of ponds and ditches. Some species are commonly found in coastal lawns. At least one species (*H. bonariensis*) is edible for humans.

PLANTS

Buttercups   *(Ranunculus* spp.)*

Above left: A typical aquatic buttercup.

Left: A typical emergent buttercup.

Distinguishing Characteristics: Height up to 1 m (3.3'). Yellow, 5-petaled flowers of most species bloom in spring and early summer. Petals of some species—especially those with the common name crowfoot—are very small. Leaves are often divided into 3 parts, and the margins are toothed, cleft, and lobed in various ways. Some species have aquatic, submerged leaves.

Habitat and Remarks: Annual, biennial, and perennial species. Many native and some introduced species. FACU–OBL, depending on species. Buttercups can be found in a variety of habitats but are most common in moist soils. Several species are found in the partial shade of bottomland forests, and some can be found in sunny meadows. Buttercups have been used medicinally in the past, but most species are considered to be poisonous. *These plants contain a poison that severely irritates mucous membranes, the digestive tract, and even the skin if handled. Be careful not to mistake a Ranunculus for the edible marsh marigold (Caltha palustris).*

Yellow Marsh Marigold (*Caltha palustris*)

Distinguishing Characteristics: Height up to 0.8 m (2.6'). Actually a member of the buttercup family (Ranunculaceae) and not related to marigolds. Its 5-petaled yellow flowers are very similar to those of other buttercups (*Ranunculus* spp.). Leaves are large, very smooth, and round to kidney-shaped, with wavy edges. Stems are quite fleshy. Flowers appear very early (March in southern range to June in far north).

Habitat and Remarks: Native. Perennial. OBL. Also called cowslip, this species inhabits woodland seeps, marshes, bogs, fens, and other wet areas. It is one of the first wetland flowers to bloom in the spring and often forms extensive patches that contrast pleasingly with the late-winter landscape. *The leaves are edible; however, they contain poisonous glycosides and alkaloids that can only be destroyed by boiling in several changes of water before eating.* Simply drop the leaves into boiling water, then pour off the water once it has started boiling again. Repeat this process twice, and then simmer until tender. Add salt, butter, and other spices as needed.

PLANTS

Sneezeweeds (*Helenium* spp.)

Distinguishing Characteristics: Height up to 1.5 m (5'). Summer/fall-blooming yellow flowers. There are 14 species of *Helenium* in the eastern U.S. All species but one (*H. amarum*) have a winged stem. Leaves are mostly alternate and lanceolate, with smooth or toothed/lobed margins.

Habitat and Remarks: Perennial. Native. FACU-OBL depending on species. Sneezeweeds are found from the edges of salt marshes to freshwater marshes and disturbed wetlands throughout the interior U.S. Common sneezeweed (*H. autumnale*) is the most widespread species, and several species are only found in the southeastern U.S. The plants' name comes from the leaves, which were once crushed to produce a powdered snuff that caused sneezing, which was thought to be therapeutic. Many sneezeweeds are relatively tough plants that are easily established in sunny wetland restoration areas and rain gardens.

Beggar's Ticks   *(Bidens spp.)*

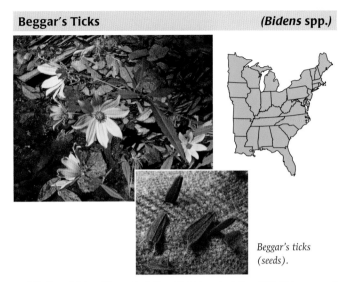

Beggar's ticks (seeds).

Distinguishing Characteristics: Height up to 1.5 m (5'). This genus of yellow asters is often collectively referred to as beggar's ticks or simply *Bidens*. Most species have conspicuous, symmetrical, many-rayed yellow flowers, but in some species the rays are greatly reduced or absent. The leaves are arranged oppositely and often have serrate margins. Leaves may be simple or compound. In winter, *Bidens* species are most readily noticed by the small, pronged "beggar's ticks" that stick to clothing and animal fur.

Habitat and Remarks: Annual/Perennial. About 17 native species in the eastern U.S. FACU–OBL, depending on the species. Many species of *Bidens* grow in moist ground in full sun, but some prefer shade. They are often found in marshes, ditches, pond/lake fringes, bottomland wetlands, and many disturbed wetlands. Waterfowl, game birds, and songbirds feed on the seeds, and rabbits feed on the foliage. Several species are important host plants for caterpillars.

PLANTS

Primrose-Willows (*Ludwigia* spp.)

Distinguishing Characteristics: Height up to 3 m (9.8'). Not actually related to tree/shrub willows (*Salix* spp.). Fleshy plants that have yellow or greenish flowers with 4 to 7 petals; some species have large, showy flowers and others have small flowers. Leaves are opposite in a few species and alternate in the majority of species. Fruits are 4-angled capsules that range from small and boxlike to more elongate fruits that are relatively square in cross section. The showier *Ludwigia* species might be mistaken for other members of the primrose family, such as the evening primrose (*Oenothera biennis*), which often grows next to ditches and disturbed wetlands.

Habitat and Remarks: Perennial/Annual. About 28 species native to the eastern U.S. and 2 introduced species. Majority are OBL; a few are FACW. Also known as water primroses, many of these plants are found in sunny, permanently inundated wetlands. They can be common in marshes and ditches, and along the fringes of ponds and lakes where they provide cover for many amphibians, fish, small mammals, and invertebrates. The seeds are eaten by ducks and the foliage is consumed by invertebrates. Dense stands of primrose-willow can be frustrating for anglers trying to fish the edges of some waterbodies, and even native primrose-willows are sometimes considered to be invasive.

Jewelweed *(Impatiens spp.)*

only orange-spotted jewelweed

both species

Above left: Orange-spotted jewelweed (I. capensis).

Left: Pale touch-me-not (I. pallida).

Distinguishing Characteristics: Height up to 1.5 m (5'). Juicy, translucent green stem. Leaves are oval shaped with wavy margins and appear silver when submerged in clear water. Ripe seeds shoot off of plant when disturbed. There are 2 native jewelweeds in the eastern U.S. Orange-spotted jewelweed (*I. capensis*) has orange flowers with black spots, and pale touch-me-not (*I. pallida*) has pale yellow flowers.

Habitat and Remarks: Annual. Native. FACW. Both jewelweeds are commonly found in shady, moist soils, often around the margins of swamps, bottomland forested wetlands, woodland seeps, and vernal pools. Orange-spotted jewelweed is widespread in a variety of geographic types, while pale touch-me-not prefers calcareous soils often found around streams of our mountains and other highlands. The shoots of both species may be eaten after boiling in 2 changes of water to remove some of the bitterness (don't drink the water). Crushed leaves and juice from the stem are well-known and effective remedies for poison ivy rash, nettle stings, and many other skin maladies. Hummingbirds love to feed from the flowers and other birds eat the seeds.

PLANTS

Bladderworts   (Utricularia spp.)

Above left: Humped bladderwort (U. gibba).

Left: Floating bladderwort (U. radiata).

Distinguishing Characteristics: Height up to 25.4 cm (10"). There are about 18 species of bladderwort in the eastern U.S. Most parts of these plants are submerged in water or rooted in damp substrate; however, the irregularly shaped flowers stand out above the water or ground on a thin, erect stalk. Most bladderwort species have yellow flowers, but a few have whitish-purple flowers. Some species, such as floating bladderwort (*U. radiata*), have inflated bladders arranged like wheel spokes under water. Others have only a diffuse network of submerged, threadlike bracts with tiny bladders scattered throughout.

Habitat and Remarks: Perennial. Most species are native. OBL. Bladderworts are found in wet meadows/savannahs and in the sunny waters of ponds, marshes, ditches, swamps, bogs, and fens. Like other carnivorous plants, they have evolved to absorb important nutrients (especially nitrogen) from tiny animals they capture. Bladderworts have a fascinating active capture mechanism: When a microcrustacean or tiny insect larva comes into contact with the sensitive hairs around the bladder, it quickly snaps open, suctioning water and the animal into it, and then snapping shut. The animal is digested within the bladder and key minerals are absorbed by the plant.

Yellow Pond-Lily (Nuphar lutea)

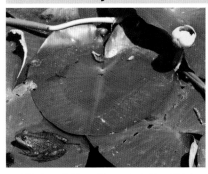

Distinguishing Characteristics: Height up to 15.2 cm (6") above the water. An emergent plant with leaves that float on the water or stick out slightly. Yellow, cup-like flowers are spherical before they open. The leaves are round or oval with smooth margins and a V-shaped cleft at the base. Some taxonomists have split this plant into a number of species based on leaf shape, size, and range; however, many of these forms were recently lumped back together under this name.

Habitat and Remarks: Perennial. Native. OBL. Also known as spatter-dock and bullhead lily, this is a familiar inhabitant of lake margins, marshes, and other sunny, shallow waters. The leaves provide shade and cover for many fish and invertebrate species. The whole plant is eaten by beavers, muskrats, and moose, while the seeds are fed upon by several duck species. The roots may be thrown into the coals of a campfire to roast. When the charred rind and mud are peeled away, the inner root has a pleasantly sweet flavor. The seeds also can be roasted and eaten.

PLANTS

Pitcherplants   *(Sarracenia* spp.)*

only purple
pitcherplant
*Sarracenia
purpurea*

multiple pitcher-
plant species

*Top left: Hooded
pitcherplant
(S. minor).*

*Bottom left:
Yellow pitcher-
plant (S. flava).*

*Left: Purple
pitcherplant
(S. purpurea).*

Distinguishing Characteristics: Height up to 1 m (3.3'). Pitcher-plants, with their cuplike leaves, are difficult to mistake for anything else. Their flowers are typically green, red, or yellow, and are also very distinctive. The relatively short and wide purple pitcherplant (*S. purpurea*) is the only species commonly found outside the southeastern coastal plain. The shape of the pitchers usually helps to identify these plants, ranging from the small, almost-closed pitcher of the hooded pitcherplant (*S. minor*) to the widely opened, large pitchers of yellow trumpet (*S. flava*).

Habitat and Remarks: Perennial. Native. There are about 9 species in the eastern U.S., but numerous hybrids and variants of species are recognized. OBL. Pitcherplants are most often found in bogs. Southeastern coastal

PLANTS

plain species also inhabit wet pine savannahs, borrow pits, ditches, pocosins, rare montane bog (or fen) communities, and marshes. They are passive carnivores, deriving nutrients from insects and other small animals that become trapped in the liquid held in the pitcher. These plants secrete enzymes that digest the trapped animals and then absorb nutrients, such as nitrogen, that are of limited availability in nutrient-poor wetlands they often inhabit. Pitcherplants and other carnivorous plants have become popular house plants and additions to bog gardens. However, take care to avoid buying a plant that was illegally collected from the wild because the habitat of these plants is often rare and fragile.

Smartweeds (*Persicaria* and *Polygonum* spp.)

Water smartweed (P. amphibium).

Distinguishing Characteristics: Plants in these genera vary from small, erect herbs to 3-meter-tall weeds and vining species. Smartweeds usually have alternate, simple, entire (smooth-edged) leaves. However, the leaves can be various shapes, including elliptical, linear, hastate (arrowhead-shaped), cordate, and obovate. A tubular sheath that encircles the stem at the base of each leaf (called an ocrea) is usually present in members of this family. Many of the species' flowers look like the one pictured, and many of their stems are reddish. These were formerly lumped together in the genus *Polygonum*, but now some sources place most of the wetland species in *Persicaria*.

Habitat and Remarks: Annual/Perennial. About 28 native and 20 introduced exotic species in our area. FACU–OBL, depending on species. Various smartweeds are found growing in small patches in many wetland types; however, large monocultures often occur in freshwater marshes, along the margins of ponds, and in other sunny, seasonally flooded habitats. Smartweeds are one of the most important groups of plants for wetland wildlife. Their seeds are essential to waterfowl and other birds, and the cover provided by smartweeds is used by huge numbers of vertebrates and invertebrates.

Swamp Milkweed   *(Asclepias incarnata)*

Distinguishing Characteristics: Height up to 1.5 m (5'). Inflorescence consists of erect umbels of small, pink-purple flowers. Each flower consists of 5 erect hoods and drooping petal-like parts. Leaves are oppositely arranged, lance-shaped, pubescent on the underside, narrower than those of many other milkweeds, and smooth along the margins. Unlike some similar-looking wetland milkweeds, the leaf veins form an acute angle with the mid-rib (in other species they form a right angle). Two of the most similar species are aquatic milkweed (*A. perennis*), which inhabits shady wetlands and has white flowers; and red milkweed (*A. rubra*), which inhabits bogs, marshes, and wet pinewoods, and has white or pinkish flowers, with glabrous leaves beneath.

Habitat and Remarks: Perennial. Native. OBL. Swamp milkweed inhabits sunny wetlands such as marshes, wet meadows, pond fringes, ditches, beaver ponds, and other canopy gaps within forested wetlands. The flowers are highly sought after by butterflies and hummingbirds, and are an excellent addition to wetland restoration projects and rain gardens. Mature parts of this plant are *toxic to humans in large quantities*. The young seed pods and very small shoots—less than 15.2 cm (6") tall—can be eaten if boiled for about 15 minutes in several changes of water, and the flowers can be boiled briefly, battered, and fried as fritters. Fibers from the stem make excellent string, but it will rot quickly if left outside.

Mallows   *(Hibiscus* and *Kosteletzkya virginica)*

hibiscus

hibiscus and kosteletzkya

Above left: Halberdleaf rosemallow (H. laevis).

Left: Saltmarsh mallow (K. pentacarpos).

Distinguishing Characteristics: Height up to 2 m (6.6'). There are about 9 species of *Hibiscus* native to the eastern U.S. Crimsoneyed (*H. moscheutos*) and halberdleaf rosemallow (*H. laevis*) are the 2 most widespread inland wetland species. Robust, shrub-like herbaceous plants with large, showy flowers (many species are white or pink, some with dark centers). Leaves are various shapes and textures. Virginia saltmarsh mallow (*K. virginica* or *K. pentacarpos*) has flatter fruits than those of the *Hibiscus* species and is restricted to coastal habitats. The large flowers of mallows are hard to mistake for any other wetland species.

Habitat and Remarks: Annual/Perennial. Many species are OBL. Mallows are found in many types of sunny wetlands, including marshes and the edges of lakes and ponds. Virginia saltmarsh mallow is typically found in coastal salt marshes, brackish marshes, and some freshwater wetlands. Mallows make a beautiful addition to wetland restoration projects. They also add value for nectar-feeding insects and birds, and provide seeds that are often eaten by birds and small mammals.

PLANTS

Meadowbeauty (*Rhexia* spp.)

Distinguishing Characteristics: Height up to 1 m (3.3'). There are 11 species of meadowbeauties in the eastern U.S. Only Maryland meadowbeauty (*R. mariana*) and handsome Harry (*R. virginica*) are found throughout most northern states. Most species have 4 pink flower petals with prominent yellow stamens, although one species (*R. lutea*) has yellow flower petals. Leaves are opposite, simple, 3-veined, and sometimes hairy. The stem is angular or winged, and the fruits are tiny, urn-shaped capsules.

Habitat and Remarks: Native. Perennial. FACW or OBL depending on species. Meadowbeauties, as their name implies, are attractive denizens of our wet meadows and marshes. They are often found in sunny areas that are not too deeply inundated. Where meadowbeauties are common, the tender leaves can be eaten cooked or raw, and some have edible tubers that can also be snacked on. They are an attractive addition to some wetland restoration projects and rain gardens.

PLANTS

Cardinal Flower   *(Lobelia cardinalis)*

Flower close-up.

Distinguishing Characteristics: Height up to 1.5 m (5'). This plant has bright red asymmetrical flowers consisting of 3 petals at the bottom and 2 petals at the top united into a long tube at the base. Leaves are alternate and lanceolate, with small teeth along the margin. They are glabrous to slightly hirsute.

Habitat and Remarks: Perennial. Native. OBL/FACW depending on region. The cardinal flower can grow under a variety of conditions, from sun to shade. It can be relatively common in wet meadows, pond/lake fringes, and canopy openings of bottomland wetlands. This plant is poisonous to humans if eaten in large quantities, but it is an excellent choice for showy wetland restorations and rain gardens. Hummingbirds are highly attracted to the flowers.

PLANTS

Purple Loosestrife   *(Lythrum salicaria)*

Distinguishing Characteristics: Height up to 2.5 m (8.2'). Long spikes of purple flowers, each with 6 petals, a green tubular calyx, and 6 or more stamens. Leaves mostly opposite or whorled, lance-shaped, clasping the stem, with entire margins, and hairy (smooth in some varieties). Stems are square-like or round in cross section and usually pubescent at the top of the plant, while more woody and smooth in the lower parts. Superficially resembles willowherb species (*Epilobium* spp.) and some members of the mint family (Lamiaceae); however, the flowers of those plants differ in shape and/or number of petals. Winged loosestrife (*L. alatum*) is similar, but has a winged stem.

Habitat and Remarks: Perennial. Introduced exotic invasive plant from Eurasia. OBL. Found in sunny habitats such as marshes, bogs, and wet meadows, and especially in disturbed wetlands. While it is found throughout the east, purple loosestrife reaches its highest abundance in the Northeast and Midwest where it often forms monospecific stands that are of little value to wildlife and smother native plants. Unfortunately, this plant is still sold in certain areas because of its attractive flowers. Small populations of this plant can be controlled by manual pulling over multiple years, but it rapidly reproduces from seeds and root/stem cuttings, so all material should be removed from the wetland. Advanced infestations require treatment with herbicide and replacement with aggressive vegetation such as smartweeds (*Polygonum* spp.).

Pickerelweed *(Pontederia cordata)*

Distinguishing Characteristics: Height up to 0.9 m (3'). An easily recognized, erect plant with a purple (sometimes white) flower. Often found growing in standing water. One leaf is not far below the flower, while the rest are at the base. The large, single leaf that accompanies the flower is deeply cleft at the base, giving the leaf the shape of an elongated heart. There are 2 varieties—1 with narrower leaves (more common in the Southeast) and 1 with broader leaves, although intermediate forms are common. The flowers of this species are similar to its invasive family member, water hyacinth; however, that species is a low-growing, floating plant with very inflated petioles and uncleft leaf bases.

Habitat and Remarks: Perennial. Native. OBL. Pickerelweed is typically found in marshes, sloughs, and sunny parts of swamps. The seeds are edible and nutlike. The young shoots can be boiled and eaten as greens. The seeds are eaten occasionally by muskrats and ducks, such as the mottled duck. The plant provides cover for many species and is a flashy addition to wetland restoration projects where it is native.

PLANTS

Water Hyacinth (Eichhornia crassipes)

Close-up of swollen petiole.

Distinguishing Characteristics: Height up to 1 m (3.3'). Often found growing as a monoculture in thick, floating mats or rooted in mud during low water. This species produces a lavender flower spike similar to pickerelweed. Water hyacinth leaves are oval shaped and lack the cleft, heart-shaped base present in pickerelweed. The leaf stalks are greatly inflated with bulbs of aerenchyma tissue that aid in flotation.

Habitat and Remarks: Perennial. Introduced exotic noxious weed. OBL. In the frost-free southern states, this species quickly clogs coastal plain marshes, canals, rivers, swamps, and other wetlands. It sometimes spreads from water gardens in more northern states but does not reach the over-abundance found in the south. Water hyacinth has some potential for water treatment because of its ability to absorb metals and excess nutrients, which might then be removed with the mats of vegetation. However, eradication of this plant is a challenge, and it should never be introduced to wetlands because of its propensity for smothering native vegetation and choking open water.

Virginia Iris *(Iris virginica)*

Distinguishing Characteristics: Height up to 0.9 m (3'). There are at least 10 other native eastern U.S. iris species and various domesticated varieties, but Virginia iris is one of the most common wetland species. The flower is made up of 3 horizontal sepals and 3 vertical petals. These are usually purple or lavender, and each sepal has a spot of yellow or orange at its midpoint. The leaves are sword-shaped blades that might be mistaken for cattails if not for the midrib usually present at least at the base of iris leaves. The leaves of sweetflag are similar, but the roots of that plant have a sweet smell.

Habitat and Remarks: Perennial. Native. OBL. Also known as blue flag, this species may grow in shaded or sunny wetlands, such as bottomland forested wetlands, swamps, pond/lake fringes, marshes, and shrub swamps. Iris is an excellent native plant for adding color to stream bank restoration projects, and is visited by hummingbirds. Its leaves can be used in weaving and cordage making; however, iris is not edible for humans.

Trees and Shrubs

NOTES ON ORGANIZATION

The trees and shrubs in this section are grouped largely by family because families tend to share many characteristics. We begin with a few woody plants that might be mistaken for herbaceous plants by the casual observer. Then we cover shrubs and trees with simple leaves, followed by species with compound leaves, and finally trees with needles or scales.

River Cane *(Arundinaria gigantea)*

Distinguishing Characteristics: Height up to 6 m (20'). Actually a member of the grass family, but likely to be thought of as a shrub because of its woody stems. An evergreen plant with a tall, straight, hollow, jointed stem. Leaves are 5–12 inches long, dark green, and sharply pointed at the tip. They occur in groups of 3 or 5 at the ends of short branches. The leaf sheath is rounded and overlapping, and is attached to the stem by a row of short hairs. Various species of non-native, invasive bamboo have been introduced and are likely to create confusion when attempting to identify river cane near human developments.

Habitat and Remarks: Native. FACW. Grows in large thickets called canebrakes along bottomland wetlands and swamps. These thickets were once a dominant part of the southeastern U.S. landscape; however, it is believed that less than 2 percent of these remain today. The biggest reasons for their decline are fire suppression and clearing for farmland. River cane (considered 2 or 3 species by some) is the only member of the bamboo family that is native to the U.S.; however, there have been many shortsighted introductions of non-native bamboo species for commercial use. These plantings will only lead to destruction of wildlife habitat and choking of native plant communities. River cane was used by Native Americans as food and fuel, and for making weapons, baskets, and flutes. River cane thickets make excellent wildlife habitat and were once used as year-round grazing for livestock. They are also important for erosion control, and have been found to be very effective at filtering agricultural runoff.

Swamp Rose   *(Rosa palustris)*

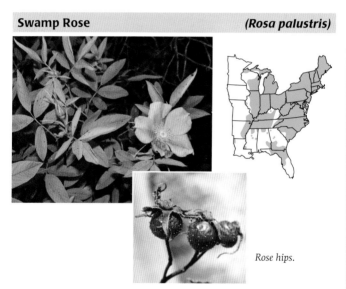

Rose hips.

Distinguishing Characteristics: Height up to 2.1 m (7'). A relatively large, erect rose. Flowers have 5 pink petals and yellow centers. Twigs are smooth or slightly pubescent with slightly curved prickles. Leaves pinnately compound and finely serrate, with 7 leaflets on most leaves. Fruits, called hips, at 1.9 cm (¾") are large for a wild rose. This is the most common wild rose found in eastern U.S. wetlands.

Habitat and Remarks: Native. OBL. Found in freshwater marshes, the margins of fens and bogs, and sunny portions of swamps. Provides nesting habitat and food for birds and small mammals. The mealy hips can be nibbled raw or used to make a tea that is very high in vitamin C.

Steeplebush and Meadowsweet   *(Spiraea* spp.)

- ▢ both
- ▢ meadowsweet
- ▢ steeplebush

Above left:
Meadowsweet
(S. alba).

Left: Steeplebush
(S. tomentosa).

Distinguishing Characteristics: Height up to 2.1 m (7'). Erect shrubs that might be confused for an herbaceous plant. At first glance they look like a pink or white goldenrod species. There are 2 species commonly found in eastern wetlands: steeplebush (also known as hardhack, *S. tomentosa*) and white meadowsweet (*S. alba*). The flowers of these 2 species are in racemes or panicles that are longer than they are wide, while other shrubs in this genus have an inflorescence that is wider than it is long (a corymb). Leaves are alternate and lanceolate, and the edges have both large and small teeth. Steeplebush usually has pink flowers (sometimes white), and the leaves are tomentose (fuzzy) on the lower surface. White meadowsweet has white flowers, and the leaves are hairless below.

Habitat and Remarks: Native. FACW. These shrubs are most common in the northern part of their range and at higher elevations farther south. They are most common in sunny wetlands such as bogs, fens, old beaver ponds, wet meadows, and the edges of marshes and lakes. The seeds and flower buds are occasionally eaten by birds, and the plant provides cover for a number of small animals. The foliage is largely avoided by herbivores.

Swamp Loosestrife *(Decodon verticillatus)*

*Swamp loosestrife
growth habit.*

Distinguishing Characteristics: Height up to 1 m (3.3'), but arching stems to 2 m (6.6'). Actually a perennial sub-shrub that dies back to the ground every year in colder climates. The lower stems are often woody, and it is likely to be thought of as a shrub. Leaves are opposite or whorled, entire, and willow-like. Flowers are pink/purple with 5 petals and 5 long, protruding stamens. The branches arch to the water where they take root and form more arching stems.

Habitat and Remarks: Native. OBL. Found in sunny habitats, such as marshes and the fringes of bogs, fens, sparsely canopied portions of swamps, and lakes/ponds. This shrub can form extensive thickets. It provides cover for wildlife and its capsules are eaten by ducks.

Cranberries *(Vaccinium macrocarpon* and *V. oxycoccos)*

Top left: Large cranberry (V. macrocarpon).

Above: Small cranberry (V. oxycoccos).

Left: Cranberry fruit.

Distinguishing Characteristics: Trailing vines with length up to 2 m (6.6'), but height is usually only up to 0.3 m (1'). Surprisingly small for a shrub, and easily mistaken for an herbaceous plant. Tiny, elliptical, evergreen (reddish in winter) leaves. The 2 major species are very similar; however, large cranberry (*V. macrocarpon*) has broader leaves with flatter edges, larger fruits, and larger bracts (>3 mm [>⅛"]) located more than halfway up the pedicel (flower stalk). Small cranberry (*V. oxycoccos*) has more elongate narrow leaves with the edges rolled under, smaller fruits, and tiny bracts (<3mm [<⅛"]) located less than halfway up the pedicel. Southern mountain cranberry (*V. erythrocarpum*) and highbush cranberry (*Viburnum opulus*) might be confusing because of their names, but these are larger woody shrubs, not creeping vines.

Habitat and Remarks: Native. OBL. Originally called "craneberries" because of the resemblance of their graceful flowers to these birds. Found in bogs, fens, constructed cranberry marshes, and a few other sunny wetland types, and often associated with sphagnum moss. Cranberries are most common in the extensive bogs of cold northern states, and are also found in cool parts of Asia and Europe. In the eastern U.S., they can also be found farther south at high elevations in the Appalachian Mountains. Cranberries were an important American Indian food, and large crops are grown commercially for cranberry juice and sauce. Natural wetlands were once used to grow cranberries, but now they are often grown in large impoundments, excavated and carefully leveled in upland areas where the water level can be manipulated with tile, dykes, and irrigation equipment.

Bog Rosemary   *(Andromeda polifolia)*

Bog rosemary flowers.

Distinguishing Characteristics: Height up to 50 cm (1.7'). Small evergreen shrub with balloon-shaped white flowers, which eventually turn pink. Leaves are alternate and strongly resemble rosemary leaves. They are thin with the edges tightly rolled under, and have a low-luster, blue-green top surface with a fuzzy, whitish surface underneath. Bog laurel is similar, except it has opposite leaves.

Habitat and Remarks: Native. OBL. One of several small evergreen shrubs of the Heath family (Ericaceae) that inhabit northern bogs. Acid-loving. Commonly found in part shade in cedar/spruce bogs. Despite its name and appearance, this species is not related to rosemary, and is in fact *poisonous. It contains acetylandromedol, which in large quantities causes symptoms such as watery mouth and eyes, low blood pressure, vomiting, paralysis, and sometimes death.*

TREES AND SHRUBS

Bog Laurel   *(Kalmia polifolia)*

Distinguishing Characteristics: Height up to 50 cm (1.7'). Small evergreen shrub with pink flowers. Leaves are opposite and narrowly elliptical, with smooth edges tightly rolled under. Bog rosemary (*Andromeda polifolia*) is found in similar habitats, but its leaves are alternate. Sheep laurel (*K. angustifolia*) is similar and found throughout the Northeast, but typically has leaves in whorls of 3. Mountain laurel (*K. latifolia*) is a widely distributed upland species often found along the fringes of mountain bogs. It is usually larger and more often has white flowers. You may see similarly shaped flowers in pocosins and wet pine forests because 3 other *Kalmia* species are found in southeastern wetlands.

Habitat and Remarks: Native. OBL. One of many small evergreen shrubs of the Heath family (Ericaceae) that inhabit bogs. Acid-loving. Leaves, bark, and wood of this species are toxic to humans.

Leatherleaf *(Chamaedaphne calyculata)*

Leatherleaf flowers.

Distinguishing Characteristics: Height up to 1.5 m (4.9′). Evergreen shrub with alternate, elliptical, leathery leaves; finely toothed at the tip with a shiny green upper surface. Unlike many similar members of the Heath family, such as huckleberries, the stem and underside of the leaves are covered in tiny brown scales. Urn-shaped white flowers hang from one side of a raceme or are found singly in leaf axils.

Habitat and Remarks: Native. OBL. This is one of several evergreen shrubs in the Heath family that is typical of sunny northern bogs; however, there are scattered populations occurring in southern montane bogs, pocosins, and peat domes. It loves acidic conditions. As trees shade these wetlands, leatherleaf becomes sparse. This is one of the first shrubs to recolonize bogs after commercial peat mining and clear-cutting. It is grazed by sharp-tailed grouse, moose, and other members of the deer family.

TREES AND SHRUBS

Bog Labrador Tea   *(Ledum groenlandicum)*

Distinguishing Characteristics: Height up to 1 m (3.3'). Evergreen shrub with oblong, alternate leaves. The leaves are curled under along the edges, and the upper surfaces are leathery green. Unlike many similar evergreen shrubs, the lower leaf surfaces are densely covered in cinnamon-brown hairs. Stems are covered in fine hairs. Flowers are tight clusters of small white flowers.

Habitat and Remarks: Native. OBL. This is one of the most common shrubs in northern bogs. The blooms are used by several butterfly species, and the leaves are browsed by moose. The leaves can be dried and steeped in hot water to produce an aromatic tea (steep until the water turns a deep orange color). This tea was used extensively as a substitute for oriental tea during the American Revolution, and has potential health benefits. However, excessive use or concentrated doses may have negative health effects as this plant contains alkaloids that are known to be toxic to livestock.

Fetterbush   *(Lyonia lucida)*

Distinguishing Characteristics: Height up to 2.7 m (9'). One species of a confusing tangle of ericaceous shrubs (members of the Heath family) often found in eastern wetlands, especially in the Southeast. Leaves are alternate, thick, leathery, elliptical, shiny green above, and dull green with black spots below. The leaf edges are smooth, and 3 light-colored veins (1 in the middle of the leaf and 1 along the very edge of each margin) contrast with the darker leaf tissue. Twigs are 3-angled and red or green, turning brown with age. Bark is covered with black scales. Flowers are pinkish-white, urn-shaped, and occur in clusters. The fruit is an ovular capsule with 5 chambers that occurs in clusters surrounding the stem. Fetterbush could easily be mistaken for many other members of the Heath family. However, the most similar species have extensive scaly tissue on the underside of the leaves, toothed margins, thinner deciduous leaves, and/or white flowers. Similar shrubs include 4 other *Lyonia* species: coastal fetterbush (*Eubotrys racemosa*), blueberries, huckleberries, and leatherleaf.

Habitat and Remarks: Native. FACW. Commonly found in swamps, wet pine savannahs, pocosins, and other southeastern wetlands. As common names such as fetterbush and staggerbush imply, this shrub can form thick tangles of vegetation that are impossible to walk through without a machete. The flowers are an important source of nectar for bees, and deer occasionally browse on the foliage.

Highbush Blueberry   (Vaccinium corymbosum)

Distinguishing Characteristics: Height up to 4 m (13.1'). Crown-forming shrub, not creeping. Leaves are elliptical, entire, with smooth to finely toothed margins, waxy above, pubescent below (at least on the veins). The 5-petaled flowers are white and urn-shaped, occurring in a cluster of 8 to 10. Twigs are glabrous when young. Berries are easily recognized by most people. This is the common, widespread blueberry bush found in eastern wetlands; however, some botanists have split this taxon into numerous species, varieties, and hybrids. Differentiation between these and all other species of *Vaccinium* is beyond the scope of this book. Young specimens might be mistaken for huckleberry species (*Gaylussacia* spp.), which have yellow resinous dots on the undersides of the leaves that leave yellow staining when wiped on paper.

Habitat and Remarks: Native. FACW. Found in sunny locations with acidic soils such as bogs, marshes, lake fringes, and swamps. This plant forms extensive, monospecific stands and is the major source of commercial blueberries. The berries are an excellent source of vitamins such as iron. The plant provides excellent wildlife cover, and the berries are also extremely important for a variety of wildlife ranging from tiny songbirds to bears.

Inkberry *(Ilex glabra)*

Distinguishing Characteristics: Height up to 3 m (10'). Small evergreen member of the Holly family (Aquifoliaceae) with black berries. Can form dense colonies of lithe suckers. Leaves are thick, glabrous, and elliptical, with smooth margins, except at the tip where they are often crenate and sometimes have small prickles. Leaves are usually 3 to 4 times as long as wide (usually <2 cm wide). Big gallberry (*I. coriacea*) is the most similar species, but its leaves are only 1.5 to 3 times as long as they are wide (often >2 cm wide). Other evergreen hollies have red, orange, or yellow berries. Superficially similar to some blueberry and huckleberry species, but their leaves do not have crenate margins or prickles.

Habitat and Remarks: Native. FACW. One of the most common shrubs in pocosins and wet pine savannahs of the Southeast, but also found around bogs, swamps, and other freshwater coastal wetlands. Important nectar plant for honey production in some areas and excellent cover for wildlife. The berries are eaten by a variety of birds *but are mildly poisonous to humans.*

Common Winterberry *(Ilex verticillata)*

Distinguishing Characteristics: Height up to 4.5 m (15'). A large, multi-stemmed shrub with showy red berries lasting from late summer through much of the winter. Bark is dark gray with raised lenticels. Leaves are thin, deciduous, alternate, and doubly serrate. There are a number of other members of the holly family that have red berries; however, many of these have thick, evergreen leaves. Winterberry can be distinguished from the other 10 red-berried, deciduous hollies such as possumhaw (*I. decidua*) and smooth winterberry (*I. laevigata*) by the following characteristics: leaves that are finely toothed and finely hairy; leaves that are broadest past the middle; a shiny fruit surface; fruit pedicels <9 mm long; 6 to 8 seeds in each fruit; smooth seed surface; and ciliate and obtuse sepals (as opposed to smooth and acute). Winterberry is the most widespread of these species, and the only one found in most of the Great Lakes region. Possumhaw is extremely similar and dominates much of the Southeast.

Habitat and Remarks: Native. FACW. Also known as black alder. Winterberry is a common shrub of northern swamps, and is found along the margins of lakes, bogs, fens, streamhead seeps, and marshes throughout the eastern U.S. It does best in sunny locations with acidic soil. This is an extremely important native shrub for landscaping, and its bright red berries provide visual appeal and wildlife food throughout the winter months. Female plants produce the red berries, while the male plants are necessary for pollination (actually, a male holly of virtually any species can fulfill this role).

Eastern Baccharis *(Baccharis halimifolia)*

Distinguishing Characteristics: Height up to 2.7 m (9'). Medium-sized shrub with tardily deciduous leaves and green twigs. In the fall female plants turn silvery with whitish bristle-tipped achenes, while male plants bloom a dull yellow. Flowers are at the ends of the branches. The leaves are alternate, fleshy, and variable in shape, often with prominent dull teeth. Silverling (*B. glomeruliflora*) is similar, but has flowers at intervals along the branches.

Habitat and Remarks: Native. FAC. Also known as sea myrtle, groundsel-tree, and consumption weed. Baccharis is found in a variety of wetlands, such as brackish marshes, high salt marshes, interdunal swales, and fresh-water marshes; however, it is also hardy enough to survive in upland areas and disturbed sites. In contrast, silverling (FACW) is usually only found in coastal wetlands.

Bayberries and Sweetgale   (Family Myricaceae)

Above: Southern bayberry (M. caroliniensis).

bayberries
sweetgale
both

Left: Sweetgale (M. gale).

Distinguishing Characteristics: Height commonly to 6 m (20'). Diameter up to 15 cm (6"). Evergreen or tardily deciduous shrubs, often with multiple stems. Leaves are elliptic or oblanceolate and coarsely saw-toothed in many species, especially from the middle of the leaf to the tip. Leaves are very aromatic in some species. Fruits of the bayberries (genus *Morella*, 4 native species in our area) are small, warty cones that look like a berry coated in bluish-white wax. Sweetgale (*Myrica gale*) lacks this waxy coating. All of these species were formerly lumped together in the genus *Myrica*.

Habitat and Remarks: Native. FAC through OBL depending on species. Southern bayberry (*Morella caroliniensis*) and scentless bayberry (*Morella inodora*) are found in wet pine savannahs, pocosins, coastal plain bogs, and other southeastern wetlands. Northern bayberry (*Morella pensylvanicum*) and wax myrtle (*Morella cerifera*) prefer drier habitats adjacent to coastal wetlands of the Northeast and Southeast, respectively. Sweetgale, also known as bog myrtle, commonly rings the shores of glacial lakes and bogs in our northern states. Colonists boiled the fruit of bayberries to separate the wax, which they used for candles. The fragrant leaves of shrubs in this family have been used as spices and insect repellent, and for various medicinal purposes.

Redosier Dogwood *(Cornus sericea)*

Redosier dogwood berries.

TREES AND SHRUBS

Distinguishing Characteristics: Height commonly to 3 m (10'). Diameter up to 7.5 cm (3"). A large, spreading, multi-stemmed shrub; rarely a small tree. Leaves are opposite, ovate or elliptical, and pointed at the tip with smooth margins. They are dull green above, whitish green and hairy below, and have 5 to 7 long, curved, sunken veins on either side of the midvein. Twigs are slender, deep, and purplish red, with hairs when young and rings at nodes. Bark is gray or brown, mostly smooth with slight furrows and flat plates. Flowers are small and white and occur in clusters. Fruit is a small whitish drupe with 2 seeds.

Habitat and Remarks: Native to the northern and western U.S., but considered invasive in some states. FACW. It is common in moist woodlands and wetlands and around the edges of ponds, lakes, and streams where it forms thickets. When branch tips lean over and touch the ground, they will root and form new shoots. It is important for erosion control on stream banks in its native range. The name "osier" comes from French, meaning "willow-like." Native Americans had many uses for different parts of the plant. They used the inner bark in tanning hides or smoked it in a tobacco mixture during ceremonies. The berries were used for medicinal purposes, and the stems were used for making dreamcatchers and arrows and for weaving baskets.

TREES AND SHRUBS

Swamp Bay   *(Persea palustris)*

Distinguishing Characteristics: Height commonly to 9 m (30'). Diameter up to 0.6 m (2'). Small tree with a compact, rounded crown and thick, upright branches. Leaves are alternate, elliptical, or lanceolate, and are thick, bright shiny green above and pale and hairy below, with smooth margins curled slightly under. Leaves are pungently aromatic if crushed. Twigs are slender, fuzzy, and dark green. Hairs on twigs and leaves are often rust colored. Bark is dark reddish brown with broad scaly ridges. Flowers are yellow and appear in many clusters at the leaf base in early spring. Fruit is up to 1.5 cm (0.6") long, oblong, and shiny dark blue with a 6-lobed cup at the base. Red bay (*P. borbonia*) is very similar, except its twigs are smooth. There are at least 2 other trees that, along with swamp bay, are collectively referred to as "bays" in our southeastern wetlands. Sweetbay (*Magnolia virginiana*) also has aromatic leaves, but has huge white-petaled flowers encircling scars on the twigs and a distinctive aggregate of red fruits similar to other magnolia species. Loblolly bay (*Gordonia lasianthus*) has smooth leaves that are not aromatic when crushed, large white flowers that are ball-like before they open, and usually at least a few red or orange leaves during any season.

Habitat and Remarks: Native. FACW. Common in a variety of southeastern wetlands including wet pine forests, swamps, interdunal swales, pocosins, and other peaty wetlands. The wood is handsome and used for cabinetry as well as for lumber. The leaves can be dried or used fresh in place of commercial bay leaves for seasoning soups and other foods. The berries are also a food source for many types of birds.

Common Buttonbush *(Cephalanthus occidentalis)*

Distinguishing Characteristics: Height up to 6 m (20'). Diameter up to 10.2 cm (4"). A shrub, or rarely a small tree, with many crooked branches, often leaning. Leaves are opposite or whorled with 3 at a node, and ovate or elliptical with pointed tips. They have round bases and smooth edges. Leaves are very late to fall. Twigs are reddish brown, usually smooth, and marked with large, corky lenticels. Flowers are small, white, and tubular, and form into dense round clusters with many flowers each. Fruit is a rough brown ball consisting of many nuts.

Habitat and Remarks: Native. OBL. Buttonbush thrives in the wettest places that a shrub will grow and is often found living in semi-permanently flooded areas. It grows in marshes, bogs, sunny gaps in swamps, and on the fringes of lakes and ponds. Ducks are very fond of the seeds. The branches, which are usually coated with vines, form a sort of platform above flooded areas and are inhabited by nesting birds, sunning snakes, and small mammals.

TREES AND SHRUBS

TREES AND SHRUBS

Mangroves   (Unrelated, except by common name)

all 3 mangroves

black mangrove only

Above left:
Black mangrove
pneumatophores.

Left: Red mangrove
prop roots.

Distinguishing Characteristics: Height commonly to 20 m (66'), but usually much shorter. This is a group of tropical trees that are not actually that closely related, but together they form a very important coastal wetland ecosystem. All of them have rather succulent, ovular leaves with smooth margins; however, each has characteristics that easily set it apart. Red mangroves (*Rhizophora mangle*) have tall, branching prop roots. Black mangroves (*Avicennia germinans*) have numerous short, aerating branches (pneumatophores) that stick up from the roots. While white mangroves (*Laguncularia racemosa*) may also have pneumatophores, they have 2 glandular bumps on the petiole of each leaf.

Habitat and Remarks: Native. OBL. The word mangrove refers both to the trees that make up the habitat and the habitat itself. These are extremely important saltwater wetlands, and may be interspersed with various salt marsh species. They provide habitat for numerous fish, crabs, reptiles, birds, and mammals. Red mangrove usually occurs closest to salt water, often taking root on tiny islands of sand. Its roots catch sediment and organic material and actually begin to build land out into the ocean. Black mangroves often inhabit the area directly landward of red mangroves, and white mangroves live landward of the black mangroves. However, they may be interspersed in various combinations. Mangroves are viviparous (bring forth live young) in that they send out very mature seedlings called propagules rather than producing a dormant seed stage. These propagules float

Above: White mangrove (L. racemosa).

Right: Red mangrove propagule.

until they become stranded in sediment where they can develop; this gives them a leg up over plants with seeds, which often have difficulty germinating while submerged.

Water Tupelo *(Nyssa aquatica)*

Left: Water tupelo leaves.

Below: Water tupelo leaves and fruit.

Distinguishing Characteristics: Height commonly to 24 m (80'). Diameter up to 1.8 m (6'). A large, aquatic tree with a long trunk, swollen base, and narrow, rounded crown. Leaves are large—often up to 30 cm (11.8") long—and slightly thickened, ovate, irregularly toothed, smooth, and shiny dark green above and paler below, with a

long, hairy leafstalk. Twigs are thick and hairy when young, and reddish brown. Bark is dark gray or brown and furrowed into long ridges. Male flowers occur in long clusters while females occur singly, usually on separate trees. Fruit is an oblong, dark purple, berry-like drupe about 2.5 cm (1") long. There are 3 other tupelo species found in and around wetlands. Ogeechee tupelo (*N. ogeche*) is the most similar, found primarily in Georgia and Florida, and has velvety twigs and leaf undersides. Black tupelo (*N. sylvatica*) and swamp tupelo (*N. biflora*) are very nondescript trees and are so similar that they are considered to be the same species by some. Their leaves hang on petioles <2.5 cm (1"), while those of water tupelo are >3 cm (1.2"), inhabit less permanently flooded areas, and have much smaller leaves and fruits than water tupelo

Habitat and Remarks: Native. OBL. A quintessential tree of southern swamps and floodplains, where they usually spend several months of the year submerged in water. The scientific name *Nyssa* is derived from that of a Greek water nymph. Tupelo comes from the Creek Indian word meaning "swamp tree." The roots of the tree are spongy and are locally used in place of cork for fishing net floats. Hollow tupelos provide habitat for many wildlife species, including large groups of bats.

Black Willow *(Salix nigra)*

Distinguishing Characteristics: Height commonly to 15 m (50'). Diameter up to 0.8 m (2.5'). Tree, usually with a divided trunk. Trunks are straight and usually leaning. Leaves are alternate, narrowly lanceolate, and usually curved to one side. They are finely toothed and smooth, shiny green above and paler below. Twigs are brownish, slender, and delicate. The bark is very dark brown to black and deeply furrowed into scaly ridges. Flowers form in catkins with hairy yellow scales. Fruit is a reddish-brown capsule that matures late in the spring. There are at least 31 other native species of willow in the eastern U.S. (even more north of the Great Lakes). Most of them are shrubby species with narrow leaves like those of the black willow. A few willows, such as pussy and Bebb's willow (*S. discolor* and *S. bebbiana*), have broad leaves. Several native willows reach more than 6 m (20') in height, but no other species form trees as large as black willows. There are also many non-native willows, especially hybrids and variations of the weeping willow (*Salix babylonica*).

Habitat and Remarks: Native. FACW or OBL depending on region. Found in virtually any damp sunny spot, including beaver ponds, pond/lake fringes, ditches, bottomland hardwood forests, and swamps. Black willow grows very fast and sometimes occurs in stands, but also is found with other mixed hardwoods. This is the only willow important for wood products. Native Americans and others use the supple shoots (called withes) in basket making. The dried inner bark can be steeped in hot water (1 to 2 teaspoons per cup of water) for about 30 minutes to produce an aspirin-like pain reliever. Willow cuttings root readily in damp soil and are used extensively for erosion control.

Eastern Cottonwood *(Populus deltoides)*

Distinguishing Characteristics: Height commonly to 27 m (90'). Diameter up to 1.5 m (5'). A large-branched tree with a broad open crown. Leaves are triangular with coarse, curved teeth and long, flattened leaf stalks that allow them to flutter in the slightest wind. Twigs are thick, yellow

TREES AND SHRUBS

brown, and angular. Buds are greenish, often with a golden resin under the scales. Bark is yellow green and smooth in young trees, becoming ash gray and thickly furrowed in old ones. The fruits, which are produced in early summer, consist of small seeds attached to cotton-like fibers that gather into small drifts in cottonwood groves. Might be mistaken for swamp cottonwood (*P. heterophylla*), an obligate wetland tree with petioles that are round in cross section; or balsam poplar (*P. balsamifera*), a northern tree with dark buds coated with reddish resin.

Habitat and Remarks: Native. FAC. Cottonwood is found along swamps, bottomland wetlands, ponds, and the fringes of wet meadows and marshes. It is one of the fastest-growing native trees and can grow up to 1.5 m (5') per year in prime habitats. It is possible for this tree to grow up to 4 m (13') tall in its first year of life. Cottonwood is a favorite beaver food, and the buds are eaten by many mammals and birds. It is relatively short lived, but this characteristic makes the cottonwood an excellent home for snag-loving species such as wood ducks, woodpeckers, and various bats.

American Elm *(Ulmus americana)*

Cross section of bark showing brown and white layers.

Distinguishing Characteristics: Height commonly to 24 m (80'). Diameter up to 2 m (6.5'). A large tree with a spreading crown. Leaves are alternate, doubly serrate, lance shaped, and asymmetrical at the base. The leaves may be smooth or rough on the upper surface, but are not as rough as those of slippery elm (*U. rubra*). The bark is rough and corky, often displaying white areas. Unlike other elms sometimes found in wetlands, such as slippery elm and water-elm (*Planera aquatica*), American elm bark consists of alternating layers of corky brown and white tissue. This is easily seen in cross section when a small chunk of the outer bark is sliced from the tree and broken in half.

Habitat and Remarks: Native. FACW (FAC in the coastal plain). Commonly found in bottomland forested wetlands, swamps, beaver ponds, the edges of lakes, and upland habitats. Less indicative of wetland conditions in the coastal plain region than in other areas. Dutch Elm Disease, a fungal disease spread by elm bark beetles (subfamily Scotytinae), has wiped out many of our larger American elms, although moderate-size trees are still common. The inner bark is very fibrous, and with the proper technique it can be folded into waterproof containers. Large plates of bark were once peeled and used to cover American Indian dwellings. The tree is edible and has various medicinal uses.

Sweetgum *(Liquidambar styraciflua)*

Sweetgum
(L. styraciflua).

Distinguishing Characteristics: Height commonly to 23 m (75'). Diameter up to 1.2 m (4'). A tall tree with a small crown. Leaves are alternate and distinctively star shaped. They have 5 to 7 deep lobes with 5 main veins and finely toothed margins, and are shiny bright green above and paler below. Twigs are round or slightly angled and commonly develop cork-like wings during the second year. Bark is gray brown, thick, and deeply furrowed with rounded scaly ridges. Flowers are very small and occur in round green clusters. Fruit is a brown ball that droops down from a long stem and is composed of several individual fruits that end in 2 long prickly points.

Habitat and Remarks: Native. FACW in the Midwest and FAC elsewhere. Lives in bottomland hardwood forests, drained beaver ponds, and along the edges of swamps and wet meadows. It is often one of the first trees to appear after clear-cutting occurs, or in abandoned fields. The wood of this tree is very important to the timber industry and is second only to the oak in hardwood harvesting quantity. Pioneers once made gum out of resin that they scraped from behind the bark of these trees. It was used for chewing, and as a remedy for multiple ailments such as cough and sore throat. It is currently an ingredient in "compound tincture of benzoin," which is available in pharmacies and has a variety of respiratory- and skin-related uses.

Alders *(Alnus spp.)*

TREES AND SHRUBS

Catkins and strobili.

hazel alder

multiple alder species

Distinguishing Characteristics: Height commonly to 9 m (30'). Diameter up to 10.2 cm (4"). Large spreading shrubs, or occasionally small trees, with many trunks. Might be mistaken for other members of the Birch family (Betulaceae). Alders are easily recognized by their small, pinecone-like fruiting structures called strobili, which can usually be found on mature specimens year round. Individual trees have both male and female flowers. Male flowers of all alders consist of yellowish drooping catkins, while female flowers are variable. Leaves are alternate, obovate or elliptical, and finely toothed, sometimes with wavy edges. The 4 native eastern U.S. species are distinguished as follows:

- **Hazel alder (A. serrulata):** only species throughout most of the Southeast but ranges north into New England; smooth bark without obvious lenticels; strobili in groups.
- **Seaside alder (A. maritime):** extremely limited range (only found in tiny areas of coastal Delaware and Maryland, northwest Georgia, and Oklahoma); smooth bark without obvious lenticels; single strobili.

Speckled alder.

- **Speckled alder (*A. incana*):** primarily a northern species; bark is red or brown and speckled with prominent whitish lenticels; female flowers droop.
- **Green alder (*A. viridis*):** primarily a northern species; young twigs with greenish bark; all bark marked with prominent lenticels, upright female flowers, unstalked buds, long-stalked strobili.

Be aware that there are also several cultivated species that may occur on disturbed sites and near developed areas.

Habitat and Remarks: Native. FACU through OBL depending on species and region. These species form thickets in a variety of habitats ranging from southern swamps to northern bogs and coastal wetlands. Alders help to replace nitrogen in the soil by fixing it from the air via a symbiotic relationship with the bacteria living on their roots (similar to the way that legumes help to replace soil nitrogen). Because of their ability to live on and improve barren soils, alders can inhabit strip-mined land, clear-cuts, and old rockslides. Alders provide browse for deer, moose, rabbits, and beavers. The buds, seeds, and catkins are also important food sources for songbirds, woodcocks, and grouse.

River Birch   *(Betula nigra)*

Distinguishing Characteristics: Height commonly to 24 m (80'). Diameter up to 0.6 m (2'). Usually a small tree with multiple leaning trunks. Leaves are alternate, sharply double-serrate, shiny dark green above and whitish and hairy below, with 7 to 9 pairs of veins. Bark is thin and yellowish, silver, or bronze, and separates distinctively into shaggy, curled, papery strips. Fruit matures in May or June and takes the shape of a cone with hairy scales and 2-winged nuts. Yellow birch (*B. alleghaniensis*, FAC) is found in some swamps and bogs in northern states and mountainous areas. It has less papery bark and twigs that are sweet smelling when rubbed. Gray birch (*B. populifolia*, FAC), which inhabits some northern bogs and wet meadows, has smooth, sooty-grayish bark and pointed triangular leaves. Bog birch (*B. pumila*, OBL) is a shrub that more closely resembles an alder than a birch and is commonly found in bogs around the Great Lakes.

Habitat and Remarks: Native. FACW. Often found in swamps, bottomland wetlands, beaver ponds, and other wetlands associated with streams. This is the southernmost birch in the U.S. and the only one that exists at low altitudes in the Southeast. The sap of all birches is edible and can be made into a syrup that is similar to molasses. The inner bark can be dried and made into flour, and the twigs can be boiled to make tea.

Wetland Oaks   *(Quercus* spp.)

Distinguishing Characteristics: Height commonly to 27 m (90'). Diameter up to 1.8 m (6'). Oaks have alternate leaves that may be lobed or entire. All oaks have buds clustered at the tips of the twigs, and all oaks have acorns. Eastern oaks can be divided into 2 major groups: red oaks and white oaks. The red oaks generally have bristle-tipped leaves, tight dark-colored bark, and acorn caps that are hairy on the inside (e.g., pin oak, cherrybark oak, willow oak, and water oak). The white oaks generally have rounded leaf lobes that lack bristle tips, peeling light-colored bark, and acorn caps that are not hairy on the inside (e.g., swamp chestnut oak, swamp white oak, and overcup oak).

Key identifying characteristics of several common eastern wetland oaks are summarized here with photos for quick reference. Note that oaks often hybridize.

Pin oak (Q. palustris): 5 to 7 bristle-tipped lobes and deep, rounded sinuses. Tight, dark bark. Long, straight trunk and nearly horizontal branches. FACW.

Cherrybark oak (Q. pagoda): Bark resembles that of wild black cherry (Prunus serotina). 7 to 11 lobes. Wedge-shaped leaf base. One side of each leaf sinus meets the mid-line at a 90-degree angle, creating a leaf shaped like a pagoda. FACW.

Willow oak (Q. phellos): Very small, willow-like, elliptical leaves with smooth edges and a tiny bristle tip. Tight bark. Most similar to swamp laurel oak (Q. laurifolia), which is uncommon, and has more leathery leaves that are broadened in the middle and persist most of the winter. FAC or FACW, depending on region.

Water oak (Q. nigra): Semi-evergreen. Tight, dark bark. Leaves are wedge-shaped with 3 short, bristle-tipped lobes at their end. FAC or FACW, depending on region.

Above: Swamp chestnut oak (Q. michauxii): Also known as basket oak. Light gray, scaly bark. Leaves are large and elliptical, with large, evenly spaced, rounded teeth along the margin. Most similar wetland species is swamp white oak, but it has less symmetrical leaf margins and very distinctive acorn stalks. FACW.

Left: Swamp chestnut oak acorns.

Above: Swamp white oak (Q. bicolor): Bark is light gray and flaky, becoming blockier at the base with maturity. Leaf margins are sparsely and often irregularly toothed. Leaf is whitish below and green above. Acorn stalk is longer than any similar wetland oak (2.5–10 cm [1–4"]). FACW.

Left: Close-up of developing acorns and last year's cap.

Overcup oak (Q. lyrata): Bark is light gray and flaky. Leaves are various irregular shapes, often with 3 rectangular lobes at the end, giving the leaf a crucifix shape. Acorns are very distinctive—large and almost completely enclosed in a thin cap. OBL.

Habitat and Remarks: Oaks are an important part of forested wetlands throughout the East. Pin oak and swamp white oak inhabit many of our northern swamps, bottomlands, and wet flatwoods, while the other species listed above and on the previous pages tend to inhabit southern wet hardwood forests and swamps. Acorns from members of the red oak group take 2 years to mature, while those of the white oak group mature in a single year. The acorns of most members of the white oak group are lower in tannins and are more palatable to wildlife and humans. However, some species in the red oak group (such as willow oak and pin oak) have small acorns that are readily eaten whole by ducks. Acorns are a hugely important winter food source for wildlife including waterfowl (especially wood ducks), squirrels, wild turkeys, deer, and songbirds. They are also edible for humans and can be ground into flour after being soaked or boiled in several changes of water to remove bitter tannins.

American Sycamore   *(Platanus occidentalis)*

American sycamore leaf.

Distinguishing Characteristics: Height commonly to 30 m (100'). Diameter up to 2.4 m (8'). A large, strikingly colored tree, with a massive straight trunk and crooked, spreading branches. Leaves are alternate and with 3 to 5 very shallow lobes, 3 to 5 main veins, and coarsely toothed margins. Twigs are slender and green, and grow in zigzag patterns. Bark is smooth and flakes off in large patches, exposing underlying layers and giving the upper trunk a very mottled appearance of white, green, brown, and gray. The base of the tree is dark reddish brown and scaly. Fruit is a brown ball, 2.5 cm (1") in diameter, on a long stalk and is made up of many tiny nutlets, each with a hair tuft.

Habitat and Remarks: Native. FACW. American sycamore inhabits various types of wetlands including bottomland hardwood forests, swamps, beaver ponds, and the edges of wet meadows and lakes. The white upper branches of sycamore are visible from far away and can often be used to locate wet areas in the distance. Sycamore is a fast-growing pioneer species that quickly takes over cleared land. It is among the largest of the eastern hardwoods, and the biggest American sycamore on record had a trunk diameter of almost 4.6 m (15'). American sycamore can be tapped like a maple tree and the sap can be boiled down to make sugar or syrup, although it takes huge amounts of sap to do this. The trunks of old sycamores are often hollow and provide habitat for variety of wildlife, including bats, raccoons, opossums, woodpeckers, and chimney swifts.

Red Maple   *(Acer rubrum)*

Distinguishing Characteristics: Height commonly to 21 m (70'). Diameter up to 0.8 m (2.5'). A large tree with a tight, rounded crown. Leaf shape, texture, and thickness vary across this species' range. Leaves are opposite, with 3 short, pointed lobes (5 in some varieties), irregularly toothed margins, 5 main veins from the base, and red leafstalks. They are dull green above and paler and hairy below. Twigs are slender and reddish brown. Bark is thin and gray when young, becoming fissured with age into long, rough ridges. Flowers are red and occur in tight clusters in very early spring. Fruit is a paired, forking samara with long wings.

Habitat and Remarks: Native. FAC. Occurs in stream floodplain wetlands and swamps, but is also quite common in upland forests in some areas. It has the largest north-to-south range of any East Coast tree species. Red maples are commonly planted for shade because of their beautiful displays of red leaves in fall and flowers in spring. However, their soft wood does make them prone to rot. Early settlers used the bark to make ink and dyes.

Silver Maple *(Acer saccharinum)*

Distinguishing Characteristics: Height commonly to 21 m (70'). Diameter up to 0.9 m (3'). A large, forked tree with an open, spreading crown, long branches that curve downward, and a short, thick trunk. Leaves are opposite, and have 5 deep lobes (with a long-pointed middle lobe), doubly saw-toothed margins, and 5 main veins from the base. They are dull green above and silvery below, with a reddish leafstalk. Twigs are long, green or brown, and droop slightly. Bark is gray and furrowed into long, shaggy ridges. Flowers occur in tight clusters in very early spring. They begin as reddish buds and then turn greenish yellow. Fruit is a paired, widely forking samara with long, broad wings.

Habitat and Remarks: Native. FACW in most regions, FAC in coastal plain. Found in wet soils along floodplain wetlands and swamps. Like red maple, it is commonly planted for shade, but has brittle limbs that are prone to wind damage. The sap can be harvested for sugar, but is low yielding.

Boxelder *(Acer negundo)*

Distinguishing Characteristics: Height commonly to 18 m (60'). Diameter up to 0.8 m (2.5'). A small- to medium-sized tree with a broad, rounded crown and a short trunk. Leaves are opposite and pinnately compound, with 3 to 7 paired leaflets (except at the tip) along a slender axis. Leaflets are elliptical with a sharply pointed tip, sharply toothed (sometimes lobed), and light green above and paler green with hairs below. Twigs are mostly green, sometimes appearing whitish or purple. Bark is thin, light gray or brown, and becomes deeply furrowed into broad ridges. Flowers are very small, greenish yellow, and clustered together on drooping stalks. The fruit is a paired samara with a flat body and long, curved wing.

Habitat and Remarks: Native. FAC. Common along the edges of swamps, ponds, and floodplain wetlands. Boxelders are easily distinguished from other maples by their pinnately compound leaves. They are fast growing and often planted for shade, but can be broken easily in wind. Native Americans collected the sap to make into sugar. The common name comes from the resemblance of its leaves to those of the elders, and its light wood to that of boxwoods.

TREES AND SHRUBS

Poison Sumac   *(Toxicodendron vernix)*

Distinguishing Characteristics: Height commonly to 6 m (20'). Diameter up to 15 cm (6"). A shrub, or small tree, with a narrow crown. Leaves are pinnately compound with 5 to 13 leaflets on a red axis. Leaflets are paired, except at the end, and ovate or elliptical with smooth margins. They are shiny dark green above and duller green and hairy below. In fall, they become bright orange or red. Twigs are red when young, and later turn gray with many orange spots. Flowers are greenish, with 5 petals, and often in long clusters. Fruit is a poisonous, waxy, one-seeded white berry that occurs in bunches. The fruit often remains attached well into the spring.

Habitat and Remarks: Native. OBL. Found in bogs, swamps and flood-plains, and shady forests. It is a dangerous plant, containing extremely toxic sap, which causes a rash on most people upon contact. Though the berries are also toxic to humans, they are not poisonous to birds and wildlife, and provide an important food source for many animals, especially in winter when food is hard to find.

Swamp Titi *(Cyrilla racemiflora)*

TREES AND SHRUBS

Distinguishing Characteristics: Height up to 9 m (30'). Diameter up to 20 cm (8"). A multi-branched shrub or small tree with a short, crooked trunk and a spreading crown. Leaves are narrow and oblong (usually widest beyond the middle), with a blunt tip and smooth margins. They are slightly thickened, dark shiny green above and paler below, and occur in clusters at the end of twigs. Twigs are slim and brown. Bark is gray and smooth when young, and becomes scaly and reddish brown with age. Flowers are white and occur in crowded, upright clusters. Fruit is round, brown or yellow, and also occurs in clusters.

Habitat and Remarks: Native. FACW. Occurs in southern floodplains and around sandy swamps. It is also native to Central and South America and the West Indies. In the mountain forests of Puerto Rico, it is known as a red tree because of the color of its bark and wood. The flowers are useful as a nectar source for bees, which use it to produce a dark honey.

TREES AND SHRUBS

Elderberry   *(Sambucus nigra)*

Above left:
Elderberry flower.

Left: Elderberry
lenticel close-up.

Distinguishing Characteristics: Height up to 5 m (16'). Diameter up to 15 cm (6"). Multi-stemmed shrub with an irregular spreading crown. Leaves are opposite and pinnately compound with 3 to 7 leaflets. Twigs are green and angular with homogeneous white pith and node rings. Bark is brown or gray with raised, dot-like growths (lenticels). Flowers form in flat-topped clusters up to 20 cm (8") wide late in the spring and are very fragrant. Fruit is a small, purple or black berry that is juicy and somewhat sweet.

Habitat and Remarks: Native. FACW. Also called American or black elder. Occurs in sunny, moist soils, often at the edges of marshes, swamps, ponds, ditches, and in wet meadows. It is a common, tough, and widespread species that does well in disturbed areas, and is an excellent choice for wetland plantings. The berries are only mildly sweet and are a little unpleasant when raw, but if prepared correctly they make delicious jellies and pies. Dry-

ing the fruit will also remove the unpleasant smell and taste, and it can be stored for later use in muffins or pies. Many species of birds and mammals also feed on the fruit. The flower clusters can be battered and deep fried. *However, the plant's greenery, roots, and unripe fruit are toxic and cause severe stomach upset.*

Green Ash *(Fraxinus pennsylvanica)*

Distinguishing Characteristics: Height commonly to 18 m (60'). Diameter up to 0.6 m (2'). Medium-sized tree with a thick, rounded, or irregular crown. Leaves are opposite and pinnately compound with 7 to 9 oblong or lance-shaped leaflets that are finely toothed. Leaflets are paired (except at the tip), shiny yellow green above and paler and slightly hairy below. Twigs are rounded, green when young, and then gray with age, and have semi-orbicular (shield-shaped) leaf scars below the buds. Fruits are yellowish with a narrow wing extending from the bottom of the seed. They hang in clusters in the fall. There are several similar ash species:

- **White ash (*F. Americana*, FACU)** is widespread but more common in uplands, and has U-shaped leaf scars that partially encircle the bud.
- **Carolina ash (*F. caroliniana*, OBL)** is found in swamps of the southeastern U.S., and has seeds surrounded by a wing (rather than just winged from the bottom).
- **Pumpkin ash (*F. profunda*, OBL)** is an uncommon species found in deep swamps throughout the eastern U.S., often with cypress and tupelo; twigs and undersides of leaflets are pubescent.

Habitat and Remarks: Native. FACW. Prefers loose, moist soils on the fringes of floodplain wetlands, wet meadows, ponds, swamps, and ditches. Several ashes prefer even wetter sites than green ash (see above and black ash), but this species is included here because is the most widespread native wetland ash. It is hardy and fast growing. Unfortunately, all ash species are susceptible to damage and eventual death from the emerald ash borer (*Agrilus planipennis*), an exotic beetle introduced to this country accidentally—probably in wood packing material—from Asia. Adult beetles eat leaves and cause little harm, but the larvae live and feed on the inner bark and disrupt the tree's ability to transport food and water from the leaves to the roots. In many states, quarantine is in effect and it is illegal to move firewood to prevent the spread of the pest.

Black Ash   *(Fraxinus nigra)*

Above: Black ash bark.

Left: Black ash bud.

Distinguishing Characteristics: Height commonly to 15 m (50'). Diameter up to 0.3 m (1'). A small- or medium-sized tree with a narrow, rounded crown. Branches are upright. Leaves are opposite, and pinnately compound, with 7 to 11 paired leaflets (except at the end). Leaflets are lanceolate, finely saw-toothed, and without a stalk. They are dark green above and paler below, with reddish hairs along the midvein. Twigs are thick and gray, and hairy when young. Bark is very soft, gray, and fissured into many narrow ridges that rub off easily. Flowers are purple and occur in small clusters. Fruit is a single, broad-winged key, which hangs in clusters until late summer.

Habitat and Remarks: Native. FACW. Usually only found in wet soils of northern swamps and bogs. It is the northernmost native ash. The name is derived from the dark heartwood. It is also sometimes called basket ash or hoop ash. Splints created by soaking and pounding the wood of this species have been used to create superb baskets, including the durable pack baskets favored by many trappers and gatherers. The wood also has been used for snowshoes, barrels, canoe ribs, and many other functions for which durability and strength are essential.

Bald Cypress (Taxodium distichum)

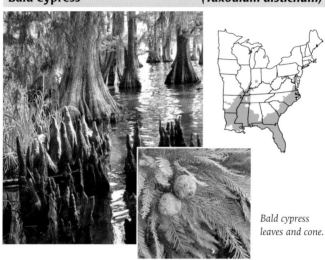

Bald cypress leaves and cone.

Distinguishing Characteristics: Height commonly to 30.5 m (100'). Diameter up to 5.2 m (17'). Deciduous, aquatic conifer with spreading branches, a flat-topped crown, enlarged trunk base, and cone-shaped "knees" growing from the submerged roots. Bark is brown or gray and fibrous, with scaly ridges that peel off in horizontal strips. Cones are round and gray and 2.5 cm (1") in diameter. They grow either singly or in pairs at the end of the twig, and contain several hard, quadrangular cone scales that are shed in the fall. Pond cypress (*T. ascendens*) has been considered to be a separate species by some, but is sometimes considered to be a subspecies of bald cypress. Bald cypress needles grow in 2 flat rows on flattened or 4-angled green twigs. Pond cypress leaves are awl- or scale-like, appressed (angled toward the twig), and overlapping.

Habitat and Remarks: Native. OBL. Bald cypress is the quintessential tree of southern swamps. It is often seen with Spanish moss

Pond cypress leaves.

(*Tillandsia usneoides*) hanging from the boughs in the blackwater swamps of the Deep South. However, the natural range of bald cypress extends northward as far as southern Indiana, and the species has been widely planted in yards and along the edges of lakes as far north as New York. Cypress can often be seen growing in the middle of a shallow body of water; however, this species does not sprout and grow underwater. It requires periodic drying or the presence of exposed hummocks in order to become established. The heartwood is resistant to decay, giving cypress the nickname "wood eternal." The lumber is used for docks and boats.

White Cedars (*Chamaecyparis thyoides* and *Thuja occidentalis*)

northern white cedar

Atlantic white cedar

both

Distinguishing Characteristics: Height commonly to 14 m (45'). Diameter up to 1.8 m (6'). Northern white cedar (*Thuja occidentalis*), and Atlantic white cedar (*Chamaecyparis thyoides*) are similar evergreen trees with soft, smooth leaves (in comparison to the sharp leaves of eastern red cedar [*Juniperus virginiana*]). Bark is fibrous and brownish red. Northern white cedar (pictured) has flattened twigs, fan-shaped sprays of leaves, and irregular scaled cones. Atlantic white cedar also has fan-shaped sprays of leaves, but the twigs are not flattened and cones are round and lumpy.

Habitat and Remarks: Native. Northern white cedar is FACW and Atlantic white cedar is OBL. The Atlantic species grows in peat swamps and bogs along the Atlantic Coast, while the northern species occupies bogs, fens, and swamps in the north and at scattered locations south to the Appalachian Mountains. The white cedars are often found in high-quality sites that are relics of larger wetlands. The foliage is a preferred browse for white-tailed deer, which can have a substantial negative effect on seedlings. The wood is extremely decay resistant and is excellent for outdoor projects ranging from fence posts to shingles to log cabins, but unfortunately it has been heavily logged. Northern white cedar is also commonly called arborvitae, and is widely planted as an ornamental.

Wetland Pines   *(Pinus spp.)*

Distinguishing Characteristics: Height commonly to 30.5 m (100'). Diameter up to 1.5 m (4.9'). The long, thin needles readily separate pines from other wetland conifers, such as spruces, cedars, tamaracks, and cypress. Bark is dark black, gray, or reddish brown, and furrowed into scaly, rectangular plates. There are 4 main species commonly found in southeastern wetlands:

Loblolly pine (*P. taeda*) is the most widespread; has needles mostly in bundles of 3 (sometimes 4); no bunches of needles sprouting from the bark; and cones that are longer than they are wide.

Example of elongate cone (loblolly pine).

Pond pine (*P. serotina*) has needles usually in bundles of 3 (sometimes 4); gnarly branching; many bunches of needles sprouting straight from the trunk bark (epicormic sprouting); and cones that are as wide as they are tall when they open (they look exactly like a chicken egg when closed).

Slash pine (*P. elliottii*) is found naturally only in the Deep South; has

Short, squat cone of pond pine.

roughly even numbers of bundles with 2 and 3 needles; no bunches of needles sprouting from the bark; and cones that are longer than they are wide

Spruce pine (P. glabra) is found only in a limited area of the deep South; has mostly 2 needles per bundle; and cones that are usually slightly longer than they are wide.

There are also a few upland pines that may inhabit wetlands in special cases. For instance, Eastern white pine (*P. strobus*, FACU)—readily identified by having 5 needles per bundle—is a dominant species in many northern swamps from Massachusetts to Minnesota. Pitch pine (*P. rigida*), which is very similar to pond pine, is occasionally found along the margins of swamps in New England and the Mid-Atlantic. The southern pines commonly hybridize, making identification of every pine specimen found in a southern wetland a difficult task.

Habitat and Remarks: Native. FACU through OBL. The southeastern U.S. has vast areas of pine-dominated wetlands. Pond pine or "Pocosin Pine" is commonly found in pocosins, savannahs, and other wetlands of the coastal plain. Loblolly pine is a wide-ranging species common in a variety of habitats from wet pine savannahs to bottomland swamps to even the edges of coastal wetlands. Slash pine is common in wet savannahs of the Deep South, but also inhabits pine plantations (which are often planted in wetlands) farther north. Several pine species are dependent on fire for regeneration because their cones remain closed until after they are exposed to fire.

Tamarack *(Larix laricina)*

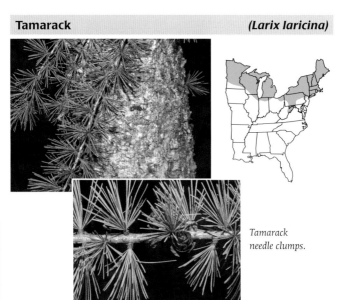

Tamarack needle clumps.

Distinguishing Characteristics: Height commonly to 24 m (80'). Diameter up to 0.9 m (3'). A small- to medium-sized tree with thin, cone-shaped crown and a tapered trunk. Branches are horizontal. Needles are deciduous, soft, and very narrow, occurring in distinctive clusters on spur twigs and also distributed along the main twig. They are light bluish green. Twigs are orange-brown, thick, and hairless with many spurs. Cones are elliptical and red, turn brown with maturity, and fall the second year. Foliage is a brilliant yellow in the fall.

Habitat and Remarks: Native. FACW. Also known as American larch. A common inhabitant of northern peat bogs and swamps, it is one of the northernmost trees and is very hardy. Native Americans used the thin roots as thread to sew together pieces of birch bark when making canoes and containers. The lumber is durable and is used in framing buildings.

Black Spruce _(Picea mariana)_

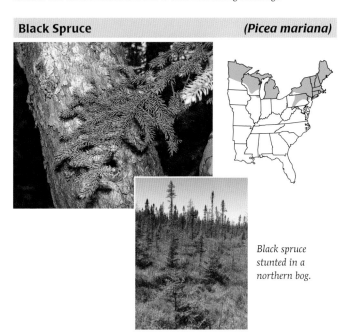

Black spruce stunted in a northern bog.

Distinguishing Characteristics: Height commonly to 18 m (60'). Diameter up to 0.3 m (1'). A small tree with an irregular, cone-shaped crown of short branches, which grow horizontally or droop slightly. Needles are evergreen, 6–15mm (¼–⅝") long, sharply pointed, spread from all sides of the twig, and have a menthol-like smell when crushed. They are 4-angled, and pale blue-green with white lines. Twigs are yellow-brown, slender, and hairy. Bark is dark brownish gray or black, and separates into thin, scaly plates, exposing brown underneath. Inner bark is yellow. Cones are up to 3 cm (1¼") long, round or egg shaped, and often clustered near the top of the tree. Two other native spruces may be found around wetlands. White spruce (*P. glauca*) has white inner bark and the foliage smells like cat urine or skunk when crushed. Red spruce (*P. rubens*) first-year twigs have a reddish coat of down; twig color is generally red-brown, and the cones are more elongate than the spherical cones of black spruce.

Habitat and Remarks: Native. FACW. One of the most widely distributed coniferous species in North America. They are common in northern bogs and are often found in the most extremely nutrient-poor and weather-exposed environments, where they have a stunted, scraggly form. In fact, a 1-inch diameter tree may be over 100 years old. The lower tree branches take root after snow pushes them to the ground, which forms rings of small trees around larger ones. The wood has several uses, but production is limited because of the small size of the tree. This species, along with red spruce, was used to make spruce gum and spruce beer.

INVERTEBRATES

Invertebrates

Invertebrates are an extremely important part of wetland ecosystems. They eat leaves and other organic matter, helping to break it down into nutrients that are useful to plants. They provide food for other invertebrates, fish, amphibians, reptiles, birds, and even carnivorous plants. Some groups, such as the dragonflies, even have bright colors that catch the human eye. The groups that we cover here are some of the most important wetland taxa. We are limited by space to the groups that have at least some aquatic stage in their life cycle. You may also notice that there is very little mention of saltwater species. This is partially because there are very few insects that have larval forms inhabiting salt water. We have included some taxa (mollusks, crustaceans, etc.) that are easily seen inhabitants of our estuaries, but do not have space for a detailed treatment of our ocean's invertebrates.

NOTES ON ORGANIZATION

Invertebrates have been loosely arranged here from the simplest body form to the most complex. This means that worms and invertebrates with worm-like larvae come first, and things that always look like "normal" insects come last.

Many of the aquatic invertebrates covered here are aquatic as larvae, and emerge to become terrestrial adults.

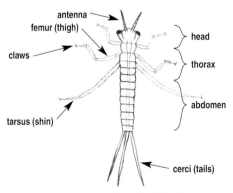

Anatomy terms useful in identifying insects.

INVERTEBRATES

Flatworms   (Class Turbellaria)

Distinguishing Characteristics: Length up to 3.2 cm (1.25"). Many species are less than 1.5 mm (0.06") long. These are flat, wormlike creatures, but often appear to be amorphous blobs, especially after being preserved. While watching flatworms slide along the clear glass of a collecting jar, you will probably see that the head region is arrowhead-shaped, and that some species have 2 light-colored eyespots. Unlike the tube-shaped aquatic earthworms, flatworms are flat on the top and bottom. Flatworms lack the suckers found on each end of leeches, as well as legs, jointed mouthparts, and segmented bodies, which separates them from other wormlike aquatic creatures. Identification of individual species usually requires dissection and mounting on a slide to investigate with a microscope.

Habitat and Remarks: There are about 200 freshwater species of flatworms in North America, but many more species can be found in marine and brackish environments. They are often called planarians because many of the larger species are in the genus *Planaria*. Flatworms are common in wetlands, where they often live among detritus and below the substrate. Flatworms can be difficult to distinguish from mud and organic matter, but if you collect some detritus and put it in a jar these worms will often begin to crawl up the sides. They can also be captured by placing some liver or an injured invertebrate wrapped in wire mesh into a wetland overnight; or by just peering into a clear vernal pool at night with a flashlight to look for some of the larger species. Flatworms feed largely on other invertebrates, detritus, diatoms, and other microscopic organisms. Flatworms are famous for their ability to reproduce asexually (basically cloning themselves). If you cut a flatworm into several pieces, many of them will produce complete new worms.

Leeches   (Class Hirudinea)

Distinguishing Characteristics: Length up to 46 cm (18"). Wormlike creatures that are usually flattened in cross section. Unlike flatworms, leeches have segmented bodies, but they lack the bundles of bristles present on aquatic earthworms. Leeches also have a sucker at each end of the body that is used in locomotion and to attach the leech to prey or host animals. They also have eyespots on the first few body segments. Leeches vary in size and shape, ranging from the large, flattened, teardrop-shaped species often found on turtles to more wormlike species that are often round in cross section. Many leech species are brilliantly colored with green, orange, red, and yellow.

Habitat and Remarks: There are about 69 species of freshwater leeches in North America, and approximately a dozen species are found along the eastern Atlantic Coast. Many wetlands are ideal environments for leeches, which prefer to live in debris and organic matter. Some kinds are parasitic, using rows of small teeth to make a puncture in the host. Their saliva contains an anti-coagulant (hirudin), which makes feeding on the fluids much easier. Leeches are quite often found attached to turtles, but also feed on fish, frogs, waterfowl, and occasionally mammals. Most leeches that are captured with a net are not parasitic. Instead, these species engulf smaller invertebrates whole, or pierce them and drain their body fluids. While the amount of blood that freely flows from a leech bite can be disconcerting, they are essentially harmless. The best method for removal is usually to use a fingernail or something similar to scrape the suckers free of the skin. Applying fire, salt, or other such methods can make the external parasite detach itself quickly, often causing it to regurgitate its stomach contents into the wound. Leeches are usually easy to avoid if you use waders or refrain from swimming around thick deposits of organic matter and plants.

Aquatic Earthworms (Class Oligochaeta)

Distinguishing Characteristics: Length up to 15 cm (6"). Similar in appearance to nightcrawlers and red worms used for fishing, but usually much longer and thinner. Aquatic earthworms are round in cross section, have many body segments, lack suckers and eyespots, and have microscopic clumps of bristles on their bodies.

Habitat and Remarks: There are about 170 species of freshwater oligochaetes in the U.S. The biomass of these worms can be extremely high within the sediments of certain wetlands, such as estuaries. Oligochaetes are capable of reproducing sexually or asexually. The majority of these worms feed on fine-grained organic matter and small organisms found in the mud, which they eat as they burrow. They are extremely important in the diet of other invertebrates and vertebrates, including fish, salamanders, and birds.

Aquatic Snails (Class Gastropoda)

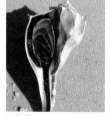

Common freshwater snails (left to right): pouch snail, ramshorn snail, and pond snail.

Whelk.

Distinguishing Characteristics: Length up to 7 cm (2.75"). Aquatic snails have a single shell that is usually either spiraled or flat and cone-shaped. Several of the most common, conspicuous freshwater snail families are described below, but there are also several species in some families (such as the Hydrobiidae) that are so tiny they are overlooked by most. The pouch snails (family Physidae) are thin-shelled species that are unique because the shell opening (aperture) is on the left side when viewed with the tip of the

Saltmarsh periwinkle snail.   *Apple snail.*

shell pointed upward. Snails in the families Lymnaeidae (pond snails, truly aquatic) and Succineidae (amber snails, semi-terrestrial) are thin shelled and similar to pouch snails, but their shell aperture is on the right. Ramshorn snails (family Planorbidae) have shells that are flattened and spiraled, resembling the coil of a sheep's horn. Although they are limited to the Deep South, the apple snails (*Pomacea* spp.) are another easily recognized freshwater group because of their size and distinctive shape.

Habitat provides an important clue to the identification of marsh periwinkle snails (genus *Littorina*). They are present in large numbers in tidal salt marshes, and are often found clinging to the stalks of cordgrass. Another easily identifiable group of estuarine snails is the whelks (family Melongenidae), which have large, very sculptured shells. There are about 500 species of freshwater gastropods in North America, and several thousand species of marine gastropods may live in estuaries or occasionally be carried in by tides.

Habitat and Remarks: Aquatic snails inhabit most kinds of wetlands. Pouch snails, ramshorn snails, and lymnaeid snails inhabit virtually any kind of freshwater wetlands. Apple snails are found mostly in marshes and other wetlands with a lot of green vegetation. The other groups listed inhabit estuaries and salt marshes. Most of the snails encountered in our wetlands eat by scraping biofilm from surfaces using their radula (a tooth-covered anatomical structure in the mouth). Some species, such as the apple snails, eat aquatic plants. Other snails, such as the whelks, actually feed on other mollusks.

Freshwater Mussels and Clams (Class Bivalvia)

Pea clam with siphons and foot exposed.

Distinguishing Characteristics: Length up to 250 mm (9.8"). These mollusks have 2 shells connected on one side by a hinge ligament. There are 2 major groups of native bivalves in our freshwater wetlands: the native mussels (superfamily Unionoidea) and the pea clams (family Pisidiidae). Freshwater mussels attain much larger sizes than pea clams, which are usually less than 25 mm (1") long. Also, the shells of pea clams have a long, linear "lateral tooth" on both sides of the umbo. Native mussels have only one of these lateral teeth or lack teeth altogether.

Habitat and Remarks: There are about 300 species of native mussels and 36 species of pea clams in North America. More mussel species are found in the flowing waters of rivers; however, some species are found in sloughs, lakes, ponds, and swamps. Pea clams—also known as fingernail clams or pill clams—are extremely common in wetlands and may reach surprising densities (up to 10,000 per square meter). The mussel species found in wetlands typically have thinner shells than their river counterparts. This prevents them from sinking into the muck. Mussels are an important food for muskrats, and pea clams are commonly devoured by wetland fish and amphibians such as sirens.

Eastern Oyster *(Crassostrea virginica)*

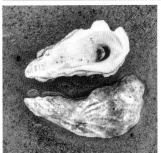

Shells of a dead oyster.

Oyster reef.

Distinguishing Characteristics: Length up to 20 cm (8"). Usually found living in a large conglomeration of shells. Oysters have 2 thick shells (valves) covered in irregular bumps and ridges. One of the shells is cemented to a hard surface, such as another oyster shell or a rock, and each shell has a purple muscle scar on the inside that can be seen in dead shells. Some other salt marsh mussels, such as ribbed mussels (*Geukensia demissa*) and blue mussels (*Mytilus edulis*), are also found in large groups, but their shells are much more regular in shape.

Habitat and Remarks: The common eastern oyster is found in estuaries from the Gulf of Mexico to southern Maine. Oysters require brackish water to survive and will perish if exposed to fresh water or marine salinity for too long. The reefs formed by the shells of this species provide habitat for colonization by barnacles, crabs, worms, fish, other mollusks, and many more organisms. Oysters are a very commercially valuable species, yet they are threatened by a number of factors including pollution, predation, disease, parasites, and changes in salinity caused by canals and inlets. Young oysters (called "spat") need a hard surface on which to develop, and many coastal communities have realized the importance of placing shells from harvested oysters back into estuaries to ensure future oyster beds.

INVERTEBRATES

Microcrustaceans (Various taxa in the Subphylum Crustacea)

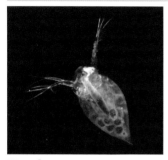

Water flea.

Distinguishing Characteristics: Length up to 2 cm (0.8"), but mostly much smaller. We have lumped members of several taxonomically distinct groups of animals into this category. Most of them are very tiny (many less than 1 mm) and defy identification with the naked eye. Water fleas (suborder Cladocera) and copepods (subclass Copepoda) look like tiny, opaque dots swimming around in the water column or moving over detritus in various types of wetlands, but closer examination or macro photography reveals their differing shapes. Ostracods (class Ostracoda) and clam shrimps (order Diplostraca, taxonomy disputed) might be mistaken for tiny mollusks, but closer examination reveals they have jointed appendages.

Habitat and Remarks: While specific identification of these groups can be difficult without a microscope, they are an extremely important part of wetland food chains. Some, such as the water fleas, can reach extraordinary abundance in small wetlands. Many larval salamanders, small fish, and invertebrates feed on these tiny crustaceans. Many of the microcrustaceans are considered to be part of the zooplankton community, which is eaten extensively by filter-feeding fish and invertebrates. These species are best captured using an aquarium net or similar type with very small mesh.

Sow Bugs and Scuds (Orders Isopoda and Amphipoda)

Sow bug.

Scud.

Distinguishing Characteristics: Length up to 22 mm (0.9"). Small, highly segmented crustaceans with 7 pairs of legs and 2 pairs of antennae. In sow bugs (isopods), 1 pair of antennae is much longer than the other; in scuds (amphipods), both pairs are about the same length. The familiar "roly-polies" often found under logs and other areas of damp soil are isopods. Isopod bodies are dorsoventrally flattened (flattened from the top and bottom, like a pancake), while amphipod bodies are laterally flattened (flattened from side to side). Isopods tend to crawl more, while scuds swim around rapidly when disturbed.

Habitat and Remarks: Isopods and amphipods are commonly found in the detritus and aquatic vegetation of many types of wetlands, where they feed on decaying organic matter, biofilms, and small invertebrates. There are approximately 130 species of freshwater isopods, but many new species (especially cave-dwelling species) are still to be described. There are approximately 150 to 175 species of freshwater amphipods in North America. Coastal wetlands have additional species of both amphipods and isopods, including some that are parasites of fish, jellyfish, and other marine life.

Fairy Shrimp (Order Anostraca)

Distinguishing Characteristics: Length of eastern U.S. species up to 3.8 cm (1.5"). Crustaceans with 11 pairs of leaf-like legs and a habit of hovering upside down in the water column, fluttering their abdominal appendages. Fairy shrimp come in a variety of colors, including translucent shades of white, red, and green. Males have a set of claspers used in mating that makes their head appear larger than that of females. Females often have a brood pouch filled with eggs at the base of the abdomen. The overall shape and means of locomotion of fairy shrimp readily separate them from similar crustaceans such as amphipods and true shrimps.

Habitat and Remarks: Fairy shrimp are most common in vernal pools and other temporary wetlands that lack fish. These shrimp filter-feed on

INVERTEBRATES

microscopic particles of algae, protozoans, and detritus. They are more closely related to other branchiopods, such as water fleas and clam shrimp, than true shrimp (class Decapoda). Fairy shrimp eggs are adapted to survive the effects of drying, freezing, and even ingestion by birds. They are typically seen in late winter or early spring.

Shrimp (Infraorder Caridea and Suborder Dendrobranchiata)

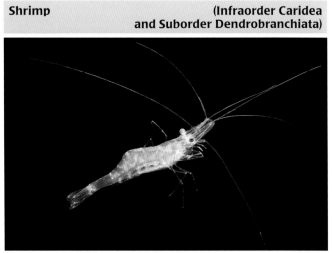

True shrimp.

Distinguishing Characteristics: Length up to 40 cm (15.7"). Five pairs of legs. Unlike most crayfish, the pincers on the first pair of legs is not greatly enlarged. Most of the "true shrimps" (infraorder Caridea) found in freshwater wetlands are small and translucent with pincers only on the first 2 pairs of legs (unlike crayfish and Dendrobranchiate shrimps). In the eastern U.S. these are often called grass shrimp or glass shrimp (family Palaemonidae). There are 2 genera and 15 species of these freshwater shrimp. The larger, more marine shrimp or "prawns" (suborder Dendrobranchiata) that support fishing off the Gulf and Atlantic coasts have pincers on the first 3 pairs of legs.

Habitat and Remarks: The terms shrimp and prawn are often used interchangeably. Shrimps of the family Palaemondiae are found in many types of wetlands, including sloughs, lake fringes, freshwater marshes, and brackish marshes. The dendrobranchiates are primarily found in marine habitats as adults, but our coastal wetlands are extremely important nursery habitats for these commercially valuable species when they are young.

Crayfish   (Family Cambaridae)

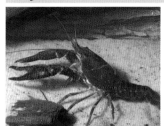

Red swamp crayfish.   *A* Cambarus *species.*

Distinguishing Characteristics: Length up to 15 cm (6"). Resemble miniature lobsters. Similar to some freshwater shrimp, except for the pincers on the first 3 pairs of legs; the first pair of legs also is usually greatly enlarged. Occasionally, the first pair of legs has been lost in a fight and may be absent or greatly reduced in size as it grows back, so it's a good idea to look at a number of individuals if you are unsure of the number of paired legs. There are about 9 genera and more than 300 species of crayfish in the eastern U.S. The genus *Cambarus* is one of the most speciose and widespread in eastern U.S. wetlands. *Cambarus* species are often robust-clawed, and males usually have short, stoutly curved gonopods (the first pair of appendages under the tail). Many of the other wetland crayfish genera, such as *Procambarus*, *Fallicambarus*, and *Cambarellus*, are most common in wetlands of the southeastern coastal plain.

Habitat and Remarks: Crayfish inhabit virtually all types of freshwater wetlands. Some species can even live in wetlands that are dry for much of the year because they burrow down to the water table, leaving telltale crayfish "chimneys." Female crayfish carry their eggs and newly hatched young under their tail. Crayfish feed on virtually anything, including invertebrates, fish, amphibians, carrion, plants, and dead organic material. The red swamp crayfish (*Procambarus clarkii*), a brilliant red species with very thin pincers, is one of our most famous wetland crayfish. It now has a virtually worldwide distribution because of its release into the wild from facilities that propagate crayfish for human cuisine. Aquarists have also capitalized on color variation to produce white and electric blue varieties of this species.

Crayfish chimneys.

Crabs   (Infraorder Brachyura)

Left: Fiddler crab.

Bottom left: Blue crab.

Below: Marsh crab.

Distinguishing Characteristics: Body length up to 22.5 cm (9"). True crabs have 4 well-developed pairs of walking legs and usually 1 pair of pincers. Common true crab species include the blue crab (*Callinectes sapidus*), fiddler crabs (*Uca* spp.), and marsh crabs (*Sesarma* spp.). Some other crabs, such as hermit crabs (Superfamily Paguroidea), are actually not true crabs and are classified in the infraorder Anomura. They have only 2 or 3 well-developed pairs of walking legs, with remaining legs vestigial and very reduced in size.

Habitat and Remarks: Crabs inhabit most saltwater and brackish habitats. Fiddler crabs (*Uca* spp.), which are easily recognized by their single, enlarged pincer, are among the most common animals seen in coastal wetlands. They inhabit salt marshes and brackish wetlands where they excavate tiny tunnels. Blue crabs (*Callinectes sapidus*) are one of our most beautiful crab species and one of the most commercially important species in Atlantic coastal wetlands. Marsh crabs (*Sesarma* and *Armases* spp.) are commonly found under leaves and driftwood. Crabs inhabit many other coastal niches, ranging from tiny parasitic species that live inside oysters to pelagic crabs that wash into wetlands from the open ocean. Coastal wetlands are important nursery areas for many crab species, even if they do not live there as adults.

True Bugs (Order Hemiptera [suborder Heteroptera])

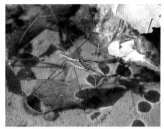 

Water striders. *Backswimmer.*

Distinguishing Characteristics: Length up to 10 cm (3.9"). Adults and larvae are very similar, except larvae lack developed wings. This order includes many common but different-looking families, but adults of all taxa typically have a triangle-shaped area in the center of the back, which is created by the folded wings. Adults and larvae both have mouthparts that have been modified into a cone or tube (called a "rostrum"), which is excellent for piercing and sucking juices out of prey. Water striders (Gerridae), which skate around on the water surface, are one of the most conspicuous families. Backswimmers (Notonectidae) swim around upside down with their oar-like elongated rear legs, while water boatmen (Corixidae) have similar oar-like legs, but swim right-side up. Occasionally, one may encounter stick-like water scorpions (Nepidae), enormous giant water bugs (Belostomatidae), the aptly named toad bugs (Gelastocoridae), toe-biters (Naucoridae), or members of several other families.

Left: Giant water bug.

Bottom left: Giant water bug male with eggs on its back.

Below: Water scorpion.

INVERTEBRATES

Habitat and Remarks: There are about 15 families and 400 species of hemipterans that inhabit North America's fresh waters. True bugs breathe air and lack gills. Because these insects do not obtain oxygen directly from the water (they surface to obtain air) they are able to inhabit salt water, low-oxygen water, and areas that have been polluted. They may be found in any kind of wetland, and even far out on the open ocean. Members of this order are often the most conspicuous invertebrates netted from the waters of ponds, marshes, and sloughs. Many of the true bugs are capable of delivering a *painful bite*. Their saliva contains poisons used to immobilize prey, but usually only cause a burning welt in humans. The saliva contains enzymes that dissolve internal parts of the prey, which are then sucked out using the straw-like rostrum. Except for water boatmen, which engulf very small prey like protozoans and algae, all true bugs are predators of other small animals. Some, such as the water scorpions and especially the giant water bugs, have been known to eat tadpoles and even small fish! Many species are capable of flying, although they seldom do so. Most lay eggs on aquatic plants or moist soil. Certain giant water bugs have an interesting egg-laying strategy—the eggs are laid on the male's back where he can protect them and maintain flowing water over them.

Caddisflies   (Order Trichoptera)

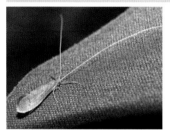

Typical adult caddisfly.

Right: Many caddisfly larvae start out with a small case made of sand grains.

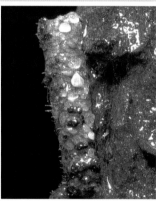

Distinguishing Characteristics: Body length of larvae up to 43 mm (1.7"), but case length up to 76 mm (3"). Adult length up to 25 mm (1"). Most kinds of caddisfly larvae build elaborate cases or nets that they live in or use to collect food, or both. Many start out with tiny cases made of sand grains or tiny pieces of leaf. Caddisfly cases, constructed of silk and debris, are highly variable. Two of the most recognizable families are pictured on the next page. However, the cases or nets are often destroyed while being collected. If cases aren't present, caddisfly larvae can be distinguished from

Northern casemaker larva.   *Giant casemaker larva.*

other small, wormlike invertebrates (such as worms, fly larvae, and beetle larvae) by the following characteristics: an obvious head region; at least the first segment of the thorax covered with a hard plate on top; 3 pairs of segmented legs originating from the thorax; a pair of claws—which may or may not be on 2 prolegs—extending from the end of the abdomen; and an abdomen that lacks other leglike appendages, although there may be single or branched gills. The somewhat mothlike adults have the following characteristics: hairy wings held together to form a peaked roof over the body; 2 sets of wings similar in length and extending past the end of the body; thin antennae projecting in front of the body; and 2 hairy appendages extending down from the head. We still do not know what many adult caddisflies look like as larvae.

Habitat and Remarks: There are about 1,400 known species and 21 families of caddisflies in North America. Caddisfly larvae are found in vernal pools, pond/lake fringes, swamps, and streamside wetlands of many types. Adults are often attracted to lights near wetlands at night. All caddisflies pupate into adults inside silk cocoons similar to those of moths and butterflies. These insects are extremely important prey items as larvae (for other invertebrates and for fish) and as adults (for amphibians, fish, birds, and bats).

INVERTEBRATES

True Flies   (Order Diptera)

Typical adult fly.

Mosquito larva.

Distinguishing Characteristics: Length of larvae up to 35 mm (1.5"); length of adults up to 60 mm (2.4"). This order of invertebrates includes some of the ugliest aquatic larvae you will ever encounter. They are usually somewhat wormlike and can be distinguished from other invertebrates by the combination of the following characteristics: no segmented legs (but there may be some fleshy appendages); no wing pads; and 2 opposing jaws or 2 fanglike mouthparts (which may not be evident to the naked eye). Adults vary in appearance from microscopic biters like no-see-ums (Ceratopogonidae) to relatively huge crane flies (Tipulidae). Adults can be identified by the combination of the following characteristics: only 1 pair of obvious wings; a pair of hindwings reduced to 2 small stalks with knobs on the ends; and mouthparts modified for piercing or sucking.

Habitat and Remarks: There are more species of Diptera than any other insect order besides beetles (Coleoptera), and Diptera has more species with an aquatic stage than any other order of insects. Out of the 108 Dipteran families, 29 (about 3,500 species) have an aquatic larval stage. Larvae live in a wide variety of habitats where they feed on particles of detritus, scrape organic matter from surfaces, or act as predators of smaller organisms. Blood-red midge larvae (Chironomidae) are easy to pick out of the debris of most wetlands, and mosquito larvae (Culicidae) are commonly found where water

Above: Midge larvae.

Right: Typical adult midge.

has been trapped in puddles or outdoor containers. Adults feed on a wide variety of things, including plant nectar and blood, but many do not feed at all as adults; instead, these species live most of their lives in the larval form, and transform into adults only to breed quickly before dying. One of the most important roles of true flies may be as prey for thousands of aquatic and terrestrial species, including carnivorous plants, true bugs, beetles, dragonflies, salamanders, frogs, bats, birds, and many other animals.

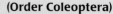

Beetles (Order Coleoptera)

Left: Typical adult beetle.

Above: Typical beetle larva.

Distinguishing Characteristics: Larval length up to 83 mm (3.25"); adult length up to 41 mm (1.6"); both lengths exclude antennae and tails. The front wings of beetles are modified into a hard, smooth carapace and meet in the middle to form a straight line. This straight midline (lacking a triangular area) and the presence of chewing mouthparts easily separate beetles from some superficially similar true bugs. Most aquatic beetle larvae found in wetlands are wormlike and may be distinguished from other aquatic invertebrates by these characteristics: a distinguishable head with a tough covering; 3 pairs of jointed legs coming from the thorax; no wing pads; a back surface usually somewhat hardened; and no hooks or prolegs on the end of the abdomen (although there may be 2 tails).

Habitat and Remarks: There are more species in the order Coleoptera than any other order of insects in the world. There are 113 families and approximately 24,000 species in North America, but only about 1,450 species—comprising 20 families—have an aquatic life stage. Aquatic beetles are found in virtually any type of wetland, ranging from very ephemeral vernal pools to swamps, ponds, and even salt marshes. They vary in diet from species that eat tiny algae to large beetles that feed on tadpoles and small fish. Predaceous diving beetles (Dytiscidae) are one of the most common families, and some species in this family can reach impressive size and sport

Predaceous diving beetle (Dytiscidae).   *Whirligig beetle (Gyrinidae).*

vibrant coloration. Water scavenger beetles (Hydrophilidae) are also very common, conspicuous beetles that are often netted from the same beds of vegetation that house predaceous diving beetles. Whirligig beetles (Gyrinidae) form very conspicuous groups, spiraling around on the water surface. There are also several families of small, inconspicuous beetles. For instance, the crawling water beetles (Haliplidae) are small as adults, and their preserved larvae are easily mistaken for the seed of some sort of rye or other grass.

Dragonflies and Damselflies   (Order Odonata)

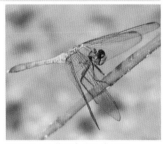

Green darner (Aeshna junius).   *Eastern pondhawk (Erythemis simplicicollis).*

Distinguishing Characteristics: Length of larvae up to 64 mm (2.5"); length of adults up to 109 mm (4.3"). All odonates have a hinged lower lip (called a labium) that can be extended to catch prey. This structure—often spoon-like in dragonflies and more flat in damselflies—readily separates odonates from other aquatic insect larvae. Unlike dragonfly larvae (suborder Anisoptera), damselfly larvae (suborder Zygoptera) are very slender and have 3 paddle-shaped tails (which are actually gills). Mayfly larvae also often have 3 tails, but theirs are long and thin like whiskers. Dragonfly larvae (suborder Anisoptera) are broader than damselfly larvae and lack gills on the end of the tail; instead, they have 3 short, pointed structures that form a pyramid-shaped valve. Most adult damselflies hold their 2 sets of wings together vertically or flat and angled slightly toward their rear when perched. Conversely, dragonflies spread their wings flat and perpendicular to the long axis of their body when perched. Many adult dragonflies can be identified quite reliably through binoculars by using their coloration, but damselflies are significantly more challenging to identify this way.

Habitat and Remarks: There are 5 families and about 130 species of damselflies in North America. There are 6 families and about 320 species of dragonflies in North America. The skimmers (family Libellulidae) are the most common dragonflies found perched or flying around most eastern wetlands, and the darners (family Aeshnidae) are the largest denizens of our marshes and swamps. Clubtails (family Gomphidae) are also fairly common around some wetlands and are easily recognized by their swollen tail tip. Many of the bright blue damselflies seen around wetlands are bluets, members of the pond damsel family (Coenagrionidae). Dragonflies and damselflies inhabit virtually any type of wetland; some wetlands, such as woodland seeps and isolated bogs, are home to rare habitat specialists that need very specific conditions to survive. Larvae of most odonates live among underwater vegetation, where they rely on their camouflaged appearance to ambush passing prey. Odonate larvae are fierce predators of invertebrates, but also will eat small fish and tadpoles! Dragonflies can remain in the larval form for up to 6 years before emerging to fly the skies. Adult odonates feed mostly on small insects, especially flies. Dragonfly watching has become very popular,

so we have provided a few plates with common wetland species on the following page. Male and female odonate adults are often different colors, adding to the beauty and colorful diversity that these creatures provide to their growing audience.

*Blue dasher (*Pachydiplax longipennis*).*

Typical adult damselfly.

Below: Dragonfly larva.

Cobra clubtail (Gomphus vastus).

Needham's skimmer (Libellula needhami).

Damselfly larva.

Eastern amberwing (Perithemis tenera).

Common whitetail (Plathemis lydia).

Fish

NOTES ON ORGANIZATION

The fish in this section are generally arranged from smaller species to larger species; however, members of the same family are kept together because they share similar characteristics.

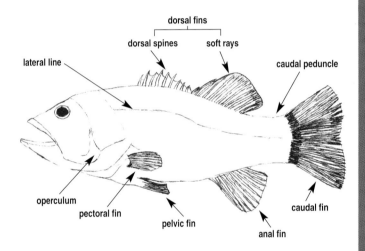

Anatomy terms useful in identifying fish.

Darters   *(Etheostoma* spp.)

Above left: Swamp darter
(E. fusiforme).

Left: Slough darter
(E. gracile).

Distinguishing Characteristics: Length up to 18 cm (7.25"), but most wetland species <10 cm (4"). Small, elongate fish that sit on the bottom, often darting along while propped up on their pelvic and pectoral fins. Darters have 2 dorsal fins—the first has spines and the second has rays. There are about 150 species of darters in the genus *Etheostoma*, but most species inhabit streams and relatively few live in wetlands. For instance, throughout most of the Northeast the swamp darter (*E. fusiforme*) is the only species commonly found in swamps and marshes. It has an incomplete lateral line that is arched at the front, a dark spot at the front of the dorsal fin, and speckles along the lower sides. The slough darter (*E. gracile*) is another common swamp species, but it is found farther south in the Mississippi River drainage, where there are many more wetland darter species. Slough darters have green squares on their sides, and males have a red band in the first dorsal fin. Spawning male darters of many stream-dwelling species are brilliantly colored; however, most of the wetland darters are comparatively drab.

Habitat and Remarks: Darters can be found in virtually any permanent freshwater habitat type in the eastern U.S. Several species are found along the fringes of lakes and ponds, but only a few inhabit the stagnant waters of swamps and sloughs. With the exception of the swamp darter, most of these wetland dwellers are found in the southeastern coastal plain and northward up the Mississippi River valley. Most darters do not have a swim bladder, allowing them to sit on the bottom where they feed on small worms, mollusks, and aquatic insect larvae.

Mudminnows   *(Umbra spp.)*

Central mudminnow.

☐ eastern mudminnow
▨ central mudminnow

Distinguishing Characteristics: Length up to 14 cm (5.5"). Resembles a topminnow or small bowfin superficially. Unlike most eastern fishes, mudminnows have a single dorsal fin located far back on the body. Topminnows and killifishes (such as the mosquitofish) also have this type of dorsal fin, but those families have upturned mouths suited for feeding from the water's surface and lack the mudminnow's black bar at the end of the caudal peduncle. There are 2 mudminnow species found in the eastern U.S.: the central mudminnow (*U. limi*) and the eastern mudminnow (*U. pygmaea*). These species are easily separated by range throughout most of the eastern U.S, but the eastern mudminnow also has 10 to 14 horizontal stripes, which the central mudminnow lacks.

Habitat and Remarks: Mudminnows inhabit swamps, sloughs, marshes, ditches, and other relatively permanent wetlands. They favor the cover provided by vegetation and organic debris. Eggs are attached to underwater vegetation. Until they grow to about 25 mm, developing young have a spinal column that extends above the caudal fin. Mudminnows are capable of surviving oxygen depletion by gulping air at the water's surface and can be found in some of the warmest, shallowest ditches. Mudminnows eat many microcrustaceans, along with amphipods, isopods, snails, and aquatic insects.

Pirate Perch *(Aphredoderus sayanus)*

Distinguishing Characteristics: Length up to 14 cm (5.5"). Small, gray fish with a large head. One of the most distinguishing characteristics is that the anus is located under the throat. However, when pirate perch are juveniles the anus is located normally; it moves forward as the fish approach maturity. Pirate perch are most easily confused with small sunfish (Centrarchidae), but unlike pirate perch, sunfish have more than 3 dorsal spines.

Habitat and Remarks: Pirate perch live in swamps, sloughs, marshes, and lake backwaters where they stick to cover provided by vegetation and organic debris. Pirate perch eat small invertebrates, such as microcrustaceans, isopods, amphipods, and fly larvae, that inhabit their sluggish-water environment.

Mosquitofish *(Gambusia affinis)*

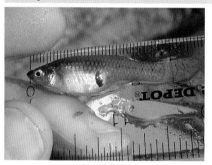 

Distinguishing Characteristics: Length up to 6.5 cm (2.5"). One of the tiniest fish you are likely to encounter in most of the eastern U.S., mosquitofish have upturned mouths designed for eating topwater invertebrates such as mosquito larvae. They have a large, blackish teardrop marking under each eye, and lack the horizontal lines present on many topminnows. Males have a long gonopodium (modified and elongated anal rays used for reproduction) extending from the front of the anal fin. Females are typically larger than males and have a black abdominal spot. The mosquitofish is the only *Gambusia* in the eastern U.S.; however, some authorities consider populations on the Atlantic slope to be a separate species—the eastern mosquitofish (*G. holbrooki*). The rainwater killifish (*Lucania parva*), a widespread species of our coastal wetlands, can look very similar, but male killifish lack a gonopodium and have a black spot at the base of the front dorsal.

Habitat and Remarks: Mosquitofish were originally native from the southeastern coastal plain northward to southern Indiana and Illinois, but have been introduced very widely. They feed on a variety of aquatic insects, microscopic crustaceans, snails, amphibians, and small fish. Mosquitofish are very tolerant of warm water and low-oxygen conditions that would kill most other fish. Therefore, they can be found in virtually any type of aquatic habitat. Three or 4 broods may be born in a single summer, and this species can reach extremely high densities quickly. Introductions of mosquitofish severely threaten fish, larval amphibians, and other species in areas where *Gambusia affinis* is not native, especially the southwestern U.S. Public health officials sometimes introduce these fish to stormwater ponds and other wetlands for mosquito control; however, this is not necessary in healthy, natural wetlands because dragonfly larvae, beetle larvae, larval salamanders, and many other predators keep mosquitoes in check.

Topminnows *(Fundulus spp.)*

Mummichog.

Distinguishing Characteristics: Length up to 18 cm (7″), but many species are smaller. Topminnows, as the name implies, are adapted for life at the water surface—the mouth is turned upward to suck insects from the water surface, the top of the body is flattened, and the eyes are large. Topminnows, especially males, are often very brightly colored, and many species have a white- or golden-colored spot on top of the head. Topminnows have a single dorsal fin located far back on the body and abdominal pelvic fins (located under the belly), but lack a lateral line and spines in the fins. Top-

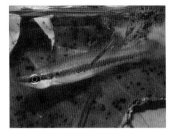 

Blackstripe topminnow (F. notatus).   *Banded killifish* (F. diaphanous).

minnows are often called mudminnows by coastal fisherman. They superficially resemble true mudminnows (*Umbra* spp.), except topminnows have upturned mouths.

Habitat and Remarks: Topminnows are often found in still water near vegetation. They inhabit many types of more permanent wetlands, and several species live in brackish marshes. Topminnows typically feed by sucking insects from the water surface, but also feast on a variety of insect nymphs, worms, and crustaceans found deeper in the water column. There are 24 species of topminnows in the eastern U.S., and many of them are found in the Southeast and along the coasts. The 2 species pictured above—blackstripe topminnow (*F. notatus*) and banded killifish (*F. diaphanous*)—are among the most wide ranging in freshwater environments, while the mummichog (*F. heteroclitus*) is one of our most widespread brackish-water topminnows and is found along the Atlantic Coast.

Golden Shiner *(Notemigonus chrysoleucas)*

Distinguishing Characteristics: Length up to 36.7 cm (14.5"). A very deep-bodied shiner, but thin when viewed from the top. The mouth is very small and slightly upturned. The color is silver in clear water, but becomes golden in water stained with tannins. Dorsal fin origin is behind the pelvic fin origin. Lateral line curves strongly downward. There is an unscaled keel along the belly from the pelvic fins to the anal fin.

Habitat and Remarks: Found mostly in swamps, sloughs, lakes, ditches, and other permanent wetlands. This species is quite tolerant of warm, low-oxygen water, helping to make it a popular bait minnow. The eggs stick to aquatic vegetation or sunfish nests, over which they are dispersed. This minnow can live up to 8 years. Golden shiners eat zooplankton, aquatic and terrestrial insects, algae, and snails. They are occasionally caught on a hook, but more often by seining or cast-netting.

Common Carp   *(Cyprinus carpio)*

Distinguishing Characteristics: Length up to 122 cm (48"). Weight up to 36.3 kg (80 lb). Often gold-colored fish with huge, thick scales and a fleshy ventral mouth modified for sucking. More than 15 dorsal fin rays. The first dorsal and anal fin elements are spiny and serrated. Members of the sucker family lack these serrated spines. Native minnows have fewer than 13 dorsal fin rays. Goldfish lack barbels. In addition to this species, new species of Asian carp seem to be continually introduced to our waters, where they cause endless harm.

Habitat and Remarks: Introduced invasive fish from Eurasia. Inhabits many freshwater wetlands, especially those that are connected to rivers and streams. Carp are very tolerant of low-oxygen and warm water. Spawning is usually stimulated by heavy rains, and eggs are deposited on submerged vegetation. Carp eat aquatic plants, various invertebrates, and even small fish. Much of their food is obtained by rooting through sediment and detritus. This activity reduces growth of native aquatic plants and contributes significantly to the turbidity of the water. The increased siltation caused by carp suffocates many native species and their eggs. Carp are often caught on hooks baited with worms, corn kernels, or dough balls. They have a tendency to feed in the shallows with half of their backs exposed, which makes them excellent targets for bowfishing. The flesh has an undeserved reputation for

FISH

bad taste. For some of the best cooking results, remove the red tissue below the lateral line, soak the meat in cold salt water for several hours, and then smoke it. It is also quite good fried in a tasty batter and then squirted liberally with lime juice.

Tadpole Madtom 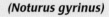 *(Noturus gyrinus)*

Distinguishing Characteristics: Length up to 13 cm (5″). This species is somewhat chubby and tadpole-shaped, with a vein-like line running down the side of the body. Like other members of the North American bullhead catfish family (Ictaluridae), tadpole madtoms have smooth skin lacking scales, 4 pairs of barbels (whiskers) around their mouth, and sharp spines in their dorsal and pectoral fins. Most likely to be confused with the bullheads (*Ameierus*); however, madtoms (*Noturus*) are different from all other catfish in that the rear edge of their adipose fin is attached to the body.

Habitat and Remarks: This is our only madtom species that is regularly found in the still waters of wetlands; most others are found in flowing streams. *Spines located in the fins can cause a painful sting. Venom is produced in the membranes covering the spines, and in glandular cells located at their base.* During the day this species typically hides among leaves, debris, and vegetation. It feeds on small insects, worms, crustaceans, and fishes.

Yellow Bullhead *(Ameiurus natalis)*

Distinguishing Characteristics: Length up to 47 cm (18.3"). Weight up to 1.65 kg (3.6 lb). Tan or yellow upper sides with light-colored belly. The rear end of the adipose fin is free from the body (unlike in madtoms), and the caudal fin is rounded (unlike in many of the larger catfish species). Flathead catfish (*Pylodictis olivaris*) have a white spot along the upper edge of the caudal fin, which bullheads lack. A yellow bullhead has yellow or white chin barbels, unlike black (*A. melas*) and brown (*A. nebulosus*) bullheads, which both have brown or black chin barbels. Three other bullhead species have a dark blotch at the dorsal fin base, which is lacking in yellow bullheads.

Habitat and Remarks: Often found over soft substrates in sloughs, ponds, swamps, ditches and other muddy wetlands. *Spines located in the pectoral and dorsal fins can cause a painful sting. Venom is produced in the membranes covering the spines, and in glandular cells located at the base of the spines.* Both the male and female may participate in hollowing out a nest cavity, but the male guards the eggs and the school of youngsters until they reach about 50 mm (2") in size. Catfish are notorious bottom-feeders, and tend to eat benthic invertebrates such as snails, pea clams, crustaceans, midge larvae, and oligochaetes. Yellow bullheads, in particular, eat quite a bit of vegetation and sediment (probably in search of benthic invertebrates). Catfish are very keyed in to olfactory cues. They use their barbels and taste buds to find food, which comes in handy because bottom-feeders are often very active at night. Bullheads are most readily caught using hook and line with the bait at or near the bottom. A variety of baits will work, including worms, dough balls, chicken livers, and "stink" baits designed to appeal to a catfish's dominant sense—smell. Because of their bottom-feeding lifestyle, many catfish accumulate toxins in their flesh from consuming chemical-laden sediments and organisms. Limit consumption where you suspect pollution.

FISH

Pygmy Sunfish   (*Elassoma* spp.)

banded pygmy
sunfish

Everglades pygmy
sunfish

spring pygmy
sunfish

multiple species
of pygmy sunfish

Top: Banded pygmy sunfish (E. zonatum). *Bottom: Everglades pygmy sunfish*
(E. alabamae).

Distinguishing Characteristics: Length up to 4.7 cm (1.75"). Tiny
sunfish. Unlike the true sunfishes (family Centrarchidae), pygmy sunfish
(family Elassomatidae) have a rounded caudal fin margin and no lateral
line. They have a large eye, protruding lower jaw, and many black specks on
the head and body. Females and non-breeding males have rather muted colors, but breeding males are blackish with deep, iridescent blue stripes and
flecks. The banded pygmy sunfish (*E. zonatum*) is the most widely distributed
species, and a number of species' ranges overlap in the deep Southeast (Florida
and nearby states). One species, the spring pygmy sunfish (*E. alabamae*), is
only found in 2 springs in Alabama.

Habitat and Remarks: Found in swamps, sloughs, ditches, springs, and
other permanent wetlands, usually among vegetation or leafy debris. They
feed on tiny worms, aquatic insects, small crustaceans, and mollusks.
Spawning males perform interesting dance displays when courting, and are
becoming popular native aquarium fishes. Eggs are laid in vegetation and on
the bottom substrate.

Bluespotted and Banded Sunfishes *(Enneacanthus* spp.)

Above left: Bluespotted sunfish (E. gloriosus).

Left: Blackbanded sunfish (E. chaetodon).

Distinguishing Characteristics: Length up to 9.5 cm (3.75"). Unlike most other sunfishes, these 3 species have a rounded caudal fin. Unlike the pygmy sunfishes (family Elassomatidae), they have 8 or more dorsal spines. The bluespotted sunfish (*E. gloriosus*) has horizontal lines of silver or blue spots on its sides. The blackbanded (*E. chaetodon*) and banded sunfish (*E. obesus*) both have prominent vertical bands along the sides of the body. Blackbanded sunfish also have black at the front of the first dorsal fin.

Habitat and Remarks: All 3 *Enneacanthus* are fishes of lakes, ponds, marshes, and sloughs, where they inhabit beds of vegetation. They can also occasionally be found in brackish wetlands. Like other sunfish, males build a saucer-shaped nest in the substrate for spawning. All age groups of these fish feed on microscopic crustaceans, midge larvae, and aquatic oligochaetes, while more mature fish also eat things like amphipods and gastropods. The small size of these fish brings them little attention in hook-and-line fishing, but they may be easily caught in a seine. They are also very attractive aquarium fishes.

FISH

Flier   *(Centrarchus macropterus)*

Distinguishing Characteristics: Length up to 30 cm (11.8"). Weight up to 560 g (1.2 lb). The flier is deep-bodied and has spines in the first dorsal fin and anal fin like most members of the sunfish family. With their tall body and broad fins, fliers' outlines are almost circular. The most striking characteristics of the flier are its large black teardrop and interrupted rows of black spots. Closer inspection reveals that unlike similar sunfish (*Lepomis* spp.) and crappies (*Pomoxis* spp.), the flier has 7 to 8 anal spines and 11 to 13 dorsal spines. Young fliers have a red-orange halo surrounding the black spot located in their rear dorsal fin.

Habitat and Remarks: Fliers are common in tannin-stained waters of swamps and sloughs, and in vegetated lakes of the southeastern coastal plain. They feed on aquatic insects and other invertebrates, especially at the water's surface. They are not highly sought-after by fisherman because of their small size, but they have excellent meat similar to that of other sunfishes.

Sunfish   *(Lepomis spp.)*

Distinguishing Characteristics: Length up to 41 cm (16.2"). Weight up to 2.2 kg (4.75 lb). Our common sunfish in the genus *Lepomis* are deep bodied, laterally compressed (thin) species. They all have 3 anal spines, unlike some other members of the sunfish family such as crappies (5 anal spines) and fliers (7 to 8 anal spines). They also have a shallowly forked caudal fin (rather than a rounded fin), which helps separate them from the pygmy sunfish (*Elassoma* spp.), mud sunfish (*Acantharcus pomotis*), and banded sunfishes (*Enneacanthus* spp.). The males have bright colors (especially during the spring/summer spawning season) that are useful for identifying species, but winter males, females, and juveniles may be quite pale. Several of the more common wetland species are listed on pages 189–91, along with distinguishing characteristics, but remember that sunfish species sometimes hybridize.

Bluegill (L. macrochirus): Complete lateral line. Bluegill have very long, pointed pectoral fins that extend past the eye when bent forward. Unlike other sunfish with this characteristic, bluegill usually have a dark spot in the second dorsal fin and paired vertical bars along the side of the body. Bantam sunfish (L. symmetricus, not pictured) is very similar, except it is chubbier, has short pectoral fins, and has an incomplete lateral line.

Green sunfish (L. cyanellus): Less deep-bodied than most members of the sunfish family. Dark back with yellowish belly. Large mouth that extends backward to the rear edge of the eye. Irregular blue or green lines on the face.

Warmouth (L. gulosus): Body is heavily mottled with dark pigment; eye may be reddish, especially in breeding males; large mouth that extends backward to the rear edge of the eye. Unlike the green sunfish, warmouth have black bars on the cheeks behind the eye and a patch of teeth on the tongue.

FISH

Pumpkinseed (Lepomis gibbosus): Long, pointed pectoral fins that reach at least to the front rim of the eye when extended forward but don't extend to base of the dorsal fin; lacks a single black spot or bold spots in the second dorsal fin; has a red, orange, or light-colored rear edge on the ear flap; and lacks silvery green sides with well-spaced orange or brown spots.

Dollar sunfish (L. marginatus): Very similar to longear sunfish (L. megalotis), which is found in streams and not usually in the swampy habitat of the dollar sunfish. Silver stripes and flecks in the black ear flap; ear flap flexible and often slanted upward; red streak along lateral line; short, rounded pectoral fins.

Redear sunfish (L. microlophus): Long, pointed pectoral fins that extend to the base of the dorsal fin; lacks a dark spot or bold spots in the second dorsal fin; has a red, orange, or light-colored rear edge on the ear flap; lacks silvery green sides with well-spaced orange or brown spots.

Orangespotted sunfish (L. humilis): Orange or reddish spots scattered on silver-green sides; long, pointed pectoral fins that reach at least to the front rim of the eye when extended forward; flexible black ear flap with a whitish edge.

Spotted sunfish (L. punctatus): Small black spots on side of head; rows of spots along sides (black spots in Atlantic populations and red/tan in more western populations); short, rounded pectoral fins; short, stiff earflap.

Habitat and Remarks: Sunfish vary in their habitat preferences. Some species, such as bluegill, pumpkinseed, and green sunfish, can be found in almost any permanent water throughout their range. Some of the others, such as dollar sunfish and orangespotted sunfish, seem to have a preference for swamps and other mud-bottomed habitats common in wetlands. These fish love beds of vegetation and tree roots. Sunfish males excavate dish-shaped nests in shallow, still water, and the male defends the eggs until they hatch. They feed on a wide variety of invertebrates, such as midge larvae, crustaceans, and insects, often slurped from the water surface. Sunfish are readily caught with live bait suspended on a hook and bobber, but may also be captured on lures, such as spinners and jigs or topwater bugs and flies.

FISH

Largemouth Bass   *(Micropterus salmoides)*

Distinguishing Characteristics: Length up to 97 cm (38"). Weight up to 10 kg (22.3 lb). Has spines in the first dorsal fin and anal fin, like most members of the sunfish family. Much less deep-bodied than members of the genus *Lepomis*, except for the green sunfish, which usually has some iridescent, irregular blue-green lines on the face that the largemouth bass lacks. May be separated from other similar fishes by the following characteristics: large mouth that extends backward past the eye; 3 anal spines; deep notch between the first and second dorsal fins that nearly separates the 2 fins; and silver or green coloring with a thick horizontal bar along the lateral line.

Habitat and Remarks: Largemouth bass can be found in ponds, lakes, swamps, and even some brackish wetlands. They are fairly tolerant of warm water and turbidity as long as there are some deeper, shady areas to escape to in summer. The male builds a shallow nest on firm substrate in shallow water. He then seeks out a female, and the pair spawns over the nest. The male guards the eggs until they hatch. Young largemouths eat zooplankton and small aquatic insects. Larger individuals feed mostly on fish and crayfish, but will take frogs, mice, birds, and virtually any other moving thing that they can catch. There has probably been more written about catching largemouth bass than any other fish, but in summary, they can be taken on a wide variety of topwater lures, jigs, rubber worms, spinners, and live baits, such as nightcrawlers, minnows, and crayfish.

Grass Pickerel *(Esox americanus)*

Distinguishing Characteristics: Length up to 38 cm (15"). A cylindrical fish with a green body and yellow eyes. Snout is shaped like a duck bill. As an adult, this species is smaller than the widely sought northern pike (*E. lucius*) and muskellunge (*E. masquinongy*). The chain pickerel (*E. niger*) is quite similar but has a chain-like pattern on the side. Unlike all of these species, the grass pickerel has a black teardrop stripe that slants backward from the eye.

Habitat and Remarks: Also known as a redfin pickerel because some individuals have reddish fins. Unlike the northern pike and muskellunge, which are found mostly in clear lakes, grass pickerel are common in swamps, sloughs, shallow lake fringes, and ponds. Grass pickerel have mouths full of sharp teeth that they use to feed on other fishes. They are often seined from slow water, and larger ones may be caught using minnows or various types of lures.

Bowfin   *(Amia calva)*

Juvenile bowfin.

Distinguishing Characteristics: Length up to 109 cm (43"). Weight up to 9.74 kg (21.5 lb). This is a robust, cylindrical fish with a mouth full of teeth. The dorsal fin extends along the length of most of the body and tail and is moved using a rippling motion like that of an eel. Adult males usually have a yellow spot with a black center at the top end of the tail, and juveniles are strikingly colored with orange, brown, and black. The bowfin is most likely to be confused with one native fish, the burbot (*Lota lota*), and a group of recently introduced exotic pest species, the snakeheads (*Channa* spp.). Unlike bowfins, burbot have 2 dorsal fins and a single barbel (whisker) in the center of the chin. The pelvic fins of snakeheads are located almost directly under their pectoral fins, while bowfins have pelvic fins located near the middle of the body.

Habitat and Remarks: Bowfins inhabit swamps, sloughs, marshes, sluggish streams, lake backwaters, and other permanent wetlands. The bowfin is the only surviving member of a prehistoric family of fishes. It has characteristics of primitive fish, including a bony "gular plate" covering its throat and a lung-like swim bladder that allows it to breathe air gulped at the water's surface. This adaptation allows the bowfin to inhabit wetlands where decomposition often removes much of the oxygen from the water. The male excavates and guards a nest in shallow water, and when the young hatch they follow him around in a tight school until they are about 10 cm (3.9") long. Young bowfins eat insects and crustaceans, and adults feed mostly on fish and crayfish, but they will also eat amphiumas (*Amphiuma* spp.) and sirens (*Siren* spp. and *Pseudobranchus* spp.). Bowfins may be caught with lures, minnows, crayfish, or cut bait. They are often caught on trotlines—but watch out for their teeth.

Longnose Gar   *(Lepisosteus osseus)*

Distinguishing Characteristics: Length up to 1.8 m (72"). Weight up to 22.8 kg (50.3 lb). Very cylindrical, long fish with an exceptionally long nose (more than twice as long as the rest of the head). All gar species have jaws lined with sharp teeth, and thick diamond-shaped scales that don't overlap. The dorsal and anal fins are located extremely far back on the body (near the caudal fin). There are 4 other gar species in the eastern U.S., but this is the most widespread. The other species have much shorter noses. The shortnose gar (*L. platostomus*) lacks spots on its paired fins. The spotted gar (*L. oculatus*) has dark spots all over its body (including paired fins) and bony plates on the isthmus (area right behind/between gill slits). Florida gar (*L. platyrhincus*) also have many spots but lack bony plates on the isthmus. Alligator gar (*Attractosteus spatula*) reach enormous size and, unlike other gar, have a double row of teeth in the upper jaw.

Habitat and Remarks: Longnose gar are the most widely distributed gar. They commonly inhabit swamps, sloughs, and even brackish wetlands. Gars are fierce predators of smaller fish such as minnows, sunfish, and shad. They are primitive fishes, and have a lung-like swim bladder that allows them to breathe air gulped at the water's surface. This allows them to live in the low-oxygen water found in many wetlands. Gar can be captured using live bait or minnows that attract their attention, but they are hard to hook.

Amphibians

NOTES ON ORGANIZATION

The amphibians in this section fall into 2 major groups: the salamanders (order Caudata) and the frogs/toads (order Anura). We begin with the most aquatic species, then move to more terrestrial salamanders before covering frogs and toads from smallest to largest.

Common Mudpuppy *(Necturus maculosus)*

mudpuppy
Necturus maculosus

various species
of "waterdogs"
Necturus spp.

Distinguishing Characteristics: Length up to 48.3 cm (19"). Brown aquatic salamander with dark spots; young ones often have 2 silver/yellowish dorsal stripes. Dark stripe through the eye. Like the larvae of many salamanders, this species has external gills, but mudpuppy gills remain present throughout life. There are several other species in the genus *Necturus*—they are difficult to distinguish, but are confined to the southeastern U.S. Unlike aquatic life stages of mole salamanders (*Ambystoma* spp.), the dorsal keel on the mudpuppy's tail only extends forward to the back leg/cloaca area.

Habitat and Remarks: Typically called "waterdogs" in the south. Mudpuppies live in a variety of wetland types, including permanent marshes, swamps, ponds, lakes, and a variety of streamside wetlands. They are mostly nocturnal, but may be active by day in murky or vegetated waters. Mudpuppies tend to hide under logs, rocks and other structures much of the time. This species eats a wide variety of animals, including crayfish, mollusks, worms, fish, and some carrion. They may be trapped in crayfish traps baited with dead fish or sometimes caught with a baited hook allowed to sit on the bottom. In warm, low-oxygen waters the gills are usually larger than those of individuals living in cool, high-oxygen waters. This allows greater surface area for absorption of oxygen in habitats where it is needed the most.

Lesser Siren *(Siren intermedia)*

lesser siren

lesser and greater
siren possible

multiple species
including
dwarf sirens

Distinguishing Characteristics: Length up to 99 cm (39"). Long, slender, eel-like salamanders with external gills and only 2 legs. Adults are distinguished from all other adult salamanders by the absence of hind legs. The presence of front legs separates them from eel-like fishes. Very young larvae of other salamanders might be mistaken for sirens because they lack hind legs, but siren larvae are much more elongate and often brilliantly colored. There are 4 species of siren in the eastern U.S. Greater sirens (*Siren lacertina*) have 4 toes on each foot; adults are typically flecked with gold and have 36 to 39 coastal grooves (grooves down the side of the body). Lesser sirens (*S. intermedia*) have 4 toes on each foot, dark spotting on the sides and head, and 31 to 34 coastal grooves. Northern and southern dwarf sirens (*Pseudobranchus striatus* and *axanthus*) are difficult to differentiate from each other, but both have 3 toes on each foot and prominent yellow and dark longitudinal stripes, which are only present in larvae of other sirens.

Habitat and Remarks: Sirens inhabit relatively permanent wetlands, but if the wetland they inhabit dries up they are capable of burrowing into the sediment, secreting a mucous cocoon, and remaining dormant until water returns. Sirens are primarily nocturnal and often associated with soft sediment/organic material and vegetation. They may be captured at night with a dipnet or in funnel traps. Sirens feed on fingernail clams, snails, small crustaceans, worms, small fish, and larval amphibians. They are eaten by bowfins, wading birds, amphiumas, water snakes, and other semi-aquatic predators.

Amphiumas   *(Amphiuma* spp.)

Distinguishing Characteristics: Length up to 116 cm (45.7"). Very long, cylindrical amphibians resembling a snake or eel with 4 tiny limbs and gill slits. Most similar to sirens, which have only the 2 front limbs and external gills. American eels (*Anguilla rostrata*) and various introduced exotic fishes such as Asian swamp eels (*Monopterus* spp.) superficially resemble amphiumas but lack tiny limbs. There are 3 species of amphiuma, identified by the number of toes on their limbs: one-toed amphiuma (*A. pholeter*), two-toed amphiuma (*A. means*), and three-toed amphiuma (*A. tridactylum*).

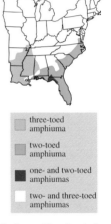

three-toed amphiuma

two-toed amphiuma

one- and two-toed amphiumas

two- and three-toed amphiumas

Habitat and Remarks: Also known as Congo eels, amphiumas are inhabitants of southern swamps, lakes, ditches, sloughs, and other reasonably permanent wetland habitats. While amphiumas are aquatic, they can be found on land on rainy nights, and also under logs—especially when females are guarding a brood of eggs. They live in burrows, which are often built by crayfish, but can also dig burrows themselves. They are nocturnal, and eat virtually anything they can catch. Amphiumas are not only the longest amphibians native to the U.S., but also have the largest cells of any vertebrate. Amphiumas are an extremely important prey item for mud snakes, and are also eaten by bowfins, great blue herons, various water snakes, and other predators.

Mole Salamanders   *(Ambystoma* spp.)

Distinguishing Characteristics: Length up to 30.5 cm (12"). The most large-bodied terrestrial salamanders in the eastern U.S. Adults are usually dark colored; some have yellow, white, or blue markings. Adults and larvae have blunt snouts, 4 toes on the front feet, and 5 toes on the rear. Unlike most other salamanders, the larvae usually have a high dorsal fin that extends from the tail up almost to the gills. Newt larvae share this characteristic, but usually have a black eye stripe, pointed snout, and reddish spots. Color patterns can be used to identify most common species (see photos below), but several of the dark and bluespotted species will require more detailed field guides and more experience to identify conclusively.

Tiger salamander (A. tigrinum): Dark with large, irregular, yellow blotches.

Spotted salamander (A. maculatum): Dark with small, round, yellow spots.

Spotted salamanders produce large, firm, distinctive egg masses.

Marbled salamander (A. opacum):
Black with large white blotches.

Marbled salamander larva, showing its distinctive dark chin and silvery "portholes" along the side of the body.

Mole salamander (A. talpoideum): Dark brown, sometimes with bluish-white flecks. Head and feet large for body size.

Smallmouth salamander (A. texanum): Dark brown or gray. Front of face (rostrum) is very short.

Jefferson salamander (A. jeffersonianum*): Blackish gray, sometimes with bluish flecks. Very long toes.*

Habitat and Remarks: Although one species is actually named the mole salamander (*A. talpoideum*), this group is usually referred to collectively as "mole salamanders" because of the terrestrial burrowing habits of the adults. They use the tunnels and trails of many small mammals throughout much of the year, but also dig their own tunnels in soft earth. From late fall through early spring, these salamanders breed in vernal pools, swamps, marshes, and other fishless freshwater wetlands. The marbled salamander is well known for its tendency to breed in the fall, waiting with its eggs in a shallow depression until fall rains bring water for its larvae. Marbled salamander larvae are often large enough to eat other amphibian larvae by the time the species hatch in early spring. Some southeastern *Ambystoma*, such as smallmouth (*A. texanum*), Mabee's (*A. mabeei*), mole, and tiger salamanders (*A. tigrinum*), can be found breeding right through the middle of winter. Other species, such as the spotted salamander (*A. maculatum*), can be quite explosive breeders. During the first warm rains of early spring, mass migrations of these salamanders can be seen moving into wetlands. In most species, males deposit whitish packets of spermatophore that are seen as the first sign of breeding activity. Females use these to fertilize gelatinous masses of eggs. *Ambystoma* salamanders feed primarily on invertebrates throughout their lives. Larvae eat tiny things, like microcrustaceans and mosquito larvae, and adults feed on earthworms, mollusks, insects, and even smaller salamanders. Some species, such as the tiger salamander, may transform into terrestrial adults or keep their gills and remain in a large larval form (called a paedomorph) for their entire life.

Ambystoma spermatophores are often the first indication of spring breeding.

AMPHIBIANS

Eastern Newt (Notophthalmus viridescens)

Eastern newt larva.

Distinguishing Characteristics: Length up to 12.2 cm (4.8"). Eastern newts have a life cycle that is fairly unique among our eastern salamanders, and they can look quite different during different stages of life. They begin as greenish larvae with a dorsal fin that extends onto the back and almost to the head, a blackish eye strip, external gills, 4 toes on the front feet, and 5 toes on the rear feet. Newts then transition into a terrestrial red eft (yellow or brilliant orange coloration) stage for a couple of years. After that, they return to the water to live and breed as aquatic adults, which are typically green with red spots or stripes bordered by black. They have rougher skin than most other eastern salamanders. Males have enlarged rear legs with blackish, horny knobs.

Habitat and Remarks: Eastern newts are often seen in vernal pools but may also be found in sloughs, swamps, pond/lake fringes, shrub swamps, and other wetlands. While the life stages described above are generally true, there are populations that retain their gills for life and some that remain in the red eft stage, only returning to the water to breed. Aquatic adults may also leave their pool if it dries, or in order to rid themselves of ectoparasites, such as leeches. Newts eat mosquito larvae, midge larvae, small mollusks, microcrustaceans, and the eggs of other amphibians.

Dusky Salamanders *(Desmognathus* spp.)

Northern dusky salamander.

dusky salamanders (*Desmognathus* spp.)

Area of extremely high *Desmognathus* diversity. Some areas have at least 6 species.

Distinguishing Characteristics: Length up to 15 cm (6"). Salamanders in the genus *Desmognathus* are collectively called dusky salamanders. Species and subspecies are extremely variable in coloration, but there is usually a light-colored diagonal line that extends from the corner of the eye to the angle of the jaw. Duskies are often brilliantly patterned with a broad, rough-edged strip down the back, but young ones may have paired spots instead of a strip. As they get older, duskies tend to become darker in color, and evidence of patterning and the diagonal jaw line may disappear.

Habitat and Remarks: There are about a dozen species of dusky salamander, but some are virtually impossible to tell apart, and some "species" may actually contain several undescribed species. The southern Appalachian mountains are the area of maximum diversity for this group. The majority of dusky salamanders live in or near small, cool streams and springs. They may be found in montane bogs (fens), woodland seeps, and southern coastal plain swamps. Eggs are usually deposited under logs, rocks, or moss near water. Both larvae and adults feed on aquatic insects, worms, sowbugs, and other small aquatic animals.

AMPHIBIANS

Four-toed salamander *(Hemidactylium scutatum)*

Distinguishing Characteristics: Length up to 10.2 cm (4"). Multi-colored orange, gray, and white salamander. Unlike any other eastern U.S. salamander, the four-toed has a combination of 3 characteristics: 4 toes on all feet, a white belly with black spots, and a noticeable constriction at the base of the tail. Like the larvae of *Ambystoma* salamanders and newts, four-toed salamanders have a dorsal fin that extends forward from the tail onto the back. However, those species have 5 toes on their hind feet.

Habitat and Remarks: This species is found in rare, disjunct, sensitive habitats throughout most of the southern portion of its range. It inhabits moist woodlands and bogs, and its egg-laying habitat requirements are quite specific. While this species sometimes lays eggs in rotting logs and grass clumps, it is most famous for laying them under sphagnum moss that is hanging over a pool of water. The moss acts as a wick, keeping the eggs moist, and the female generally stays to guard them. Eventually, the larvae hatch and fall into the water. Four-toed salamanders are commonly eaten by shrews, snakes, and other small predators.

Eastern Narrowmouth Toad *(Gastrophryne carolinensis)*

Distinguishing Characteristics: Length up to 3.2 cm (1.3"). Very small frog with a plump body and pointed face. Easily distinguished by general body shape, but also has a distinctive fold of skin across the back of the head, which similar eastern frogs and toads lack. Smooth, moist skin unlike true toads. Dark coloration. Males usually have a dark throat; female throats are light colored. Call sounds like the bleat of a lamb and lasts up to about 4 seconds.

Habitat and Remarks: Eastern narrowmouth toads inhabit bottom-land forests, swamps, pine flatwoods, and the margins of ponds and lakes. They are seldom seen and spend most of their time in the moist shelter under logs and leaf litter. Even while looking for them under logs, it can be difficult to spot them because they blend in so well with mud. They feed mostly on tiny insects such as ants, and can sometimes be found near ant-hills at night. The fold of skin at the back of their head can move forward to wipe away any insects attempting to attack their eyes. Eastern narrow-mouths breed during the summer, but may breed earlier or later in the southern part of their range.

True Toads   (*Anaxyrus* spp.)

Above left: Southern toad (A. terrestris).

Left: American toad (A. americanus).

Below: Strings of toad eggs.

Distinguishing Characteristics: Length up to 11.4 cm (4.5"). Rough-skinned, warty toads with large parotoid glands (warty, glandular growths that secrete toxins to protect the toad from predators) on the back of the head. Members of this genus can be various shades of green, brown, and red, usually with splotches of darker color. American toads (*A. americanus*) tend to

have 1 or 2 warts per splotch, while Fowler's toads (*A. fowleri*) have 3 or more warts per splotch. Throughout most of their ranges, these are the only species of rough-skinned toads. However, the southern toad (*A. terrestris*) predominates in the deep Southeast, and the Gulf Coast toad (*Incilius nebulifer*) is the major species along the western coast of the Gulf of Mexico. There are also several more localized species. To complicate things further, many of these species interbreed occasionally. Calls range from the high-pitched trill of the American toad to the short, nasal, slightly annoying *waaaaaa* of the Fowler's toad.

Habitat and Remarks: True toads are found in all kinds of habitats, including many types of wetlands. They range relatively far from wetlands, into forests, fields, and even urban yards. However, they generally return to wetlands to breed. Toad tadpoles develop rapidly, and they can use very short-lived mud puddles for breeding. They can be found in vernal pools, swamps, marshes, wet meadows, streamside wetlands, and pond/lake fringes. The tiny, black tadpoles scrape algae, bacteria, and other organic matter off underwater surfaces, while adults feed on insects and other small invertebrates.

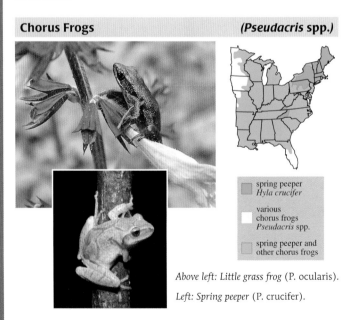

Chorus Frogs *(Pseudacris* spp.*)*

spring peeper
Hyla crucifer

various
chorus frogs
Pseudacris spp.

spring peeper and
other chorus frogs

Above left: Little grass frog (P. ocularis).

Left: Spring peeper (P. crucifer).

Distinguishing Characteristics: Length up to 3.8 cm (1.5"). Small frogs with poorly developed discs on the toes and little webbing between toes. This genus contains our smallest North American frog, the little grass

Left: Chorus frog eggs.

Below left: Spring peeper metamorph.

Below: Western chorus frog (P. triseriata).

frog (*P. ocularis*), which is often mistaken for a tiny grasshopper or other insect as it leaps through wet meadows. Most species have a white line along the upper lip. Some have distinctive markings, such as the X-shaped mark found on the back of the spring peeper (*P. crucifer*). Many of the other species and subspecies have dark lines or lines of dark spots, and there is often a broad, dark band running through the eye. Several of the most common, widespread chorus frog species were once considered to be a single species—the western chorus frog (*P. triseriata*). However, several species have since been separated from *P. triseriata*. There are currently about 13 recognized species of chorus frogs. In some areas it is virtually impossible to tell the different species apart, so we will discuss them generally. Many chorus frog calls sound like a fingernail being run up the teeth of a comb (*crreeeeeeeek*), but there are also species that make various flute-like and insect-like sounds. Spring peepers give a loud, repetitive *peep!*

Habitat and Remarks: Chorus frogs are the first frogs to begin calling in winter or early spring. They are often found in very temporary pools, grassy swales, wet meadows, marshes, vernal pools, pond/lake fringes, and many other types of wetlands. Eggs are laid in loose gelatinous clumps, usually attached to underwater vegetation. Tadpoles feed on algae and adults eat spiders, flies, beetles, moths, and many other kinds of insects.

Cricket Frogs   *(Acris* **spp.***)*

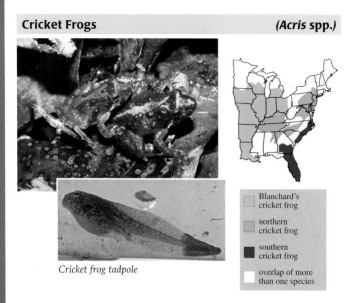

Cricket frog tadpole

Blanchard's cricket frog

northern cricket frog

southern cricket frog

overlap of more than one species

Distinguishing Characteristics: Length up to 3.2 cm (1.25"). Small frogs with pointed snouts. Their skin is moist but usually has some warts. The southern cricket frog (*A. gryllus*), Blanchard's cricket frog (*A. blanchardi*), and northern cricket frog (*A. crepitans*) are all variable in coloration and difficult to distinguish. All 3 species often—but not always—have a dark triangle between the eyes and a dark stripe on the rear side of the thigh. Some chorus frogs can also have the dark triangle but lack the thigh stripe. Coloration varies greatly, even within a single species or subspecies. The body is often gray, tan, or blackish with a wash of orange-tan or neon green on the back. Tadpoles of these species often have distinctive, black-tipped tails. The *click-click-click* call of a cricket frog is often the first indicator of its presence. The call sounds like pebbles or marbles being clicked together repeatedly.

Habitat and Remarks: Cricket frogs are often the only frogs calling during the hottest days of summer. They inhabit marshes, wet meadows, floodplain wetlands, swamps, ditches, pond/lake fringes, and many other areas. Their eggs are typically attached singly or in small groups to vegetation or to the bottom of fish-free waters. As tadpoles, cricket frogs feed on algae and other organic matter scraped from underwater surfaces. They are insectivores as adults. The tadpole's black tail tip is thought to direct the attention of small predators such as dragonfly larvae away from the tadpole's head and vital organs.

Treefrogs

(Hyla spp.)

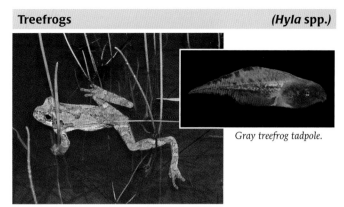

Gray treefrog tadpole.

Gray treefrog (H. chrysoscelis/versicolor): *Light spot below eye, orange wash on inner thigh. Call is a slow trill.*

Distinguishing Characteristics: Length up to 9 cm (3.5"). Treefrogs have long limbs and enlarged toe discs that aid in climbing. Chorus frogs (*Pseudacris* spp.) are sometimes mistaken for treefrogs because of their small size, but their toe discs and webbing between the toes are much less developed. There are 7 native species found in the eastern U.S. This group is more often heard than seen. Calls range from the trill of gray treefrogs (*H. chrysoscelis/versicolor*) to honks, barks, squirrel scolds, and bird calls of other species. The only distinctive, native eastern species not pictured on pages 209–211 is the Pine Barrens treefrog (*H. andersonii*), a rare and beautiful species found in scattered locations in New Jersey, the Carolinas, and the Florida panhandle.

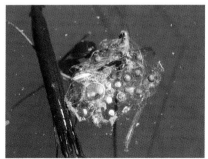

Gray treefrog egg mass.

Bird-voiced treefrog (H. avivoca): *Light spot below eye, yellowish-green wash on inner thigh. Call is a repetitive, bird-like note.*

Pine woods treefrog (H. femoralis): *Camouflage brown or gray pattern with no light spot under eye and small orange, yellow, or white spots on inner thigh. Call is a machine-like call sometimes sounding like Morse code.*

Green treefrog (H. cinerea): *Green, usually with white stripe. Call is a loud honk.*

Barking treefrog (H. gratiosa)*: Large, with many dark, rounded spots. Call sounds like the barking of distant hounds (deep honk).*

Squirrel treefrog (H. squirella)*: Nondescript. May look like a green treefrog without the white strip or a gray treefrog without the light spot under the eye. Call is a raspy note that can sound like a scolding squirrel.*

Habitat and Remarks: Some treefrogs disperse into upland forest canopy until it's time to return to vernal pools for breeding, while some species inhabit swamps and marshes full time. A few species, such as the widespread gray treefrog and the pine woods treefrog (*H. femoralis*), call from high in the trees much of the time. Others, such as the green treefrog (*H. cinerea*), are often found clinging to cattails and grasses. Tree frogs find shelter from the drying effects of the sun under loose bark, in rotting logs, and in grass clumps. They are often found at night around outside lights that draw insects, especially in the southeastern U.S. Treefrog choruses are often at their best before and during summer rains.

True Frogs   *(Lithobates* spp.)*

Distinguishing Characteristics: Length up to 15.2 cm (8"). Large-bodied frogs with smooth, moist skin. Coloration varies by species. See photos below for more characteristics and calls of widespread species. Note that there are many additional races and species with restricted ranges.

Green frog (L. clamitans)*: Green frog with bright green upper lip and a ridge down each side of the back (dorso-lateral ridges). Call is a sharp, single bow note that is sometimes repeated several times rapidly. Overlaps with the similar mink frog* (L. septentrionalis) *in the far north. Mink frogs smell very musky.*

Bullfrog (L. catesbeiana)*: Often huge, greenish frog lacking dorso-lateral ridges. Longest rear toe extends well beyond webbing. Overlaps with some lookalike species in the Deep South. Call is a deep* jug-o-rum.

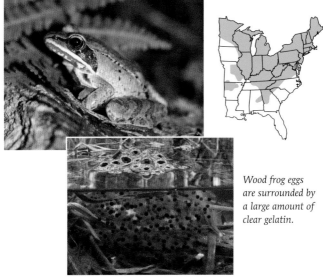

Wood frog eggs are surrounded by a large amount of clear gelatin.

Wood frog (L. sylvatica): *Tan or brown frog with a black facemask behind eyes and dorso-lateral ridges. Call is a squawk, sounding like angry ducks.*

Northern leopard frog (L. pipiens): *Tan or green frog with dark, round spots rimmed with lighter color. No light spot in tympanum (ear membrane). Call is a low snore interspersed with cackling notes.*

Southern leopard frog egg mass.

Southern leopard frog (L. sphenocephalus): Tan or green frog with dark, round spots. Coloration highly variable. Usually a light spot in the center of the tympanum. Call is a loud series of squawks and cackles.

Pickerel frog (L. palustris): Tan to greenish frog with squarish spots, light-colored dorso-lateral ridges, and a yellow-orange wash on the inner thigh surface. Call is a low snore.

Habitat and Remarks: Commonly seen along the edges of virtually any wetland type; therefore, several of the most common species are pictured here. Eggs vary from a film floating on the water surface to globular clusters attached to an underwater structure. Tadpoles graze on algae, but large tadpoles occasionally eat small invertebrates. Adults eat mostly insects, though some species also eat small mammals, birds, reptiles, and amphibians. Bullfrogs are a commercially important source of frog legs but are wreaking havoc by eating smaller native frogs where bullfrogs have been introduced outside their native range. Wood frogs are quite notable for their ability to survive being frozen solid for long periods during northern winters, allowing them to occur farther north than any other North American reptile or amphibian. All true frog species are important in the diets of wetland predators such as herons and mink.

Reptiles

NOTES ON ORGANIZATION

The reptiles below are organized according to taxonomic group, beginning with the turtles (order Testudines), followed by the snakes (order Squamata), and ending with a crocodilian (order Crocodilia).

Common Musk Turtle *(Sternotherus odoratus)*

Common musk turtle plastron.

Distinguishing Characteristics: Length up to 14 cm (5.5"). Small turtle with a high-domed, rounded shell (although shell is slightly keeled when very young). Common musk turtles are most likely to be confused with the eastern mud turtle (*Kinosternon subrubrum*) throughout much of their range, and with several other species of mud and musk turtles. Common musk turtles have the following combination of distinguishing characteristics: a one-hinged plastron; 2 obviously triangular scutes in front of the hinge; 2 light stripes on the head; and barbels on the chin and throat.

Habitat and Remarks: Inhabitant of swamps, marshes, ponds, and ditches. Its capability of producing a malodorous musk when threatened has earned this turtle the nickname "stinkpot." Musk turtles often sun on rocks and logs, and are known for their tendency to ascend fairly high into small, leaning trees. This species eats a variety of foods, including plants, fish, carrion, mollusks, and various other invertebrates.

REPTILES

Eastern Mud Turtle   *(Kinosternon subrubrum)*

Eastern mud turtle plastron.

Distinguishing Characteristics: Length up to 12.2 cm (4.8"). Small turtle with a high-domed, rounded shell. Unlike the very similar common musk turtle, the mud turtle's plastron is double hinged and it lacks lines on its face. The 2 scutes in front of the front hinge on the plastron are rectangular.

Habitat and Remarks: The eastern mud turtle appears to be declining throughout much of its range because of wetland drainage and habitat loss. Mud turtles prefer muddy swamps, freshwater marshes, and even brackish marshes, but they may also be found relatively far from permanent water in vernal pools. They often move relatively far from water to lay eggs and hibernate, making conservation of uplands next to streams and wetlands a priority for management of this species. Like the musk turtle, this species forages along the bottoms of waterbodies for plants, fish, crustaceans, mollusks, insects, and other invertebrates.

Painted Turtle   *(Chrysemys picta)*

Distinguishing Characteristics: Length up to 25.4 cm (10"). There are 4 recognized subspecies of this turtle, although they are all relatively similar in appearance. The shell is smooth and more highly domed than those of many aquatic turtles. There is a pattern of red and black along the margin of the carapace, which will also help to separate this species from map turtles, cooters, and sliders. The head, the legs, and the margins of the shell are often painted with a wonderful array of black, olive, yellow, and red. The shell coloration sometimes becomes obscured by algae. The southern subspecies of this turtle is marked with a prominent red dorsal stripe.

Habitat and Remarks: Painted turtles are commonly seen basking on logs or along the banks of swamps, marshes, ponds, and virtually any other wetland with some deep, permanent water. In northern parts of its range, this is the only species of aquatic turtle that is commonly seen basking. Painted turtles, like pond sliders, have the habit of stacking on top each other when sunning. They have an omnivorous diet consisting largely of plants, fish, carrion, insects, and mollusks. Like many other brightly colored aquatic turtles, this species has been collected extensively for the pet trade. Many species of aquatic turtles commonly carry harmful bacteria such as *Salmonella*; therefore, take great care to sterilize your hands after handling them.

REPTILES

Pond Sliders   *(Trachemys scripta)*

Distinguishing Characteristics: Length up to 29.2 cm (11.5"). There are 3 subspecies found in the eastern U.S.—yellowbelly, red-eared, and Cumberland sliders. The head coloration of the red-eared subspecies (pictured) generally makes this one easy to separate from other aquatic turtles, but it sometimes lacks the characteristic red ears. Unlike painted turtles, sliders have fairly flat shells with keeled scutes. Unlike those of map turtles, the roofs of their mouths are ridged—touch them on the nose with a stick to see this. And unlike cooters, sliders have chins that are rounded on the bottom rather than flat. Intergradation of the subspecies, algal growth, and variation in the amount of dark pigment (melanin) can almost completely obscure the shell pattern at times. Some individuals are completely black.

Habitat and Remarks: Except in the far northern U.S., this is usually the most common species of basking turtle. They may be found in swamps, ponds, and many other wetland types that have some deep, permanent water. Individuals sometimes stack themselves 2 or 3 high in popular sunning spots, but they are surprisingly wary and will topple into the water if approached too closely—especially in areas where they are not accustomed to seeing humans. Sliders eat a variety of aquatic invertebrates as juveniles, but adults are vegetarians and feed on many types of plant matter.

Cooters and Redbellies   (Pseudemys spp.)

Distinguishing Characteristics: Length up to 43.2 cm (17"). These turtles resemble pond sliders (Trachemys spp.), but often reach much larger sizes. Similar to sliders, the shell is somewhat flattened with keeled scutes and the roof of the mouth is ridged, but the chins of cooters and redbellies are flat on the bottom. The species of turtle within this genus can be difficult to distinguish. Throughout most of the East, the eastern cooter (*P. concinna*) is the most common species, particularly in rivers and floodplain wetlands. In the southeastern coastal plain, the Florida cooter (*P. floridana*) is also quite widespread in wetlands and other permanent bodies of water. The redbelly turtles (*P. rubriventris*, *alabamensis*, and *nelsoni*) are mainly found in the eastern coastal plain and piedmont, and can be distinguished from cooters by their reddish belly coloration and a notch in the tip of their upper jaw with a cusp on each side.

Habitat and Remarks: These wary turtles enjoy basking, and sometimes climb on top of each other in prominent sunning locations. Often, the only clue to their identification is a glimpse of a huge pond slider-like turtle as it splashes into the water. Like pond sliders, cooters are largely vegetarian, eating many submerged aquatic plants and algae. However, they also consume small fish, crayfish, snails, and aquatic insects.

Diamondback Terrapin　　　(*Malaclemys terrapin*)

Close-up of face.

Distinguishing Characteristics: Length up to 22.9 cm (9"). Shell has strong concentric rings on each scute, and the head and limbs are usually light gray with dark spots. Coloration of this species is highly variable, and 7 distinct races are recognized over its range. One of the best characteristics is habitat, as this is one of the few turtles commonly encountered in salt marshes.

Habitat and Remarks: Usually found in salt water and brackish marshes. Often seen basking on banks and mudflats exposed by tides. Terrapins were once highly sought after for food, and their numbers were severely diminished by market hunters who provided them to gourmet restaurants. Terrapin numbers have recovered well in recent decades as their delicacy status has been forgotten by most. They feed on mollusks, fish, crustaceans, insects, and other invertebrates.

Common Snapping Turtle   *(Chelydra serpentina)*

Distinguishing Characteristics: Length up to 49.3 cm (19.4"). Weight up to 34 kg (75 lbs). This fierce-looking turtle has a long tail and a body that is too large for it to retreat into its shell. It snaps fiercely when molested. Young snappers have prominently keeled scutes on top of their shells, and are often mistaken for baby alligator snapping turtles (*Macroclemys temminckii*), a species that can weigh over 136 kg (300 lbs)! However, in the common snapper these keels become rounded with age, and the alligator snapper has an extra row of small scutes along the lower edge on each side of the shell. Also, the common snapper has a long tail with large sawteeth on the dorsal surface, which separates it from most other turtles.

Habitat and Remarks: Common snapping turtles can be found in almost any reasonably permanent body of fresh water and are also very common in the brackish water of coastal marshes. This species and the alligator snapping turtle are both capable of snapping off human body parts, so be careful with them. The common snapper's neck is almost long enough to reach to the back of the body. Snapping turtles eat fish, amphibians, invertebrates, carrion, a variety of other animals, and some plant matter. This species does not bask as often as most other turtles, and spends a significant amount of time buried in muck or under logjams and undercut banks.

REPTILES

Softshell Turtles   *(Apalone* **spp.)**

Spiny softshell turtle.

spiny softshells

smooth softshells
and spiny softshells

Florida softshell

Distinguishing Characteristics: Length up to 43 cm (17"). The smooth softshell (*A. mutica*), Florida softshell (*A. ferox*), and spiny softshell (*A. spinifera*) species are relatively similar in appearance. Their long necks and flat, round shells can be recognized from a great distance while the turtles are floating at the water's surface or sunning on a log or sandbar. With practice, you may even be able to distinguish their drag marks in the sand of popular sunning spots from the marks of other turtles. However, distinguishing among species requires close examination. Spiny softshells have spines on the front edge of the carapace, a sandpapery shell, small spots on the shell, and a horizontal ridge in each nostril. Smooth softshells may have some speckling, but lack all of the other characteristics mentioned above. The Florida softshell has an elongate shell with flattened bumps on the front of the carapace, and a ridge in the nostrils.

Habitat and Remarks: Softshell turtles are often found in wetlands near streams and ditches. The Florida softshell is usually found in marshes, lakes, and ponds. They spend a fair amount of time buried in sand with only their heads extended, waiting to ambush prey. Their extremely long necks and tubular noses allow them to reach air at the water's surface while their bodies remain buried. Softshells feed primarily on animals such as fish, amphibians, and aquatic insects.

Northern Water Snake   *(Nerodia sipedon)*

Distinguishing Characteristics: Length up to 150 cm (59"). This snake is highly variable in color and pattern, and there are at least 4 recognized subspecies, including the northern, midland, Carolina, and Lake Erie water snakes. When young, this species is usually strongly patterned with shades of brown and orange. As the snake ages, its back may darken to almost solid black. Unlike plainbelly water snakes, this species has a belly patterned with crescents or squares, and lacks the black diagonal eye stripe of southern water snakes. Unlike cottonmouths (*Agkistrodon piscivorous*), northern water snakes have round pupils.

Habitat and Remarks: This is one of the snakes most commonly seen basking on rocks and logs around virtually any aquatic habitat of the eastern U.S. below 4,500 ft in elevation. It is the only water snake throughout much of the northeast. This species, like most water snakes, has a tendency to flatten its body when agitated, giving the snake a fat appearance and causing the head to appear more diamond shaped. This makes water snakes look remarkably similar to members of the venomous pit viper family, such as copperheads (*Agkistrodon contortrix*) and cottonmouths. Although they are harmless in terms of venom, most water snakes bite ferociously when handled, and the saliva has anticoagulant properties that can cause quite a bit of bleeding and make the bite appear worse than it is. This species feeds primarily on frogs, fish, invertebrates, and small mammals.

REPTILES

Southern Water Snake   (*Nerodia fasciata*)

Above left: Broad-banded subspecies.

Left: Florida subspecies showing the distinctive eye line of the banded water snake.

Distinguishing Characteristics: Length up to 159 cm (62.5"). Also referred to by common names for the 3 subspecies: banded, broad-banded, and Florida water snakes. Sometimes banded with bright red rimmed in black, or with broad bands of dark brown and narrower bands of tan. Occasionally almost entirely black with some red or light-colored spots along the lower sides. The coloration of some subspecies is quite similar to the northern water snake, and the 2 species sometimes hybridize. However, the southern water snake typically has a dark, diagonal stripe extending from the eye to the angle of the jaw, helping to distinguish it from northern and other species of water snakes found within its range.

Habitat and Remarks: Common in swamps, marshes, sloughs, and ponds primarily in the coastal plain. Like other water snakes, it is commonly mistaken for a cottonmouth, but is harmless. They are usually seen sunning, and are active both day and night during warm weather. Like other water snakes, they give birth to live young. Their diet consists primarily of fish and amphibians.

Plainbelly Water Snake (*Nerodia erythrogaster*)

Distinguishing Characteristics: Length up to 158 cm (62"). As an adult, this snake has a solid black or brown back (except for the blotched subspecies, which retains the juvenile pattern). The belly coloration varies by subspecies (i.e., redbelly, yellowbelly, and copperbelly subspecies) and even within a subspecies to some degree, but all plainbelly water snakes lack the checkers, stripes, crescents, or other patterns found on the undersides of other species. However, in the copperbelly subspecies (federally listed as threatened) dark coloration does encroach onto the belly.

Habitat and Remarks: This is primarily a snake of lowland swamps, shrubby wetlands, beaver ponds, and sloughs. This snake tends to wander farther from water than other water snake species, and is commonly found cruising through bottomland forests. Plainbelly water snakes are particularly fond of climbing into trees and shrubs to sun. They can reach fairly high population densities in good habitat, and feed primarily on frogs, tadpoles, salamanders, crayfish, fish, and other small animals.

Diamondback Water Snake (*Nerodia rhombifer*)

Distinguishing Characteristics: Length up to 160 cm (63"). A greenish-tan snake with a darker, chainlike pattern on the back. The light areas within the pattern sometimes vaguely resemble diamonds. Adults can become massive, thick-bodied snakes. Most similar to brown water snakes (*N. taxispilota*), which have dark squares down the center of the back and are found east of the diamondback water snake's range. Also similar to the Mississippi green (*N. cyclopion*) and Florida green (*N. floridana*) water snakes, but those species typically lack any discernible pattern on their backs. Unlike other water snakes, the male diamondback has many raised papillae on the undersurface of its chin.

Habitat and Remarks: Diamondback water snakes are common in swamps, sloughs, marshes, and ponds. They feed primarily on fish. They are commonly mistaken for cottonmouths, but are not venomous. Like other water snakes, they bite fiercely and musk profusely when picked up. They are commonly seen sunning on logs, and also climb into tree and shrub branches. Unless they are in an area where humans typically tread without bothering them, such as a nature boardwalk, water snakes typically dive from their perches as humans approach.

Mud Snake (*Farancia abacura*)

Distinguishing Characteristics: Length up to 207 cm (81.5"). A shiny black snake with a red or pink belly. Red encroaches onto the sides of the snake, and black encroaches onto the belly, forming some checkerboard patterning. Eyes are usually red. The tip of the tail has a hardened point. Not likely to be mistaken for any other snake. A small mud snake might be mistaken for the black swamp snake (*Seminatrix pygaea*), but that species has a solid red belly and the red does not encroach onto its sides. The related rainbow snake (*F. erytrogramma*) lives in similar habitats, but has longitudinal black and red stripes.

Habitat and Remarks: Mud snakes inhabit swamps, sloughs, and other muddy wetlands inhabited by their favorite prey. They feed extensively on amphiumas, but also eat leeches, fish, sirens, and amphibian larvae. Mud snakes are highly secretive, often remaining below ground in deep, mucky soils. They are occasionally found beneath half-submerged logs, and are rarely seen sunning. Unlike most other water snakes, they lay eggs in a nest excavated by the female in moist soil. When captured, they have a curious habit of poking their captor with the hardened end of their tail. This habit has led to legends about stinging snakes, but mud snakes are not venomous and usually do not even bite when handled.

Eastern Garter Snake *(Thamnophis sirtalis)*

Distinguishing Characteristics: Length up to 132.1 cm (52"). There are many species and subspecies of garter snakes, but this is the most widespread and commonly encountered species. Coloration is highly variable, but a green and black checkered pattern is common. There is usually a light stripe along the lower sides of the body that is confined to the second and third rows of scales above the belly. The eastern ribbon snake (*T. sauritus*) is similar and also fairly common. It is very slender and has 3 well-defined light stripes, the lowest of which is confined to the third and fourth scale rows above the belly.

Habitat and Remarks: Garter snakes are closely allied with water snakes. Garter snakes are often found in wet meadows, marshes, pond/lake fringes, and many upland habitats. They have a generalist diet, which has allowed them to become the most widespread snake in North America. They are one of the few snakes that may be found in urban developments, at high altitudes, and in far northern climates. In northern areas, this species is known for its tendency to hibernate in large groups. Garter snakes feed on frogs, salamanders, tadpoles, fish, small mammals, and invertebrates such as earthworms and leeches.

REPTILES

Cottonmouth *(Agkistrodon piscivorous)*

Distinguishing Characteristics: Length up to 189.2 cm (74.5"). Thick-bodied, semi-aquatic snake. When agitated, this species cocks its head back and displays the cottony inside of its mouth. The triangular head, sharply angular face, and vertical, catlike pupils separate this species from non-venomous snakes. However, many snakes flatten themselves when threatened, making their bodies appear fatter and their heads more triangular. Young cottonmouths are usually strongly patterned with white-edged orange and brown bands, but individuals usually become darker with age and some appear to be almost pure black.

Habitat and Remarks: *This is an extremely dangerous snake. Do not handle it!* Cottonmouth venom is primarily hemotoxic (attacks the tissue rather than the nervous system), and commonly leads to the amputation of fingers and toes where bites occur. Cottonmouths, or "water moccasins," are found in swamps, marshes, sloughs, ditches, ponds, lakes, and even brackish wetlands in the southeast coastal plain. In northern parts of their range, they often migrate to nearby uplands for hibernation. Like other water snakes and vipers, cottonmouths give birth to live young. The latin name *piscivorous* means "fish-eating," but this species will feed on many animals, including fish, frogs, salamanders, lizards, mammals, birds, baby turtles, and even baby alligators.

Alligator *(Alligator mississipiensis)*

REPTILES

Distinguishing Characteristics: Length up to 5.8 m (19'). Weight up to 1,040 lbs. The only large crocodilian in fresh waters of the U.S. The broad, rounded snout separates this species from the American crocodile (*Crocodylus acutus*), which is primarily found in the saltwater wetlands of southern Florida. Alligators are often seen sunning on the banks of waterbodies or swimming with just their eyes and tail out of the water. Alligators make prominent slides down the banks of streams, lakes, and wetlands, and tail drags and claw marks are often evident.

Habitat and Remarks: Habitat loss and hunting reduced numbers of this species to the point that it was placed on the U.S. Fish and Wildlife Service's list of threatened and endangered species; however, alligators have recovered to stable population levels today. The American alligator inhabits swamps, ponds, lakes, marshes, and other areas with relatively permanent water in the southeastern coastal plain. It will feed on any animal it can get in its mouth, including turtles, fish, amphibians, mammals, birds, and invertebrates. This species lays its eggs in a nest made of decomposing vegetation, which the female protects. The alligator is an important ecosystem engineer in some areas like the Everglades. This large species excavates wallows that are often the only aboveground source of water left during drought summers. Adult alligators have no natural predators except for humans, and perhaps introduced Burmese pythons (*Python molurus bivittatus*).

MAMMALS

Mammals

NOTES ON ORGANIZATION

The following mammals are loosely arranged from smallest to largest species; however, families are kept together because they share many characteristics.

Eastern Bats   (Order Chiroptera)

Eastern red bat (L. borealis).

Distinguishing Characteristics: Eastern bats range in size from the hoary bat (*Lasiurus cinereus*), with a wingspan of 41 cm (16"), to the tiny eastern small-footed bat (*Myotis leibii*), which often has a wingspan of less than 25 cm (10"). They also vary in color. Some species can be recognized in flight. For instance, the long wings and reddish fur of eastern red bats (*Lasiurus borealis*) make it possible to identify them with the aid of a good light. Many of the small, nondescript brown bats that may be found around wetlands are members of the genus *Myotis*, the most common being the little brown bat (*M. lucifugus*). Identification of individuals to the species level is unlikely because of their nocturnal flying habits, but several species are pictured here.

Little brown bat (M. lucifugus).   *Big brown bat* (E. fuscus).

Habitat and Remarks: There are about 20 bat species found east of the Mississippi. More species are found in the Deep South than in northern states, with only about 9 species common throughout most of the Midwest and Northeast. Almost all bats use wetlands to some extent, and are mostly nocturnal. Bats can often be seen drinking from pools as they skim low over the water at dusk, and they feed extensively on the flying insects that emerge from wetlands. Bats typically eat more than half their body weight in insects every night, while reproductive females match their weight, eliminating tons (literally) of agricultural pests and bloodsucking mosquitoes. Several bat species hibernate in caves during the winter, and roost in trees, barns, and other structures during summer. Others live in trees year round, some burying themselves in leaves at the base of a tree during the winter. Large, hollow tupelo and cypress trees are important roosts for several species of southeastern bats. Some bat species roost under the bark of shaggy-barked tree species or under the sloughing bark of dead trees, while others roost among the leaves of trees. Bat guano can sometimes be found under bridges, at the base of hollow trees, and in old barns. Cave-dwelling bat populations are in serious peril. Many of these bats have recently been infected with a disease called white-nose syndrome caused by a fungus (*Geomyces destructans*) inadvertently introduced to caves in the U.S. To date, this disease has killed more than 5.5 million bats, including 90 to 100 percent of the bats that once inhabited some caves in the Northeast.

Deer Mice *(Peromyscus* spp.)

Distinguishing Characteristics: Length up to 17.8 cm (7"). There are about 15 species of deer mice native to the U.S, and 5 of these are in the eastern U.S. They are difficult to differentiate. Most eastern U.S. *Peromyscus* are brown with white underparts as adults, and gray with white underparts when young. They have large eyes and a tail covered in short fur. The white-footed mouse (*P. leucopus*), the cotton mouse (*P. gossypinus*), and the deer mouse (*P. maniculatus*) are the most common and widespread species found near eastern wetlands. The deer mouse has a tail that is more sharply bicolored than that of the white-footed mouse, and these 2 species are found through-out most of the East. The cotton mouse is quite large for a *Peromyscus*, has large hind feet, and is only found in the southeastern U.S. The golden mouse (*Ochrotomys nuttallii*), a mostly arboreal species, is similar but has dense, soft, golden fur that is much different from the coarser brown fur of deer mice. Voles and lemmings have much shorter tails. Harvest mice (*Reithrodontomys* spp.) are smaller, are usually only found in meadows, and have grooved incisors.

Habitat and Remarks: *Peromyscus* species are the most common mice found in many eastern forests. In addition to many upland habitats, they frequent swamps, bottomland forests, wet meadows, marshes, lake/pond fringes, and most other wetland types. They live in hollow parts of trees, inside fallen logs, and under rocks, and often build a nest by adding a roof to a bird nest. During floods, deer mice, like many other small mammals, retreat to the safety of trees and shrubs. They feed on seeds, fruits, leaves, and insects. Deer mice are a very important prey source for mammalian predators, snakes, birds, and occasionally fish and amphibians. The most notable signs of their presence are gnawed seeds and nuts, nests, and tiny scats.

Southern Bog Lemming *(Synaptomys cooperi)*

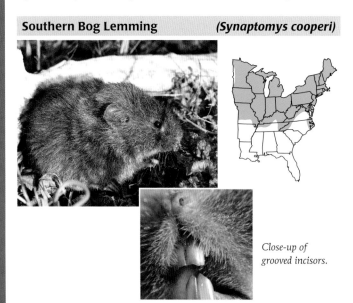

Close-up of grooved incisors.

Distinguishing Characteristics: Length up to 12.7 cm (5"). Small, vole-like animal with a very short tail, tiny ears, and a large head. Easily mistaken for a vole (*Microtus* spp.), most of which have slightly longer tails. Also, unlike eastern voles, the southern bog lemming has grooves in the incisors, which are evident in skulls collected from owl pellets or in carefully held live lemmings. The northern bog lemming (*S. borealis*) occurs in northern Minnesota and northern New England. It is extremely similar, except for the buffy hairs it often has at the base of the ears.

Habitat and Remarks: While bog lemmings do inhabit bogs, they also live in wet meadows, marsh fringes, and upland grasslands. Their tunnels and trails can often be seen cut through thick grass near the ground, and individuals are sometimes found under old boards and pieces of tin lying in grassy areas. Bright green droppings and grass stem cuttings are good indicators of this species' presence, although it often shares its habitat with vole species. Bog lemmings primarily eat grass, and sometimes eat invertebrates. They are eaten by snakes, raptors, weasels, and many other predators.

Marsh Rice Rat *(Oryzomys palustris)*

Distinguishing Characteristics: Length up to 22.9 cm (9"). A slender rat with a tail as long as the head and body combined. The appearance of this species is more similar to a very large deer mouse than the introduced vermin rat species (*Rattus* spp.) often found around human habitation. Throughout much of its range, the marsh rice rat shares habitat with the hispid cotton rat (*Sigmodon hispidus*). The cotton rat has long, coarse, grizzled fur, a blunter face more similar to that of a vole, blackish feet, and a tail that is shorter than the combined head and body length.

Habitat and Remarks: Found in marshes, swamps, lake fringes, coastal marshes, and other grassy wetlands. This species is capable of extensive diving and swimming. It feeds on insects, mollusks, crabs, eggs, seeds, and succulent plant parts. It builds nests in ground depressions or suspended in shrubs and small trees in wetter habitats. This species is preyed upon by snakes, raptors, and various mammalian predators. In some areas marsh rice rats and hispid cotton rats are equally common, but cotton rats appear to be more active during the day, which may make it easier for the 2 species to share a similar niche.

Muskrat *(Ondatra zibethicus)*

Distinguishing Characteristics: Length up to 55.9 cm (22"). Medium-sized brown mammal with a naked, relatively round tail (slightly laterally flattened). In southern Georgia and Florida this species is replaced by the round-tailed muskrat (*Neofiber alleni*). Might be mistaken for the introduced, invasive nutria (*Myocastor coypus*) in some areas, but that species is larger and has a squared-off nose with a whitish muzzle.

Habitat and Remarks: Most often found in marshes, but muskrats also inhabit pond/lake fringes, swamps, and other permanently flooded wetlands. Muskrats eat the roots and shoots of many aquatic plants, such as cattail, bulrush, and arrowhead. This species also eats a variety of animal matter, including mussels, snails, fish, and crustaceans. There are numerous signs that indicate the presence of muskrats. Their tracks resemble a smaller version of beaver tracks, except the much narrower tail often shows up in tail drags. Their pill-shaped scat can be found in prominent locations such as logs or rocks that stick up out of the water. They build small lodges out of cattails and other vegetation, or burrow into earthen banks. Feeding platforms, consisting of piles of vegetation and roots, and huge "midden piles" of mussel shells sometimes accumulate at muskrat burrow entrances or near prominent feeding locations.

Above: Muskrat feeding platform.

Right: Muskrat tracks.

American Beaver   *(Castor canadensis)*

Distinguishing Characteristics: Length up to 109.2 cm (43"). Sometimes weighs more than 34 kg (75 lbs). North America's largest rodent. Large, brown animal with a flat, scaly tail and protruding incisors. Might be mistaken for the introduced, invasive nutria, but that species has a rounded tail and a whitish muzzle. Beavers have 5-toed rear feet that are about 15 cm (6") long, with webbing that usually shows up in the tracks. The front feet have 4 toes and no webbing.

Habitat and Remarks: Beavers live in bank burrows or lodges created from mud and sticks. Beaver dams provide ponds where these semi-aquatic mammals can build lodges, cache food, and remain relatively safe from terrestrial predators. They also are responsible for the creation of vast areas of wetland. Some extensive marshes, fens, and swamps are maintained or expanded by the activity of generations of beaver. Prior to European settlement it is likely that there were many more wetlands located in our eastern stream bottoms, but this habitat was lost to early trappers, and now beaver-eradication efforts aimed at reducing flooding and timber damage. Beavers prefer to eat the inner bark of sweet, soft hardwood trees such as willow, cottonwood, and boxelder; however, they will eat a variety of other trees and vegetation. They are most often seen at dawn and dusk, and slap

Above: Small stream valley filled with wetland because of beaver activity.

Right: Beaver gnawing.

their tails loudly on the water surface when alarmed. The most obvious signs of beaver presence are their gnawings, dams, and lodges. Beavers also push up territorial markers that they make from mud and debris and cover with a strong-smelling musk (castoreum) secreted from their castor gland.

Cottontail *(Sylvilagus* spp.)

Marsh rabbit.

Right: Swamp rabbit latrine.

swamp rabbit

marsh rabbit

Distinguishing Characteristics: Length up to 50.8 cm (20"). Brown rabbits, with small, cotton ball-like tails. Cottontails are the most common rabbits throughout most of the eastern U.S. They might be confused with snowshoe hares (*Lepus americanus*) in the summer, but hares are only found in far northern states and at high elevations in the Appalachians. Hares also have huge hind feet and turn white in winter. Differentiation of cottontail species is difficult and perhaps easiest to accomplish using habitat and range.

Habitat and Remarks: The eastern cottontail (*S. floridanus*) is the most widespread species in our area. It is found along the fringes of some wetlands, but mainly inhabits old fields and brushy uplands. Two southern cottontail species are truly adapted to wetland habitats. The swamp rabbit (*S. aquaticus*) is a large species that inhabits swamps and marshes in central southern states. It often swims across pools of water, and has the curious habit of depositing its scat on prominent logs. Marsh rabbits (*S. palustris*) are more eastern than swamp rabbits, and unlike most other cottontails, the underside of their tail is brownish. Marsh rabbits also swim, and sometimes float momentarily with only their eyes exposed. They are found in cattail marshes and brackish marshes, and occasionally in swamps. Two other species of cottontail occur in New England and scattered locations in the Appalachian Mountains, but these species are difficult to differentiate from eastern cottontails and are not particularly associated with wetlands.

Common Raccoon   *(Procyon lotor)*

Distinguishing Characteristics: Length up to 101.6 cm (40"). The bandit mask and ringed tail of this species make it difficult to mistake for any other animal in the eastern U.S.

Habitat and Remarks: Raccoons are curious, roaming animals that may be found in nearly any habitat, but they prefer to be near forest and water. They may even be seen in the middle of cities, where they often use storm sewers as travel corridors. This species spends most of the day sleeping, often in a tree cavity, on a large branch, or in a burrow. During prolonged cold spells, raccoons hole up for several days at a time but do not go into a state of true hibernation. Raccoons are omnivorous—they eat animals such as crayfish, amphibians, small mammals, fish, insects, and mussels, and also feed heavily on fruit such as persimmons, pawpaw, and wild black cherry. The tracks resemble small human hand and foot prints, except with claw marks. The scat is often deposited in conspicuous piles next to prominent trees or on logs that have fallen across streams. Scat is usually filled with crayfish parts, fish scales, or whatever type of fruit is in season.

Raccoon tracks.

Mink   *(Mustela vison)*

Distinguishing Characteristics: Length up to 68.2 cm (27"). Typically dark brown with a white patch under the chin, but coloration varies somewhat by region and between individuals. Lacks the white or yellowish underparts of smaller weasels.

Habitat and Remarks: Mink are found near practically any kind of wetland, but perhaps reach their greatest abundance near marshes. They can be almost as playful as otters at times, bounding, swimming, and sliding down snowy slopes on their bellies. Mink feed extensively on muskrats and other small mammals, but also eat fish, amphibians, crayfish, and other invertebrates. Mink mostly live in muskrat lodges or bank burrows, which they dig themselves or steal from muskrats after eating the inhabitants. Tracks are similar in size to those of tree squirrels, but are more asymmetrical and have 5 toes on all feet (although the inside toe of each foot often does not register). Their bounding track pattern is similar to that of a miniature river otter. Scat is usually tight, twisted, and folded, like that of many other weasels, but the shape varies according to its contents.

Mink scat.

Northern River Otter (Lontra canadensis)

Distinguishing Characteristics: Length up to 111.8 cm (44"). A very skilled and playful swimmer, often found in groups. Unlike other large eastern semi-aquatic mammals, river otters have a large, round, furred tail. They are several times larger than mink.

Habitat and Remarks: Otters are found in marshes, swamps, lakes, and wetlands associated with streams. After European colonization, otters were almost exterminated by trappers who sought their densely furred pelts. Pollution and habitat loss also took a toll on this species, but otter populations are now rebounding across much of their former range. Otters feed primarily on aquatic organisms such as fish and crayfish, but also eat insects, mussels, frogs, and small mammals. They typically live in bank dens, but can also be found in natural cavities and beaver lodges. Good tracks show 5 toes in front and back, and webbing can often be seen in soft mud. Imprints of the toes are shaped like a Hershey's Kiss or a candle flame. The tracks are quite asymmetrical compared to the similar-sized tracks of bobcats, coyotes, and beaver. Scat is often green or reddish in color and is usually made up of fish scales and crayfish parts. Piles of scat and smears of musk can often be found near slides on muddy banks.

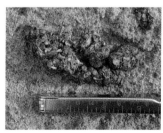 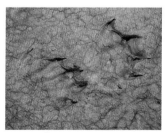

Otter scat.   Otter tracks.

Moose *(Alces americanus)*

Moose track.

Distinguishing Characteristics: Up to 2.1 m (6.9') tall at the shoulder. The largest member of the deer family (Cervidae). Moose have a humped back, and males (bulls) have distinctive palmate antlers during much of the year. Like other deer, moose shed their antlers (usually in winter) and regrow them each year.

Habitat and Remarks: Moose are an iconic part of our northern bogs, swamps, and lake fringes. They are intolerant of hot temperatures, and spend much of the summer submerged in cool lakes and rivers feeding on aquatic plants. They also feed on bark, twigs, lichens, and grasses, and can eat 40 to 70 pounds of vegetation a day. Moose populations have recently declined in much of the Great Lakes region. The decline may be because of habitat loss, increasing temperatures, brain parasites carried by deer (which have expanded their range into moose country), ticks, or a combination of factors.

Birds

NOTES ON ORGANIZATION

Birds in this section are loosely organized from smallest to largest; however, important groups are kept together for ease of identification. We begin with the smaller passerine birds often seen perching on plants and trees. Next, we cover shorebirds, rails, ibises, waterfowl, raptors, and wading birds, respectively. This is not the taxonomic order favored by most bird guides, but it should help the novice skim through similar-looking birds with similar habitat preferences.

Summer

Winter

Year-round

Migration

Key to the colors used in the bird range maps.

Marsh Wren   *(Cistothorus palustris)*

Distinguishing Characteristics: Up to 13 cm (5") tall. A small, brownish songbird with a thin bill, a dark cap, and a white eye line extending backward toward the back of the neck. There are bold black and white stripes on the back. The belly is whitish, and the sides are buffy. These birds sing at all hours of the day and night. Their song is a liquid, rattling trill, and the alarm call is a harsh *tusk*, often in pairs. The sedge wren (*C. platensis*) is a similar-looking species, but the streaking on the back is finer and the cap is also streaked with white. The Carolina wren (*Thryothorus ludovicianus*) lacks the dark cap and streaking on the back, and has a bolder white eye stripe and a bit of white on the wings. The house wren (*Troglodytes aedon*) lacks the streaking on the back and the white eye stripe. The Bewick's wren (*Thryomanes bewickii*) lacks the dark cap and streaking on the back, and has a whiter breast and throat and white spotting on the edges of the tail.

Habitat and Remarks: This is a common inhabitant of marshes full of reeds and cattails. Marsh wrens build football-shaped nests of grasses and attach them to cattail reeds. Their diet consists primarily of insects and spiders, which they glean from plants and from just under the water's surface. This is a widespread species, and there is some variation between eastern and western birds. In general, western birds are drab and sing much less musical songs. There is some question about whether or not eastern birds and western ones are actually different species.

Prothonotary Warbler *(Protonotaria citrea)*

Distinguishing Characteristics: Up to 14 cm (5.5") tall. Large for a warbler, but still a rather small bird. This is a striking bird with a deep yellow-orange head and breast. It has a greenish back and steely blue wings without wing bars. The belly and undertail are white, and there are some white spots in the tail. The song is a loud one-pitch *tweet, tweet, tweet*.

Habitat and Remarks: Can be found in wooded areas near water such as flooded bottomland forests, swamps, and the edges of large rivers and lakes. Its diet consists mostly of insects it forages for on the bark of trees. It is 1 of only 2 species of warbler that nest in cavities. It is named for the clerks in the Roman Catholic Church, whose robes were bright yellow.

Swamp Sparrow (Melospiza georgiana)

Distinguishing Characteristics: Up to 13 cm (5") tall. A small song-bird with a gray chest, a white throat, and an unstreaked whitish belly. The wings and back are dark, rusty, and streaked with gray. It has a reddish cap and a gray face. The voice is a trill, sometimes simultaneously using 2 or more pitches, and its call is a hard *chip*.

Habitat and Remarks: As the name suggests, swamp sparrows are often found in swamps, but they can also be found in a variety of other wetland habitats such as marshes and bogs. Their diet consists of seeds, fruit, and aquatic invertebrates. Occasionally they will stick their heads underwater to catch prey. This species also has longer legs than other sparrows, allowing them to wade for food. They nest in dense grass, shrubs, or cattails.

Red-winged Blackbird (Agelaius phoeniceus)

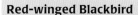

Male.

Female.

BIRDS

Distinguishing Characteristics: Up to 24.1 cm (9.5″) tall. Males are glossy jet black with red and yellow shoulder patches. Females are brownish overall with dark, well-defined streaking and often a whitish eyebrow. Females look like very large sparrows, but still have the sharp, pointed bill typical of blackbirds. Males stay more visible on high perches while females tend to stay hidden in lower vegetation. Their song is a loud *konk-la-ree*.

Habitat and Remarks: Red-winged blackbirds are perhaps the most abundant native bird in North America. They are found most often in marshes where they breed, but may be seen in virtually any wet or grassy habitat. Females build elaborate nests by wrapping wet vegetation around several upright plant stems, filling the inside with mud to make a cup, and then lining it with dry grass. They are ground foragers whose diet is composed mostly of insects in the summer and seeds in the winter. Red-winged blackbirds will sometimes use their long, sharp beaks to pry wetland plants apart at the base and eat whatever insects they might find inside. In the winter, they gather into huge flocks with other blackbirds and starlings to roost and search for food.

Belted Kingfisher *(Megaceryle alcyon)*

Female.

Male.

Distinguishing Characteristics: Up to 33 cm (13″). A medium-sized bird with a large head, a bushy crest, and a large, thick bill. It has a white throat, collar, and belly, and are blue-gray above with a blue-gray band across the chest. The female has a reddish band across the chest below the blue one. In males, there can be some red in the bluish chest band or on the flanks. The call is a loud, harsh rattle.

Habitat and Remarks: A common resident along streams, the belted kingfisher can often be seen hovering over the water and then diving head-first to catch a meal. It nests in burrows that it digs into the walls of stream banks. Often it will share these burrows with swallows, which dig rooms within the tunnel walls to nest. Its diet consists mostly of fish, but it will also eat aquatic invertebrates, insects, and small vertebrates. It flies the meal back to its perch where it pounds the prey to kill it. The kingfisher will dive into water to escape being eaten by predators.

Killdeer   *(Charadrius vociferus)*

Distinguishing Characteristics: Up to 25 cm (10") tall. Lanky birds with long tail and wings. Killdeer are brown on top with a white belly and a white chest with 2 black bands. The face is brown with black and white patches, and they have a buffy orange rump that is most visible in flight. The call is a loud *kill-deer*! There are many species of similar shorebirds that inhabit marshes and mudflats, especially during spring and fall migrations. Identification of all of these sandpiper and plover species (often informally called "peeps") is beyond the scope of this book; however, the 2 black bands on the chest of the killdeer distinguish it from all other shorebirds in the eastern U.S.

Habitat and Remarks: Killdeer can be found on river banks, mudflats, and sandbars, as well as in dry places. They are a very vocal species and will call insistently when startled or when they fear their nest is in danger. Killdeer are ground nesters and will pretend to be injured to lead predators away from their nests. They feed mostly on invertebrates, such as worms, crayfish, and aquatic insect larvae, but will also eat seeds from agricultural fields, and sometimes frogs and minnows.

BIRDS

Wilson's Snipe *(Gallinago delicata)*

Distinguishing Characteristics: Up to 27 cm (10½") tall. Medium-sized, stocky, brown shorebirds. Their heads and backs have bold, dark stripes. The underparts are white, with dark bars on the blanks. They have very long bills and fairly short legs. The call is a harsh *tuk-a-tuk-a-tuk*. American woodcocks (*Scolopax minor*) are similar in shape but lack bold stripes on their back and have a plain, buffy breast.

Habitat and Remarks: These birds are very well camouflaged to blend in with their grassy marsh habitat and are usually not seen until they scurry away or burst into flight. They use their long beaks to probe for small invertebrate prey in the mud. The tips of the bill are flexible and can be opened and closed without any movement from the base of the bill. Sensors in the tips of the bill allow them to feel their prey under the mud and water. They also sometimes eat seeds and vegetation. Nests are placed in a grassy clump near or surrounded by water. Males make a low whistle called "winnowing," a sound made by air flowing over the tail feathers as they beat their wings, rather than being vocal. The winnowing sounds like a hollow *hu-hu-hu*.

Willet *(Catoptrophorus semipalmatus)*

Distinguishing Characteristics: Up to 38 cm (15"). A large, plump shorebird with long legs; a long, thick bill; broad, round wings; and a short, blunt tail. It is heavily mottled grayish brown in summer, and more uniform gray in winter. In flight, there is a distinct black and white stripe along the underside of each wing. Its song is *pill-will-willet*.

Habitat and Remarks: Common around open beaches, marshes, and mudflats in the winter, and in salt marshes and along barrier islands during breeding season. These birds forage by probing the ground with their long, sturdy bills, and eat crabs, clams, worms, and other invertebrates. The tip of their bill is sensitive enough to allow them to forage at night as well as during the day. Nests are scraped into the ground near water, and both parents help to incubate, though it is the male that sits on the nest overnight. If threatened, the adults will act injured and limp off, dragging a wing to get the attention of a possible predator away from the nest and the young. They used to be hunted for meat and eggs, and before the Migratory Bird Treaty Act had all but vanished north of Virginia. They have since made a comeback.

Yellowlegs *(Tringa* spp.)*

Above left: Lesser yellowlegs (T. flavipes).

Left: Greater yellowlegs (T. melanoleuca).

Distinguishing Characteristics: Two very similar shorebirds are the greater yellowlegs (*T. melanoleuca*) and the lesser yellowlegs (*T. flavipes*). They are mottled brownish above and lighter below. The head, neck, and breast are heavily streaked during breeding season, and the sides and belly are barred. In winter, they are more 2-toned and the streaking is less conspicuous. The greater yellowlegs is larger, up to 36 cm (14") tall, with a longer, thicker, slightly upturned, blunt bill that is often gray at the base. The call is a loud series of descending notes occurring in sets of 3 or more: *tew, tew, tew*. The lesser yellowlegs is smaller, up to 27 cm (10.6") tall, and has a bill that is straight, thin, sharp, and black. The call is higher and shorter than the greater yellowlegs, consisting of between 1 and 3 notes: *tew*.

Habitat and Remarks: Greater yellowlegs breed in bogs with small tree stands; lesser yellowlegs breed in boreal forests with scattered wetlands. Both species winter in almost any type of wetland. Greater yellowlegs are one of the least-studied shorebirds because they breed at low densities in habitat that is difficult to traverse. They forage in the water, picking out what they see and sweeping their bills from side to side to catch prey by feel. Lesser yellowlegs mostly pluck prey they see from the water, and sometimes chase after prey on land. Both species feed on small invertebrates, fish, and frogs, and sometimes on seeds and berries.

Sora *(Porzana carolina)*

Distinguishing Characteristics: Up to 22 cm (8¾") tall. A small bird with a triangular body and a short, thick, yellow or greenish-yellow bill. The body is slate gray, with a brown head and back coarsely streaked with black. The face, throat, and breast are black. The black face and throat are less obvious in winter. The call is a descending whinny or a 2-noted *sor-ah*, with a higher second note.

Habitat and Remarks: These are very secretive marsh birds that breed in shallow wetlands with much emergent vegetation. You are much more likely to hear their distinctive, descending whinny call than to actually see the bird. Nests are made on floating vegetation. They forage on the ground for seeds and aquatic invertebrates.

Virginia Rail   *(Rallus limicola)*

Distinguishing Characteristics: Up to 24 cm (9½") tall. A small bird with a laterally compressed body, stout legs, and a long bill, curved slightly downward. It is chestnut brown above with black mottling on the back, and has gray cheeks and a rufous breast. It makes long series of pig-like grunts and a repeated *kid-dik*.

Habitat and Remarks: These are secretive birds that move stealthily through their marsh habitat. They live among the dense emergent vegetation, primarily in freshwater marshes but occasionally in salt marshes. They use their long, curved beak to probe the mud and water for aquatic invertebrates, frogs, crustaceans, small snakes, and insects. They weave a basketlike nest of vegetation, often covered, on the ground near shallow water to raise their young. They also build several "dummy" nests in addition to the one in which they place their eggs, as a defense against predators. The forehead feathers of the Virginia rail are specially developed to prevent wear from wading through dense vegetation. Rail species also have a greater ratio of leg to flight muscles than any other bird.

Common Gallinule *(Gallinula galeata)*

Distinguishing Characteristics: Up to 36 cm (14") tall. A dark bird with an olive-brown back, grayish belly, a white stripe on the flanks, a red forehead shield, and a triangular red bill with a yellow tip. The legs and feet are yellow. In winter, the forehead shield and the bill are brownish. The purple gallinule (*Porphyrio martinicus*) is similar in size and shape, but has a bright, iridescent purplish-blue head, neck, and belly; a greenish back; and a pale blue forehead shield. Gallinules make an array of sounds, including clucks, squawks, and cackles.

Habitat and Remarks: Common gallinules are the most widespread members of the rail family and are very vocal and conspicuous birds. They inhabit fresh and saltwater marshes with tall vegetation. Their long toes enable them to walk on soft mud or floating vegetation, and they are excellent swimmers although they don't have webbing between the toes. They feed prima-

Purple gallinule for comparison.

rily on seeds from grasses and sedges, and also sometimes on snails. Nests are usually anchored to emergent vegetation. Gallinule babies have spurs on their wings that enable them to climb into the nest.

American Coot (Fulica Americana)

Distinguishing Characteristics: Up to 39 cm (15½") tall. A small, plump, chicken-like bird, dark gray or black, with a rounded head, a sloping white forehead with a small red spot, a white bill, greenish legs, and red eyes. The toes are lobed instead of webbed. These birds are very vocal, and give an array of grunting, croaking, and squawking sounds.

Habitat and Remarks: Common on almost any body of fresh water, but they prefer to nest in areas with dense stands of aquatic vegetation and deep water. They can also be found in saltwater marshes and inlets. They forage while walking and swimming, and sometimes by diving under the water's surface. They feed primarily on aquatic plants but also on insects, crustaceans, and sometimes small vertebrates like tadpoles. Nests are floating, shallow basketlike structures anchored to exposed vegetation. In the winter, they can be found in groups numbering into the thousands, and in groups of mixed waterfowl.

Limpkin (Aramus guarauna)

Distinguishing Characteristics: Up to 66 cm (26") tall. A large, chocolate-brown bird with dense white streaking on the head, neck, back and breast, long legs, large unwebbed feet, and a long bill that curves slightly

BIRDS

downward and sometimes to the right. The call is a loud, screaming *krr-oww*, mostly heard at night.

Habitat and Remarks: Locally common in freshwater marshes, swamps, and the shallows of rivers and ponds. Only found in Florida in the U.S., which is the northern border of their range. Limpkins feed almost exclusively on apple snails, probing the ground and catching them with their specialized bill. They nest in a variety of sites, on the ground and on tree branches, where they build a platform of sticks and vegetation. The common name comes from their distinct, limping gait. They are the only member of their taxonomic family and are thought to be most closely related to cranes and rails.

White Ibis   (Eudocimus albus)

- ■ all year
- ☐ summer

Distinguishing Characteristics: Up to 64 cm (25″) tall. A large wading bird that is mostly white with black wing tips, bright reddish-pink skin on the face, red legs, and a long, red, down-turned bill. The call is a loud, nasal *urnk*. Juveniles might be mistaken for the other 2 ibises, but juvenile white ibis have a white rump and belly. The glossy ibis (*Plegadis falcinellus*) is a similar species in form, but is smaller and has dark, iridescent purple and green plumage and gray facial skin. The legs are green with reddish joints. The white-faced ibis (*Plegadis chihi*) is very similar to the glossy ibis, but has a red eye, red legs, and a distinct white border around the exposed skin on its face. It is mostly a western bird and only extends into the range of the white and glossy ibises in southern Louisiana, and occasionally up the East Coast.

Glossy ibis for comparison.

Habitat and Remarks: The white ibis is locally common in salt marshes, swamps, marshes, and mangroves. It forages by probing the ground for insects with its long, down-turned bill. White ibises nest in trees, while glossy ibises nest on the ground.

Pied-billed Grebe *(Podilymbus podiceps)*

Distinguishing Characteristics: Up to 34 cm (13.5") tall. A small, stocky bird with a short, thick, chicken-like beak, and a white, tufted rump. A breeding adult is brown above with a paler belly, black throat, and a white bill with a black ring around it. In the winter, the bill loses its ring, and the throat is white with a slight rufous tinge. Juveniles resemble non-breeding adults, with redder throats and white streaking on the head and neck. When in flight, almost no white is visible on the wing.

Habitat and Remarks: Although they can fly, pied-billed grebes are not often seen in flight. They usually escape predators by diving underwater, and migrate during the night. They do not have webbed feet like ducks; instead, they have an extra flap of skin around each toe to help provide more surface area for swimming. They feed on fish, crayfish, and aquatic insects, which they catch by diving from the surface of the water. They breed on ponds and lakes with heavy vegetation, building their nests in floating clumps of it, and winter in most types of wetlands.

Ruddy Duck   *(Oxyura jamaicensis)*

Male.

Female.

Distinguishing Characteristics: Up to 38 cm (15") tall. A small, chunky duck with a broad bill and large head with large, white patches on the cheeks. Breeding males are bright, rusty red on the body with a lighter belly, a black cap on top of the head, a blue bill, and a long spiked tail often held straight up. Females are more brownish all over, darker on the back and the top of the head, and have a dark horizontal stripe across the cheek. They are normally silent except in breeding season when males make popping noises.

Habitat and Remarks: Common in freshwater ponds and marshes in breeding season, and in saltwater marshes or inland lakes and ponds during winter. They are diving ducks, feeding on underwater vegetation, aquatic insects and larvae, and occasionally crustaceans and fish. They nest on the ground in stands of dense vegetation, which they sometimes pull over the top of the nest for concealment.

Bufflehead *(Bucephala albeola)*

Female.

Male.

Distinguishing Characteristics: Up to 34 cm (13½") tall. A small duck with a large head, a steeply sloped forehead, and a small gray bill. Males have black backs, black wings with a white spot, white underparts, and a dark, iridescent greenish-purple head with a very large white spot covering the entire back of the head. Females are duller, dark above with brown heads and grayish below. They have a white spot on each side of the face. They are usually silent, but offer a variety of sounds at different times of the year. Males squeal and growl in late winter and early spring, and females cluck when searching for nest sites. They have a deep chatter during breeding.

Habitat and Remarks: Found in freshwater ponds and small lakes in Canada in the summer; and along shallow marshes and in lakes and rivers in the U.S. in winter. They are the smallest diving duck in North America, and feed mostly on insects, crustaceans, and mollusks. They almost always nest in tree cavities dug out by northern flickers, and occasionally by pileated woodpeckers *(Dryocopus pileatus)*. Unlike most other duck species, they are usually monogamous, and pairs will remain together for several years. They lay their eggs slowly, and there is commonly a 2-to-3-day span between each egg.

Ring-necked Duck *(Aythya collaris)*

Female.

Male.

Distinguishing Characteristics: Up to 43 cm (17") tall. A medium-sized duck with a peak toward the back of the head and a bold white ring around the bill, just before the tip. Males are mostly black with gray sides and a white stripe that extends up the shoulder, separating the breast and sides. They also have a rusty purple-colored collar that is hard to see. Females are mostly grayish-brown with a paler gray face and a darker gray crown. They also have a white eye ring and sometimes a pale line extending toward the back of the head from the eye. They are usually silent ducks, but do give growly mating calls.

Habitat and Remarks: This is the most common diving duck found on small ponds during migration. They nest on the ground near freshwater marshes and wooded ponds or lakes. In the winter, they also can be found in coastal marshes. Their diet consists mainly of plants that they forage by diving under water. Both the scientific and the common name of the ring-necked duck come from the collar around its neck, which happens to be its most inconspicuous characteristic in the field, indicating that the first people to describe this species probably did so from dead specimens.

Lesser Scaup **(Aythya affinis)**

Distinguishing Characteristics: Up to 42 cm (16½") tall. A medium-sized duck with a slight bump on the back of the head and a bluish bill with a small black spot on the tip. Males have black heads, chests, and tails, with gray wings and white sides. Females are brownish all over (darker on the head and back) with a distinct white patch at the base of the bill. Males whistle a faint *whe-o* and females make a scratchy *garf*.

Habitat and Remarks: One of the most populous and widespread duck species in North America. They are common on lakes and ponds, preferring fresh water, but will winter in brackish areas. Their diet consists of aquatic insects, crustaceans, plants, and seeds, which they forage by diving underwater. They nest either on the ground or in floating vegetation in a grassy bowl lined with down. The chicks are capable of diving the day they hatch, but only for a moment because they are so light. By 5 weeks, they can stay under for up to 25 seconds.

Redhead **(Aythya americana)**

Distinguishing Characteristics: Up to 48 cm (19") tall. A medium-sized duck, distinguished from the canvasback by a more rounded head and shorter, tricolored bill. Males have a bright, rust-colored head, gray sides and back, black chest and rump, and a bluish bill with a white patch before the black tip. Females are brownish all over with darker crowns. Their bills are similar to males, except slightly darker. The male call during courtship is catlike.

Habitat and Remarks: Redheads are locally common in freshwater marshes, lakes, and ponds. They are diving ducks and feed primarily on aquatic plants. Nests are placed in floating vegetation; however, many redheads do not build their own nests. They are known to lay their eggs in the nests of other redheads or species of ducks, and even in the nests of American bitterns and northern harriers. Many of these parasitically laid eggs do not hatch. Redhead populations are currently declining in the eastern U.S.

Canvasback *(Aythya valisineria)*

Distinguishing Characteristics: Up to 53 cm (21") tall. A large duck with a long forehead that slopes to a long, black bill. In males, the head and neck are rust colored, the sides are white, and the breast and rump are black. Females have light brownish heads and necks and pale brownish-gray bodies. Males coo during courtship and females give a soft *krrr-krr*

Habitat and Remarks: Canvasbacks breed in prairie potholes and spend winters in coastal marshes. They are diving ducks and their diet consists mostly of plants, snails, and insect larvae. The species name of the canvasback (*valisineria*) comes from the scientific name of wild celery (*Vallisneria americana*), a preferred winter food.

Wood Duck   *(Aix sponsa)*

Distinguishing Characteristics: Up to 47 cm (18.5") tall. The male is one of the most brilliantly colored ducks in the U.S. The orange bill and green head coloration remain even during the drab non-breeding plumage. The female's crested gray head and white teardrop are distinctive. Call is a nasal, ascending *oo-eeek*, and the wings whistle in flight.

Habitat and Remarks: Wood ducks require fairly large trees with cavities for nesting. They nearly went extinct because of unregulated hunting and the loss of many bottomland forests to logging and agriculture. However, wood ducks have recovered and become the waterfowl species most often seen on our eastern woodland streams. This recovery is thanks to widespread nesting box installation, hunting regulation, and preservation of forested wetlands in conservation lands such as our National Wildlife Refuge system. Wood ducks are known to "parasitize" the nests of other females by laying eggs in them, causing some nests to end up with 40 or more eggs. Wood ducks feed on a variety of seeds, fruits, and invertebrates.

Green-winged Teal *(Anas crecca)*

Female.

Male.

Distinguishing Characteristics: Up to 37 cm (14.5") tall. Breeding males have a deep chestnut head with a green patch outlined in white over the eye and down the side of the head; a gray body; a pinkish speckled breast with a vertical white stripe; and a yellow tail stripe. Females are brownish and mottled all over with a white belly, a faint eye ring and a dark, horizontal line through the eye, and a yellow tail stripe. Non-breeding males look similar to females, and all adults have a bright green patch on the wings. Males whistle, a single note at a time, and females quack.

Habitat and Remarks: This species prefers shallow ponds with abundant vegetation inland, and tidal creeks and marshes along the coast. They are the smallest of the dabbling ducks and feed in shallow water on seeds and plant matter. They are fast, agile flyers and travel in flocks that appear to move like shorebirds.

Blue-winged teal   *(Anas discors)*

In flight.

Distinguishing Characteristics: Up to 39 cm (19") tall. A mottled brown duck. Males have a purplish-gray head with a white crescent in front of the eye. Females' heads are paler than the rest of the body, but still brownish and mottled with a prominent broken eye ring. Both sexes have blue and green wing patches.

Habitat and Remarks: These are dabbling ducks that inhabit shallow lakes and ponds, where they nest among grasses and other vegetation and forage for food. Their diet consists mostly of aquatic invertebrates and crustaceans during laying season, and seeds in winter.

American Wigeon *(Anas americana)*

Female.

Male.

Distinguishing Characteristics: Up to 48 cm (19") tall. A medium-sized duck with a small, dark-tipped, bluish-gray bill and a large white shoulder patch, which is visible in flight. Males have a white forehead and a green stripe down each side of their heads. Females are mottled brownish all over with grayish heads. The call of the male is a high, squeaky, 3-note whistle, with the second note at a higher pitch. Females quack softly.

Habitat and Remarks: A resident of shallow wetlands, ponds, and freshwater marshes. They were previously called "baldpate" because of the resemblance of the white stripe on the male's head to the head of a bald man. They nest among tall grass or bushes, often far from the water, in a lined depression on the ground. They are dabblers and feed mostly on aquatic vegetation, with the occasional insect or mollusk during breeding season. Though rare, they are the species of dabbler that is most likely to leave the water to forage for food in farm fields. In the 1980s, their numbers declined sharply because of drought in prairie regions, but they have since recovered.

Mallard *(Anas platyrhyncos)*

Distinguishing Characteristics: Up to 71.1 cm (28") tall. The male (drake) mallard is easily distinguishable thanks to a shiny green head with no crest and a white ring around the base of the neck. The body is grayish with a rusty brown chest, a white tail, and a yellowish bill with a black tip. Female mallards are mottled brown all over with white tails and yellowish-orange bills patched with black. Both sexes have orange feet and iridescent bluish wing patches. In the flying female, this patch is lined on both sides with a white stripe. The male voice is a low *kwek*, while females quack rambunctiously. Mottled ducks (*A. fulvigula*), found mainly in Florida, and black ducks (*A. rubripes*), found throughout the eastern U.S., are very similar to female mallards, but they lack the white line on the trailing edge of the colorful patch on the wing (the speculum). Usually mottled ducks have a green speculum, and black ducks have a dark body with a lighter head and light undersurfaces of wings.

Habitat and Remarks: The mallard is one of the most common ducks. It is found in all kinds of wetland habitats, including city park ponds. Like many other ducks, it filter-feeds at the surface, tips up to reach food below it in shallow water, and occasionally dives in deeper water. Its diet consists of aquatic plants, invertebrates, insects and larvae, seeds, and even acorns.

Above: Mallards (left) vs. black ducks (right).

Right: Mottled duck for comparison.

BIRDS

Gadwall   *(Anas strepera)*

Female.

Male.

Distinguishing Characteristics: Up to 51 cm (20") tall. Males mostly gray with a paler gray head, a black hind end, chestnut on the wings, and a gray bill. Females are mottled brown above with a white belly, and have a gray upper mandible with orange on the sides. Both sexes have a white wing patch that may or may not be visible when swimming and can help to identify birds in flight. Female quack is similar to that of a mallard, but more raspy and nasal. Courting males give a low, nasal *mepp*, sometimes combined with a quiet, high squeak.

Habitat and Remarks: Common in shallow ponds and marshes with lots of plants. They breed and nest on the edges of these wetlands, and form smaller flocks than other types of ducks. Gadwall are dabblers, feeding on the surface and tipping up to reach food below them. Their diet consists mostly of plants.

Northern Shoveler   *(Anas clypeata)*

In flight, displaying wing coloration.

Distinguishing Characteristics: Up to 48 cm (19") tall. A medium-sized duck with a large, spoon-shaped bill that is longer than the head. Males have an iridescent green head, white breast, rusty sides, and a black bill. Females are grayish brown all over with light edging on dark feathers and an olive-gray bill with orange edges. Males are usually quiet, with the exception of nasal braying on breeding grounds. Females give various soft quacks.

Habitat and Remarks: Breed in shallow, open wetlands, and are common in both fresh and saltwater wetlands in winter. Pairs are monogamous and stay together longer than other species of dabblers. Their diet consists of plants, aquatic invertebrates, and some seeds, which they feed on by filtering water through fine, comb-like projections along the edges of their bill. The nest is placed on the ground near water, with vegetation around at least 3 sides of it.

BIRDS

Northern Pintail *(Anas acuta)*

Distinguishing Characteristics: Up to 66 cm (26") tall. A slim duck with a long, graceful neck. Males have a chocolate-brown head atop a white neck, with a slim white line extending to the head. Back and sides are gray, with some black streaking on the wings and black lower back feathers with paler edges. Black tails are bordered by tan patches. They have very long central tail feathers that extend far past the rest of their wedge-shaped tails. Females are mottled brown all over with lighter edges on tail and rump feathers. Head and neck are paler, with a whitish chin. Central tail feathers are the longest, but not as long as the male's. Males whistle and females give a harsh quack.

Habitat and Remarks: One of the earliest-nesting ducks in North America, pintails nest on the ground near shallow wetlands, in open areas with low vegetation. Their diet consists of grains, seed, aquatic invertebrates, crustaceans, snails, and plant matter. They feed on the surface of the ground or by dabbling in the water.

Hooded Merganser *(Lophodytes cucullatus)*

Distinguishing Characteristics: Up to 48 cm (19") tall. A small duck with a long, sharp bill and a fan-shaped crest. The male's head, neck, and back are black. The crest has a large white patch within it that is bordered by black. The breast is white and bordered on each side by 2 black stripes. The wings have a white patch, and the belly is brown. In the female, the crest is shaggy and brown. Both sexes have yellow eyes. The voice is a low grunt or croak.

Habitat and Remarks: Can be found in wooded streams and wetlands where they breed, but also in other types of wetlands during migration and wintering. This species typically nests in tree cavities. Mergansers are divers that look for their food underwater. They are even capable of adjusting their vision underwater to see more clearly, and have a transparent third eyelid that helps them swim with their eyes open. Their diet consists of fish, aquatic insects, and crayfish.

Common Loon *(Gavia immer)*

Distinguishing Characteristics: Up to 81 cm (32") tall. A large bird with a thick bill slightly curved on top. Bill is black during breeding season and blue-gray with the top ridge remaining black in winter. Breeding adults have dark heads, backs, and sides. Back is patterned with large, rectangular white spots, and there are broad patches of white stripes on either side of the neck and a smaller one under the chin. Breast and belly are white. In winter, they become paler all over, with less-conspicuous patterning on the back and neck. The white breast color extends upward to the eye. Loons are famous for their eerie calls. The *tremolo* is a wavering call used to announce its presence to others or alarm; the *yodel* is the call of a territorial male, with each male having his own distinct variation; the *wail* is the famous "haunting" call used to figure out where others are located; and the *hoot* is a short, soft call used to keep in contact with others.

Habitat and Remarks: Loons are water birds, preferring areas with open, crystal-clear water, and only come ashore to mate or incubate eggs. They have solid bones, unlike other species of birds, which allow them to dive deep into the water where they catch fish. It is estimated that 2 adult loons and their 2 chicks are capable of eating nearly a half ton of fish during the 12 or so weeks that they are together. Their size and weight require them to have up to a quarter mile of space to flap their wings and gain enough speed to fly. However, once in the air, they are quite fast, and have been clocked up to 70 miles per hour. They have a complex migration pattern. Juveniles migrate south a few weeks after their parents and spend their first 2 years on coastal waters. The third year, they return north to breed, usually within 10 miles of the lake they were born on. Pairs are monogamous with bonds usually lasting around 5 years. The male chooses the nest site, usually close to the water since they don't walk well on land, and both parents build the nest. They often reuse the same nest site, simply refurbishing it the following year.

Snow Goose *(Chen caerulescens)*

Distinguishing Characteristics: Up to 84 cm (33") tall. A medium-sized goose with a stout pink bill and a long, thick neck. The bill has a black line along it, sometimes referred to as a "grinning patch" or "black lips." The snow goose can be distinguished from the smaller Ross's goose by its larger pink bill with "grinning patch," longer neck, and flatter head. It also flies with slower wingbeats than the Ross's goose. Snow geese occur in 2 color morphs. White morphs are almost entirely white bodied, with black coverts that are hardly visible on the ground but are noticeable in flight. Blue morphs have dark gray bodies, a white head, white under the tail, and white and black streaking near the wingtips. Snow geese are extremely noisy, and their main call is a loud, nasal honk. Parents and families also use a series of calls and notes to communicate with each other. In flight, there is a constant chorus of honks, quacks, and shrill calls.

Habitat and Remarks: Snow geese breed in large colonies in the arctic tundra near ponds, shallow lakes, and coastal marshes. After the chicks hatch, they move to brooding areas with much grass and vegetation, sometimes walking up to 50 miles to get there. They migrate in very large flocks and spend their winters on both coasts, and in some inland locations near marshes and ponds. They are vegetarians that feed on grasses, sedges, rushes, and other wetland plants. They will consume practically every part of the plant. Females spend up to 18 hours per day foraging for food upon their arrival at the breeding grounds, in preparation for their fast when they are incubating the eggs. The nest is placed on the ground, and the female builds it by herself.

Canada Goose *(Branta canadensis)*

Distinguishing Characteristics: Up to 114 cm (45") tall. A large-bodied, long-necked goose with a wide, flat bill, a brown back, a lighter tan chest, and a black head and neck with a white chinstrap extending from ear to ear. Large, dark wings, white underside of tail, and white, U-shaped rump band are visible in flight. The voice is varied and includes loud, musical honks, rapid cackling, and hisses.

Habitat and Remarks: Canada geese are the most familiar and common goose throughout the U.S. with at least 11 recognized subspecies, and a 20-inch height difference between the smallest and largest. They tend to get smaller the farther north into their range you go. Biologists have observed that the species uses a behavior called "assortative mating," in which each bird chooses a mate of similar size. They live in many habitats near water, and have become pests in some urban and suburban areas. They are attracted to manicured lawns with wide, open views for safety from predators. Their diet consists of grasses, seeds, berries, and grain. They also dabble in shallow water for the plant matter below. Recently, some geese have not been migrating as far south as in the past, which is attributed to a constant food supply from farm fields and changing weather patterns. They mate for life and nest on the ground where the female incubates the eggs, with the male standing guard. They congregate into large flocks in winter and assume the V formation when flying.

BIRDS

Barred Owl   *(Strix varia)*

Distinguishing Characteristics: Up to 61 cm (24") tall. Barred owls are grayish brown with large brown eyes and round heads. They are very fluffy in appearance. The chest is white with dark bars, and the belly is white with dark streaking. They have yellowish beaks and feet. The call is a series of 8 hoots, usually in 2 groups of 4 followed by a very characteristic *aw* at the end of the second group: *hoohoo-hoohoo, hoohoo-hoohooaw.*

Habitat and Remarks: Barred owls inhabit all types of forest, from wetlands and marshes to upland forest habitats. They prefer large, uninterrupted wooded areas. They consume small mammals, birds, reptiles, and invertebrates. One food of choice is crayfish, and the owls can be seen wading in water to catch their prey. Occasionally, the belly feathers can appear pink as a result of eating large amounts of crayfish. As in all owls, the edges of their feathers are frayed to make them silent fliers. They are able to stalk and catch prey without being heard.

Red-Shouldered Hawk **(Buteo lineatus)**

In flight.

Distinguishing Characteristics: Up to 61 cm (24") tall. A medium-sized, fairly robust hawk. They are brownish above, and adults have red patches on the shoulders, reddish barred bellies, and distinct black and white barred tails. The call is a screaming *kee-yer*; this is one of the most vocal species of hawks.

Habitat and Remarks: Red-shouldered hawks are found in open-canopied forests, usually near rivers, streams, and swamps. Their diet consists of small birds, reptiles, mammals, and crayfish. Often they can be seen in flight with crows. American crows regularly mob and try to steal food from red-shouldered hawks, but the reverse also happens. Sometimes the 2 species band together to chase larger predators such as owls from the hawk's territory.

BIRDS

Northern Harrier   *(Circus cyaneus)*

Female.

Male.

Distinguishing Characteristics: Up to 61 cm (24") tall. A slim hawk often seen gliding low over marshes and fields. It is the only species of hawks in which the male and female look very different. Males are light gray above with whitish bellies and some slight barring on the tail. Females have dark brown on the back, white bellies with brown streaking, and brown tails with dark bars. Both sexes have a prominent white patch on the rump. They have long wings and tails. The call is a soft whistle *pee, pee, pee.*

Habitat and Remarks: Sometimes referred to as the marsh hawk, northern harriers are often seen in open habitats, especially marshes. They also like meadows, fields, and pastures. Their diet consists of mostly mice, other small mammals, and birds, but they will also eat reptiles and frogs. Harriers sometimes catch larger prey such as rabbits, and have been known to kill them by drowning. They find prey by soaring low, and use both sight and hearing. Their faces show a defined facial disc (like an owl), which helps to concentrate sound. They nest on the ground in open fields.

Osprey *(Pandion haliaetus)*

Distinguishing Characteristics: Up to 62 cm (24.5") tall. Ospreys have a wingspan between 1.4 and 1.8 m (4.5 to 6'). They are dark brown or blackish on the back, wings, and tail, and have a white chest and belly. The head is also mostly white, but they do have a dark stripe across the cheek and down the back of the neck. Ospreys are very vocal and speak in sharp whistles: *cheep, cheep.* Because they build large nests and have white heads, they are sometimes mistaken for bald eagles, but that species lacks the osprey's white breast and belly.

Habitat and Remarks: Fish make up 99 percent of an osprey's diet; therefore, they are almost always found near water, including marshes, swamps, ponds, lakes, rivers, and streams. They nest in large trees or on a variety of man-made structures such as telephone poles. Ospreys are the only species of raptor in North America that will dive into the water for a meal. They fly above the water, sometimes hovering over it looking for prey, and then dive in feetfirst to catch fish. Ospreys have rough pads on the bottoms of their feet to help them grip slippery fish.

Bald Eagle *(Haliaeetus leucocephalus)*

BIRDS

Distinguishing Characteristics: Up to 109.2 cm (43") tall. Wingspan up to 2.3 m (7.5'). The adult has a black body and bright white head and tail, with a huge yellow bill, feet, and legs. The voice is a loud scream during flight and a series of chirps while resting.

Habitat and Remarks: Bald eagles are found near mid-size and large rivers, wetlands, and lakes, where they breed and nest in nearby forested areas. Their nests are large, constructed of sticks and placed in a large tree, often a pine. They use the same nests for many years, and nests can eventually consist of thousands of pounds of material. Bald eagles prefer fish, but also eat birds and mammals and scavenge for roadkill. They are soaring birds, but will engage in dramatic flight displays when courting. A mated pair will fly to a great height, lock talons, and tumble nearly to the ground before releasing each other.

Double-crested Cormorant *(Phalacrocorax auritus)*

Distinguishing Characteristics: Up to 81 cm (32") tall. A large bird with a long body and neck; a dark blunt beak, hooked at the tip; and a rounded yellow throat patch. Adult plumage is dark blackish all over with an iridescent sheen above. Breeding adults have backward-curving tufts starting behind each eye. Juveniles are more brownish above and paler below, with some yellow on the beak. The kinked neck in flight can help distinguish it from other cormorants. The call is a deep grunt.

Habitat and Remarks: The most common and widespread of the North American cormorants, they can be found in most types of aquatic habitats. Their diet consists primarily of fish, but they will sometimes eat other aquatic animals and insects. They hunt by diving into the water and catching prey in their beaks. They nest on the ground and in trees near water, in large stick nests that usually contain debris and even dead bird parts. Rocks can often be found in the nests as well—the birds will treat them as eggs. Youngsters in colonies of ground nesters will leave their nests and form groups with each other, returning to the nest to feed.

Anhinga *(Anhinga anhinga)*

Distinguishing Characteristics: Up to 89 cm (35") tall. A large, dark bird with a long, thin neck; long, sharply pointed bill; and long, fan-shaped tail. Males are black with a greenish sheen and silvery patches and streaks on the wings and upper back. Breeding males develop pale plumes on the back of the head and neck and brightly colored facial skin and bills. Females are similar to males, with a paler, buff-colored head, neck, and chest. Juveniles look similar to adult females. The profile view in flight looks headless. The voice is a raspy croak.

Habitat and Remarks: Anhingas are birds of southern swamps that often swim with only their head and neck exposed, resulting in their nickname of "Snakebird." They cannot waterproof their wings like other water birds. While this aids in their ability to dive while hunting, they must sit in the sun with their wings spread out to dry after a swim. They feed in freshwater, primarily on fish that they spear through the side with their sharp beaks. They are primarily freshwater birds but will sometimes breed in saltwater colonies. Males begin building nests before they pick a mate. They gather all of the material, and the females will complete the building process. Anhingas are graceful in flight and sometimes soar on thermals like raptors.

Green Heron *(Butorides virescens)*

Neck stretched in a bittern-like pose.

Distinguishing Characteristics: Up to 46 cm (18") tall. A short, squat heron with a long neck often kept drawn back close to its body, a long dark beak, long greenish-yellow or orange legs, and a shaggy crest most visible when the neck is extended. The back is dark with a blue-green tint, and the neck is dark chestnut. The voice is either a series of *kucks* or a loud squawking. The least bittern (*Ixobrychus exilis*) is a very similar species, but has a light-colored wing patch.

Least bittern for comparison.

Habitat and Remarks: The green heron is a wading bird found in marshes, ponds, creeks, streams, and swamps. It stands motionless over the water, waiting for small fish, invertebrates, or frogs to come close enough to grab out of the water. The green heron also frequently uses bait such as worms or feathers to lure its prey within striking distance. It nests in trees, usually over water.

American Bittern   *(Botaurus lentiginosus)*

BIRDS

Typical camouflaged view.

Distinguishing Characteristics: Up to 71 cm (28") tall. A fairly large, heavy-bodied bird with a long, tapered neck, pointed beak, relatively short legs, and slightly pointed wings. Plumage is rich brown above and buff below with bold reddish-brown streaking and black streaks on either side of the neck. Juveniles lack these stripes. Flight feathers are dark and sharply contrast with paler coverts. The song—a deep, hollow, repeating *oonk-a-lunk*—is usually heard at dusk. When flushed, it makes a loud *kok, kok, kok*. The green heron is often mistaken for this species, but it is darker and less robust, and has a dark cap.

Habitat and Remarks: American bitterns are secretive and can be hard to spot. They breed in freshwater marshes where they are well camouflaged among the tall reeds. In the winter, they move to waters that do not freeze, and may occasionally use brackish marshes during this time. Their diet is varied and consists of insects, fish, shellfish, amphibians, reptiles, and small mammals. They walk very slowly as they forage, and usually hunt in low light. They nest among cattails and sedges emergent from shallow waters. When frightened, they may freeze with their beak pointed straight up before flushing with rapid wing beats. They are almost clumsy in flight.

Little Blue Heron *(Egretta caerulea)*

Distinguishing Characteristics: Up to 61 cm (24") tall. A slender, medium-sized, slate-blue heron with a purplish head and neck, long dark-green legs, and a thin, dark bill. During the height of breeding season, the head and neck become reddish and the feet and legs become black. Immature little blue herons are whitish with dull grayish-yellow legs, a thick gray bill with a dark tip, and gray skin in front of the eyes. They are often mistaken for snowy egrets, which have black legs, a thin blackish beak, and yellow skin in front of the eye. The call is a loud, nasal squawk when they are threatened.

Habitat and Remarks: Immature little blue herons are tolerated in close proximity by snowy egrets better than by the blue adults. It is suggested that this is the reason little blue herons stay white for the first year— they can catch more fish and gain more protection when integrated into snowy egret flocks. They are wading birds that forage in the shallows of marshes, swamps, and lakes. They prey upon fish, aquatic invertebrates, and amphibians, which they catch with their long, thin bills. They nest on platforms of sticks placed in trees or shrubs. Unfortunately, populations are declining because of habitat loss and other changes made to local water dynamics.

Great Egret   *(Ardea alba)*

Distinguishing Characteristics: Up to 97 cm (38") tall. A large, slender, white heron. It has a long, straight yellow bill and long black legs and feet. The voice is a low-pitched croak or a *cuk, cuk, cuk*. The snowy egret (*Egretta thula*) is similar, except it is smaller and has black legs with yellow feet.

Habitat and Remarks: Great egrets nest in large groups with other species in trees over water and on islands. They can be found in swamps, tidal streams, lakes, marshes, rivers, ponds, and even flooded fields. They feed on fish, reptiles, amphibians, birds, invertebrates, and small mammals. Like other herons, they wade through shallow water to stalk their prey. They stand, leaning forward with their neck extended, and quickly stab prey with their long sharp beaks.

Snowy egret for comparison.

BIRDS

Great Blue Heron *(Ardea herodias)*

Distinguishing Characteristics: Up to 121.9 cm (48") tall. Large gray-blue bird with a long neck and usually a white crest or white face. One variety found in the Florida Everglades area has white plumage, but it has yellow legs, separating it from the great egret, which has black legs. Voice is a rough croak usually repeated several times, especially when alarmed.

Habitat and Remarks: Great blue herons spend their time stalking frogs, fish, snakes, and other aquatic creatures on the edges of streams and other water bodies. They sometimes venture into uplands in search of small mammals. This species is known for its tendency to nest in large colonies, called rookeries, which are usually built in large sycamores or other trees near streams or lakes. On the coast they may be found in large mixed rookeries with other wading birds.

Sandhill Crane   *(Grus canadensis)*

Distinguishing Characteristics: Up to 122 cm (48") tall. A very large, gray bird with a long neck, long legs, a red forehead, white cheeks, and tufted rump feathers. The gray body may be stained slightly reddish. The call is a deep trumpeting or rattling *gar-oo-oo*.

Habitat and Remarks: They breed in marshes, bogs, and wet meadows and grasslands, and forage in grain fields and marshes. Their diet consists mostly of grain and seed, with insects and small invertebrates as well. Nests are large mounds of plant material that float in the water or are attached to aquatic vegetation. Breeding pairs are monogamous and stay together year round, migrating south as a family in winter. They gather into very large groups during migration. The red staining in some individuals is the result of iron deposits in mud that is rubbed on the feathers when the birds preen with muddy bills.

Protecting Wetlands

In 1972, Section 404 of the Clean Water Act (CWA) established a means for protection of wetlands. While there are numerous other state and local protections, the CWA has remained the driving force behind wetland stewardship for several decades. However, this act does not provide a complete shield for all wetland areas, and recent lawsuits have undermined its protection for wetlands that are isolated from major bodies of water. Summarized below are a few of the ways that wetlands continue to be affected and some things that we can do to protect them.

IS INTENTIONAL WETLAND DESTRUCTION STILL ALLOWED?

The most obvious, direct way that wetlands are still being affected is through filling and draining. The federal, state, and regional regulations that protect wetlands often have provisions that allow for wetland destruction. There are provisions for land development, mining, agriculture, silviculture, and many

Rare wetland habitats have to be protected in order to save endangered species like this bog turtle.

other activities. In general, getting permits to fill or disturb a wetland requires one to document the extent of wetland destruction that will be required, and why it is necessary. Some form of mitigation is also usually required in order to be allowed to destroy a wetland. For instance, if a company needs to fill an acre of wetland in order to build a housing development, they might be required to restore or create three acres of wetland somewhere else and preserve that wetland in perpetuity. This is often done by planting trees and plugging ditches on a piece of land that was cleared and drained long ago. In theory, this would be a net gain for wetland conservation; however, there will almost always be a temporary loss of wetland habitat. Trees take time to grow, and wetland fauna may take many years to populate the site. It may be hundreds of years before the mitigation site resembles the wetland that was lost.

*Efforts are ongoing to restore whooping crane (*Grus americana*) populations from a low of just twenty-one birds in the 1940s. Wetlands are essential for their continued existence.*

Some wetlands, such as salt marshes and bogs, may have thousands of years of built-up organic matter or other physical characteristics that cannot be quickly replaced. It is unlikely that any mitigation can replace the functions of such a wetland, and we should avoid losing any more of this habitat. However, certain types of emergent marsh, some shrubby wetlands, and various types of human-made wetlands are relatively easy to replace, and mitigation may be a good option to obtain a net conservation gain.

IN WHAT OTHER WAYS ARE WETLANDS BEING AFFECTED?

Not all of the things happening to our wetlands are as obvious as draining and filling. More subtle changes in hydrology, nutrient content, and patterns of disturbance can also have a negative effect. Canals and ditches can reduce the amount of water that wetlands hold or change the salinity in coastal areas. New developments may increase the amount of sediment and chemicals flowing into wetlands. Road salt may be increasing the salinity of our wetlands to the point that they are less inhabitable by amphibians. Many wetlands that are traditionally nutrient poor, such as bogs and the Florida

Everglades, are being flooded with nutrients from fertilizers and sewage. This upsets a delicate balance and paves the way for invasive plants to strangle the species that are highly adapted to living in nutrient-poor environments. While we may not be losing as much wetland acreage directly these days, many would-be wetlands are destroyed when beaver dams are removed from small streams. Certain wetlands, such as pine savannahs and marshes, need fire to maintain their most diverse condition. However, we have suppressed fires in many of these areas, removing an important source of disturbance.

WHAT CAN YOU DO TO PROTECT WETLANDS?

Wetland conservation has come a long way in the last several decades. Many people now understand that we depend on these habitats for clean water, seafood, storm protection, waterfowl, and even simple enjoyment. One of the first steps anyone can take toward furthering wetland conservation is education. You may spark a lifetime of wetland advocacy just by showing a child some tadpoles or introducing a friend to the joys of looking for birds, reptiles, amphibians, dragonflies, and other wetland creatures. You may also want to join the efforts of a conservation organization, such as The Nature Conservancy or Ducks Unlimited, or spend time volunteering at your local National Wildlife Refuge. Some of you may even want to create vernal pools in your backyards.

Regardless of whether or how you choose to protect wetlands, the first step is to go explore them and learn more about your local environment. There is no better advocate for conservation than one who is fueled by knowledge and inspiration gained in the natural world.

Glossary

Achene. A small, dry, one-seeded fruit that does not crack open upon ripening.

Acuminate. In plants, usually refers to a leaf tip that is distinctly pinched at the tip into a small point or "drip tip."

Adipose Fin. Small, fleshy fin located on the back of fish between the dorsal fin and the caudal fin.

Aerenchyma. The space in the leaves, stems, and roots of some plants that allows the passage of gases between the plant and the root.

Alternate leaf pattern. Leaf pattern in which a leaf occurs singly at each node along the main stem (not paired with another leaf).

Aquatic. Consisting of, relating to, or living in water.

Astringent. A substance that constricts body tissue, usually after being applied topically.

Benthic. Bottom-dwelling.

Biofilm. A film of algae, diatoms, bacteria, and other matter that often adheres to hard underwater surfaces.

Bipinnate. A leaf with leaflets arranged alongside stems that grow opposite each other on a main rachis.

Bract. A modified leaf, often reduced in size, that is usually associated with a flower.

Carapace. A bony covering on the back of an animal, such as the shell on a turtle's back.

Carolina bay. Elliptical depressions along the mid-Atlantic seaboard. Some are lakes or open water scattered with cypress; others are

pocosins with vegetation floating on peat mats.

Catkin. A cylindrical flower cluster, often drooping, with very small or no petals, made up of many typically unisexual flowers.

Caudal. Posterior; situated near the tail.

Circumboreal. Distributed throughout boreal regions.

Cloaca. A posterior opening in certain animals that is the only opening for the intestinal, urinary, and reproductive tracts.

Compound leaf. Refers to a leaf made up of several smaller leaflets.

Cone. A usually woody fruit with overlapping scales.

Cordate. Heart-shaped.

Corymb. A flower cluster in which the individual flower stalks grow upward from different points on the main stem to nearly the same height, giving the cluster a flat-topped appearance.

Crest. A tuft of feathers on the head of a bird.

Deciduous. A tree or shrub that loses its leaves seasonally.

Detritus. Particles of non-living organic material.

Dorsal. Toward the top of the body.

Dorsolateral ridge. A ridge located toward the sides of an animal's back.

Doubly serrate. A leaf with double-toothed margins and small teeth upon larger ones.

Elliptical. Oval-shaped.

Ephemeral stream. A stream that flows only after precipitation, remaining dry most of the year.

Evergreen. A tree or shrub whose leaves remain attached through all 4 seasons.

Exuviae. The cast-off skin or covering of various organisms; the exoskeleton of invertebrates.

Facultative (FACU, FAC, FACW). Exhibiting an indicated lifestyle under certain environmental conditions; as opposed to an obligate lifestyle exhibited at all times.

FAC, Facultative plant. Equally likely to be found in wetlands and uplands.

FACU, Facultative upland plant. Usually occurs in uplands, but occasionally found in wetlands.

FACW, Facultative wetland plant. Usually occurs in wetlands, but occasionally found in uplands.

Forb. An herbaceous plant that is not grass-like.

Fragipan. Altered soil layers below the surface that restrict the flow of water and root penetration through the soil.

Genera. Plural of genus.

Genus. A taxonomic level indicating a group of organisms linked by common characteristics.

Glabrous. Smooth; free of hair.

Gland. In plants, a small dot-like protuberance on a leaf that usually secretes liquid.

Globoid. Globe-shaped

Grady pond. Elliptical depressions in the Gulf of Mexico coastal plain in Mississippi and Alabama; essentially the same as a Carolina bay, with the exception of their geographical location.

Guano. The feces of bats and certain other animals.

Herbaceous. A plant with little or no woody tissue, whose leaves and stems die back to ground level over the winter.

Hirsute. Covered with coarse, stiff hairs.

Hydric. Relating to, characterized by, or requiring considerable moisture.

Hydrology. The study of the properties, movement, and distribution of water.

Hydroperiod. A period during which soil is saturated with water.

Impermeable. Not allowing fluid to pass through.

Inflorescence. A cluster of flowers arranged on a branch.

Inundated. Flooded.

Karst. A special landscape formed by the dissolution of layers of soluble rock, often resulting in caves, sinkholes, and springs.

Keeled. Having a central ridge, like that on the keel of a boat.

Key. As it is used here—a winged, one-seeded fruit.

Lanceolate. Shaped like a spear point—rounded at the base, broadest toward the middle, and tapering to a point at the tip.

Lateral. Toward the sides of the body.

Laterally flattened. Flattened from side to side.

Lateral line. An organ in aquatic organisms used to detect movement and vibration in surrounding water.

Leaf scar. The mark left behind when a leaf falls off a twig.

Leaflet. One of the small blades that make up a compound leaf.

Lenticel. A corky growth on bark that serves as a pore, allowing air to reach inside a twig or branch.

Ligule. A small protrusion extending from the top of the leaf base where the leaf meets the stem. This is a useful structure in identification of grasses.

Lobe. A clear anatomical division, somewhat rounded, of a leaf.

Margin. As it is used here—the edge of a leaf.

Minerotrophic. Plants and soils whose water supply comes from streams or springs.

Monoculture. A single plant species occurring over a large area.

Monospecific. Composed of one species.

Montane. Of, or growing in the mountains.

Native. As it is used in this guide—a plant or animal naturally found in the eastern U.S. prior to European colonization.

Non-vascular plant. Plants without vascular systems, that cannot retain water or deliver it to other parts of the plant body, but instead must absorb it from the surrounding air or environment.

OBL, obligate. Almost always occurs in wetlands.

Obovate. Egg-shaped, with the broader end toward the tip (refers to leaves).

Ombrotropic. Plants or soils that receive all of their water from precipitation.

Operculum. A lid-like structure, such as that found over the shell openings of some snails and covering the gills of fishes.

Opposite. Occurring in pairs at each node along the stem.

Orbicular. Flat and circular.

Organic matter. Matter that has come from an organism that was once alive.

Ovate. Shaped like a longitudinal section of an egg, broader at the base and tapering toward the end.

Palmate. Refers to a leaf with lobes or leaflets radiating from 1 central point; shaped like an open hand.

Panicle. A compound inflorescence made up of many racemes of flowers.

Pedicel. In plants, this is a small stalk that attaches flowers to the main stem of the inflorescence.

Peduncle. A narrow part by which some larger part of the body is attached, such as a stalk that supports a flower or the caudal peduncle that supports a fish's caudal fin.

Peritoneum. Connective tissue that forms the lining of the abdominal cavity.

Pinnae. As it is used here—a leaflet of a pinnately compound leaf.

Pinnate. Refers to a leaf with leaflets arranged along both sides of a main rachis.

Pinnatifid. A term describing a leaf with very deep pinnate lobes that remain attached to each other so that they are not actually separate leaflets.

Plastron. A hard plate covering the ventral surface of animal, as in a turtle's breast plate.

Pneumatophore. A specialized respiratory root of certain aquatic plants that grows upward.

Pocosin. An inland wetland, lacking flowing water, with deep, acidic, sandy peat soils that are saturated for most of the year; an Algonquian Indian name meaning "swamp on a hill."

Proleg. Small, foot-like appendages that serve in place of legs for various species of insect larvae.

Pubescent. Covered in small hairs; often having a velvety or fuzzy texture.

Race. This word is often used as a synonym for the word subspecies. However, race usually implies a less-formally separated subgroup within a species, similar to the way the word variety is applied to plants.

Raceme. An un-branched inflorescence made up of a main stalk with flowers attached by a pedicel.

Rachis. As it is used here—the main stem of a compound leaf.

Redoximorphic features. Features of soil that form by reduction, translocation, and/or oxidation of iron and manganese, usually under hydric, anaerobic conditions.

Rhizoid. A simple, hair-like protuberance that anchors a bryophyte to the surface on which it is growing.

Rhizome. A horizontal plant stalk usually found underground that sends out shoots and roots from nodes.

Rostrum. A nose, or nose-like protrusion located on the face.

Run. A part of a stream where the water is fast moving but deeper and slower than a riffle.

Samara. A winged tree fruit.

Scape. A leafless flower stalk growing directly from the ground.

Scute. A hard external plate, as in the plates that cover a turtle shell.

Serrate. Having a toothed margin.

Shrub. A woody plant with multiple stems, less than 20 feet tall.

Simple. In plants, this refers to a leaf made up of a single blade.

Sinus. As it is used here—the space between 2 lobes of a leaf.

Slough. A river inlet, backwater, or creek in a marsh or tidal flat.

Snag. A term often used to describe dead standing trees.

Soil matrix. The portion of any given soil having the dominant color.

Sp. A single species (abbreviation).

Spadix. A spike-like flower cluster with many tiny flowers on a fleshy stem.

Spathe. A leaf-like bract that encloses a flower cluster.

Spike. A type of inflorescence in which a group of flowers is attached directly to a central stem (unlike racemes, in which flowers are attached via a pedicel).

Spp. More than one species (abbreviation).

Stipule. Small, usually paired appendages at the base of the leaf-stalk in certain plants.

Strobilus. A cone-like structure with many overlapping sporophylls arranged spirally along a central axis.

Subterminal. Located not quite at the end.

Swim bladder. A gas-filled organ that helps a fish control its buoyancy and stay at a specific water depth without wasting energy swimming.

Terminal. Located at the end of something.

Terrestrial. Relating to or occurring on land.

Thallus. A plant body not differentiated into distinct parts.

Topography. The study of the shape and features of the Earth.

Tree. A woody perennial plant with many branches supported off the ground by a single or forked trunk that is clearly dominant over other branches and is at least 15 feet tall and 2 inches in diameter.

Tubercles. Small, rounded, sometimes warty growth.

Turbidity. A measure of the cloudiness of a liquid. In streams, this is usually a measurement of the amount of suspended sediment and/or algae in the water.

Ubiquitous. Constantly occurring.

Umbel. Inflorescence with flower stalks that arise from the stem at the same point (like an umbrella).

UPL, obligate upland plant. Almost always occurs in uplands. The only reason it is in the list of wetland plants is because it occurs in wetlands in another region.

Vascular plant. A plant with a vascular system capable of transporting food and water to different parts of the plant body.

Vein. Threads of tissue in a leaf through which food and water pass.

Venation. The arrangement of veins in a leaf.

Ventral. Toward the bottom side of the body.

Whorled. Refers to a leaf arrangement in which 3 or more leaves occur at each node along the stem.

References

GENERAL WETLAND ECOLOGY

Cowardin, Lewis M., Virginia Carter, Francis C. Golet, and Edward T. LaRoe. *Classification of Wetlands and Deepwater Habitats of the United States.* U.S. Fish and Wildlife Service, 1979.

Environmental Laboratory. *Corps of Engineers Wetlands Delineation Manual.* U.S. Army Corps of Engineers, 1987.

Mitsch, William J., and James G. Gosselink. *Wetlands, 4th Edition.* Hoboken, NJ: John Wiley and Sons, 2007.

Tiner, Ralph. *Wetland Indicators: A Guide to Wetland Identification, Delineation, Classification, and Mapping.* Boca Raton, FL: Lewis Publishers, 1999.

———. *In Search of Swampland: A Wetland Sourcebook and Field Guide,* 2nd Edition. New Brunswick, NJ: Rutgers University Press, 2005.

U.S. Army Corps of Engineers. *Regional Supplement to the Corps of Engineers Wetland Delineation Manual: Atlantic and Gulf Coastal Plain (Version 2.0),* ed. J. S. Wakeley, R. W. Lichvar, and C. V. Noble. U.S. Army Engineer Research Development Center, 2010.

U.S. Army Corps of Engineers. *Regional Supplement to the Corps of Engineers Wetland Delineation Manual: Eastern Mountains and Piedmont Region (Version 2.0),* ed. J. F. Berkowitz, J. S. Wakeley, R. W. Lichvar, and C. V. Noble. U.S. Army Engineer Research Development Center, 2012.

U.S. Army Corps of Engineers. *Regional Supplement to the Corps of Engineers Wetland Delineation Manual: Great Plains Region (Version 2.0),* ed. J. S. Wakely, R. W. Lichvar, and C. V. Noble. U.S. Army Engineer Research Development Center, 2010.

U.S. Army Corps of Engineers. *Regional Supplement to the Corps of Engineers Wetland Delineation Manual: Midwest Region (Version 2.0),* ed. J. S. Wakely, R. W. Lichvar, and C. V. Noble. U.S. Army Engineer Research Development Center, 2010.

U.S. Army Corps of Engineers. *Regional Supplement to the Corps of Engineers Wetland Delineation Manual: Northcentral and Northeast Region (Version 2.0),* ed. J. S. Wakely, R. W. Lichvar, and C. V. Noble. U.S. Army Engineer Research Development Center, 2011.

PLANTS

Brown, Lauren. *Grasses: An Identification Guide.* New York: Houghton Mifflin, 1979.

Duncan, Wilbur H., and Marion B. Duncan. *The Smithsonian Guide to Seaside Plants of the Gulf and Atlantic Coasts.* Washington, DC: Smithsonian Institution Press, 1987.

"Flora of North America." http://efloras.org

"Flora of the Southeast." University of North Carolina Herbarium. 2010. http://www.herbarium.unc.edu/seflora/firstviewer.htm

Foster, Steven, and James A. Duke. *Peterson Field Guides: A Field Guide to Medicinal Plants*. New York: Houghton Mifflin, 1990.

Little, Elbert L. *The Audubon Society Field Guide to North American Trees: Eastern Region*. New York: Alfred A. Knopf, 1980.

Martin, Alexander C., Herbert S. Zim, and Arnold L. Nelson. *American Wildlife & Plants: A Guide to Wildlife Food Habits*. New York: Dover Publications, 1951.

"Native Plant Information Network." Lady Bird Johnson Wildflower Center, The University of Texas at Austin. 2010. http://www.wildflower.org/

Newcomb, Lawrence, with Gordon Morrison. *Newcomb's Wildflower Guide*. Boston, MA: Little, Brown and Company, 1977.

Peterson, Lee Allen. *Peterson Field Guides: Edible Wild Plants*. Boston, MA: Houghton Mifflin, 1977.

"Plants Database." U.S. Department of Agriculture. 2010. http://plants.usda.gov/index.html

Preston, Richard J. Jr. *North American Trees*, 4th Edition. Ames, IA: Iowa State University Press, 1989.

Sibley, David Allen. *The Sibley Guide to Trees*. New York: Alfred A. Knopf, 2009.

"U.S. County-Level Atlas of the Vascular Flora of North America." 2010. Chapel Hill, NC: The Biota of North America Program (BONAP). http://www.bonap.org/MapSwitchboard.html

INVERTEBRATES

Dunkle, Sidney W. *Dragonflies through Binoculars: A Field Guide to Dragonflies of North America*. New York: Oxford University Press, 2000.

Merritt, R. W., K. W. Cummins, and M. B. Berg. *An Introduction to the Aquatic Insects of North America*, 4th Edition. Dubuque, IA: Kendall/Hunt Publishing Co., 2008.

Nikula, Blair, and Jackie Sones, with Donald and Lillian Stokes. *Stokes: Beginner's Guide to Dragonflies and Damselflies*. Boston, MA: Little, Brown and Company, 2002.

Smith, Douglas Grant. *Pennak's Freshwater Invertebrates of the United States: Porifera to Crustacea*, 4th edition. New York: John Wiley and Sons, 2001.

Taylor, Christopher A., and Guenter A. Schuster. *The Crayfishes of Kentucky*. Special Publication No. 28. Champaign, IL: Illinois Natural History Survey, 2004

Thorp, James H., and Alan P. Covich, eds. *Ecology and Classification of North American Freshwater Invertebrates*, 2nd Edition. San Diego, CA: Academic Press, 2001.

Voshell, J. Reese Jr., with Amy Bartlett Wright. *A Guide to Common Freshwater Invertebrates of North America*. Blacksburg, VA: McDonald and Woodward, 2002.

FISH

Breining, Greg, and Dick Sternberg. *Fishing Tips & Tricks*. Minnetonka, MN: Cy DeCosse, 1990.

Etnier, David A., and Wayne C. Starnes. *The Fishes of Tennessee*. Knoxville, TN: University of Tennessee Press, 1993.

Froese, Rainer, and Daniel Pauly, eds. "Fishbase." 2010. www.fishbase.org.

Hauptman, Cliff. *Basic Freshwater Fishing*. Mechanicsburg, PA: Stackpole Books, 1988.

Machacek, Heinz. "World Records Freshwater Fishing." 2010. http://www.fishing-worldrecords.com/

Page, Lawrence M., and Brooks M. Burr. *Peterson Field Guides to Freshwater Fishes of North America North of Mexico,* 2nd Edition. Boston, MA: Houghton Mifflin, 2011.

REPTILES AND AMPHIBIANS

Behler, John L., and F. Wayne King. *National Audubon Society Field Guide to North American Reptiles and Amphibians*. New York: Alfred A. Knopf, 1995.

Conant, Roger, and Joseph T. Collins. *Peterson Field Guides: Reptiles and Amphibians: Eastern/Central North America*. New York: Houghton Mifflin, 1998.

Martof, Bernard S., William M. Palmer, Joseph R. Bailey, and Julian R. Harrison III. *Amphibians and Reptiles of the Carolinas and Virginia*. Chapel Hill, NC: University of North Carolina Press, 1980.

Mitchell, Joe, and Whit Gibbons. *Salamanders of the Southeast*. Athens, GA: Universtiy of Georgia Press, 2010.

MAMMALS

Bowers, Nora, Rick Bowers, and Kenn Kaufman. *Kaufman Field Guide to Mammals of North America*. New York: Houghton Mifflin, 2004.

Reid, Fiona A. *Peterson Field Guides: A Field Guide to Mammals of North America*, 4th Edition. New York: Houghton Mifflin, 2006.

BIRDS

"All About Birds." The Cornell Lab of Ornithology. 2010. http://www.allabout birds.org/guide/search

Dunn, Jon L., and Jonathan Alderfer. *National Geographic Field Guide to the Birds of North America*, 5th Edition. Washington, DC: National Geographic Society, 2006.

eBird. http://ebird.org

"Field Guide to Birds of North America." Whatbird.com. 2010. http://identify.whatbird.com/mwg/_/0/attrs.aspx

Peterson, Roger T. *Peterson Field Guide to Birds of Eastern and Central North America*, 6th Edition. New York: Houghton Mifflin Harcourt, 2010.

Sibley, David Allen. *National Audubon Society: The Sibley Guide to Birds*. New York: Alfred A. Knopf, 2000.

ANIMAL TRACKS AND SIGNS

Elbroch, Mark. *Mammal Tracks & Sign: A Guide to North American Species*. Mechanicsburg, PA: Stackpole Books, 2003.

Elbroch, Mark, with Eleanor Marks. *Bird Tracks & Sign: A Guide to North American Species*. Mechanicsburg, PA: Stackpole Books, 2001.

GENERAL RESOURCES

Animal Diversity Web. University of Michigan Museum of Zoology. http://animaldiversity.ummz.umich.edu/site/index.html

Integrated Taxonomic Information System. http://www.itis.gov/

Acknowledgments

Many people helped in the completion of this field guide. First of all, we would like to thank our parents, Tim and Jayne Brown and Royce and Kaye Delk, for their ever-present support in our lives. Our children, Jolie and Bristol, provide constant inspiration and challenge us to do as much as we can with our time on this earth. Our extended family has often provided us with help in the field and places to stay. Thank you, Derek and Lyndsey Norman, for putting up with us and the little biologists during our many trips to west Tennessee's swamps. Thank you, Judy and Joe Thagard, for helping us make it to the Everglades and to many birding hotspots.

Beyond our family, many others have provided help as well. Thank you, Mr. Claude Grady, for allowing us to capture and photograph animals on your land. Thank you to the personnel at all the national wildlife refuges, nature preserves, state parks, and other natural lands that we visited during the course of putting this book together. Thank you Phil Colclough, Michael Ogle, and Stephen Nelson of the Knoxville Zoo for your help with the bog turtle photo. Thank you Lee Droppelman for a week to work on this project. Thank you Nick Burgmeier, Jason Butler, Chris Chandler, Terry Derting, Ray Eaton, Adam Green, Barry Nichols, Robert Oney, Scott Slankard, and Ward Wilson for reviewing sections of the guide. A special thanks to Mark Allison for making this project a reality and to Brittany Stoner for all your hard work on the guide.

Index

Page numbers in italics indicates illustrations.